ASIAN AMERICAN BIOGRAPHY

ASIAN AMERICAN BIOGRAPHY

Volume 2
M-Z

Helen Zia and Susan B. Gall, *Editors*

An imprint of Gale Research Inc.,
an International Thomson Publishing Company

Changing the Way the World Learns

NEW YORK • LONDON • BONN • BOSTON • DETROIT • MADRID
MELBOURNE • MEXICO CITY • PARIS • SINGAPORE • TOKYO
TORONTO • WASHINGTON • ALBANY NY • BELMONT CA • CINCINNATI OH

ASIAN AMERICAN BIOGRAPHY

Helen Zia and Susan B. Gall, *Editors*

Staff

Sonia Benson, *U•X•L Developmental Editor*
Carol DeKane Nagel, *U•X•L Managing Editor*
Thomas L. Romig, *U•X•L Publisher*

Shanna P. Heilveil, *Production Associate*
Evi Seoud, *Assistant Production Manager*
Mary Beth Trimper, *Production Director*

Mary Krzewinski, *Art Director*
Cynthia Baldwin, *Product Design Manager*

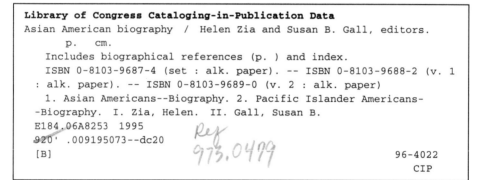

```
Library of Congress Cataloging-in-Publication Data
Asian American biography / Helen Zia and Susan B. Gall, editors.
      p.    cm.
   Includes biographical references (p. ) and index.
   ISBN 0-8103-9687-4 (set : alk. paper). -- ISBN 0-8103-9688-2 (v. 1
: alk. paper). -- ISBN 0-8103-9689-0 (v. 2 : alk. paper)
   1. Asian Americans--Biography. 2. Pacific Islander Americans-
-Biography. I. Zia, Helen. II. Gall, Susan B.
E184.06A8253 1995
920' .009195073--dc20
[B]                                                    96-4022
                                                           CIP
```

CONTENTS

READER'S GUIDE

Asian American Biography profiles more than 130 Americans who trace their ancestry to Asia and the Pacific Islands. Included are prominent men and women of Asian Indian, Cambodian, Chinese, Filipino, Native Hawaiian, Hmong, Japanese, Pacific Island, Pakistani, Taiwanese, and Vietnamese descent, both living and deceased. Profilees are notable for their achievements in fields ranging from civil rights to sports, politics to academia, entertainment to science, religion to the military. Early leaders in Asian American as well as contemporary figures are among those included. A black-and-white photograph accompanies most entries, and a list of sources for further reading or research is provided at the end of each entry. Cross references to other profiles in these volumes are noted in bold letters within the text. The volumes are arranged alphabetically and conclude with an index listing all individuals by field of endeavor.

theater, and sports. The volume contains more than 70 black-and-white photographs and maps, a glossary, and a cumulative subject index.

Asian American Chronology explores significant social, political, economic, cultural, and professional milestones in Asian American history. Arranged by year and then by month and day where applicable, the chronology spans from prehistory to modern times and contains more than 50 illustrations, extensive cross references, and a cumulative subject index.

Asian American Voices presents full or excerpted speeches, sermons, orations, poems, testimony, and other notable spoken works of Asian Americans. Each entry is accompanied by an introduction and boxes explaining some of the terms and events to which the speech refers. The volume is illustrated with black-and-white photographs and drawings and features a cumulative subject index.

Related Reference Sources:

Asian American Almanac explores the history and culture of the major ethnic groups comprising Asian America. The *Almanac* is organized into 15 subject chapters, including immigration patterns, women and family, religion, employment, civil rights and activism, education, literature and

Comments and Suggestions

We welcome your comments on *Asian American Biography* as well as your suggestions for persons to be featured in future editions. Please write: Editors, *Asian American Biography,* U•X•L, 835 Penobscot Bldg., Detroit, Michigan 48226-4094; call toll-free: 1-800-877-4253; or fax: 1-313-961-6348.

Advisors

Special thanks are due for the invaluable comments and suggestions provided by U•X•L's Asian American advisors:

Patricia Baird and Patricia Fagel
> Librarians, Media Resource Center
> Shaker Heights Middle School
> Shaker Heights, Ohio

Jeanne Dubose Goka
> Curriculum Director
> St. Michael's Academy
> Austin, Texas

Lin Look
> Librarian, Tenley Friendship Branch
> District of Columbia Public Library

James W. Miller, Teacher
> Woodrow Wilson Middle School
> Newton, Massachusetts

PHOTO CREDITS

The photographs used in *Asian American Biography* were received from the following sources:

On the covers: Margaret Cho: **Courtesy of Margaret Cho**; Amy Tan: **Courtesy of G. P. Putnam's Sons**; Lance Ito: **AP/Wide World**.

AP/Wide World Photos: pp. 31, 83, 105, 139, 142, 152, 176, 179, 181, 260, 273, 289, 304, 340, 378, 381; **Courtesy of Daniel K. Akaka:** p. 2; **Photo by Frank Ockenfels 3,** ©1993 Sony Music, courtesy of Columbia Records: p. 4; **Courtesy of Benihana:** p. 7; **Courtesy of George R. Ariyoshi:** p. 10; **Courtesy of Simon and Schuster:** p. 13; **Photo by Liane Enkelis Photography, courtesy of Kavelle Bajaj:** p. 16; **Courtesy of Atlanta Ballet:** p. 19, 20; **Courtesy of Lynda Barry:** p. 22; **Filipino American National Historical Society Collection, used by permission:** p. 25; **Photo by Ackerman Photography, courtesy of Phyllis J. Campbell:** p. 29; **Courtesy of Subrahmanyan Chandrasekhar:** p. 33; **Photo by Russ Adams Productions, courtesy of Michael Chang:** p. 37; **Photo by Christian Steiner, courtesy of ICM Artists:** p. 41; **Courtesy of Elaine Chao:** p. 43; **Courtesy of Stephen Chao:** p. 46; **Photo by Roland Neveu, courtesy of Warner Bros. Productions Limited:** p. 48; **Courtesy of William Shao Chang Chen:** p. 52; **Photo by ILM, courtesy of Doug Chiang:** p. 55; **Courtesy of NASA:** p. 57; **Courtesy of Margaret Cho:** p. 59; **Courtesy of Vernon Chong:** p. 62; **Courtesy of Harmony Books:** p. 64; **Photo by Tony Esparza, courtesy of CBS Inc.:** p. 67; **Courtesy of New England Patriots:** p. 70; **Harry Langdon Photography, courtesy of March Fong Eu:** p. 72; **Courtesy of Hiram Fong:** p. 75; **Photo by Dianne Fong-Torres, courtesy of Hyperion:** p. 78; **Courtesy of John L. Fugh:** p. 81; **Courtesy of Lillian Gonzalez-Pardo:** p. 87; **Photo by Hideo Yoshida, courtesy Philip Kan Gotanda:** p. 89; **Courtesy of James Hattori:** p. 91; **Courtesy of David Ho:** p. 93; **Courtesy of David Henry Hwang**: p. 96; **Courtesy of Daniel K. Inouye:** p. 99; **Courtesy of Paul Isaki:** p. 102; **Courtesy of H.W. Pak:** p. 109; **International Swimming Hall of Fame:** pp. 112, 114; © 1990 Capital Cities/ABC, Inc., used with permission: p. 117; **Courtesy of Elaine H. Kim:** p. 119; **Courtesy of Jay Kim:** p. 122; **Courtesy of San Francisco Giants:** p. 126; **U.S. Army Center of Military History:** p. 131; **Courtesy of Maxine Hong Kingston:** p. 135; **Courtesy of Harold Hongju Koh:** p. 137; **Asian Law Caucus:** p. 145; **Courtesy of Paul Kuroda:** p. 148; **Courtesy of Fred Lau:** p. 155; **Photo by Robert Zuckerman, courtesy of *A. Magazine*:** p. 157; **Photo by Columbia Pictures Industries, courtesy of *A. Magazine*:** p. 161; **Photo** © Norman Studios, courtesy of Knopf: p. 164; **Photo by Marty Umans:** p. 167; **Courtesy of Roosevelt University Library:** p. 171; **International Swimming Hall of Fame:** p. 173; **Photo by Ascherman, courtesy of The Cleveland Orchestra:** p. 185; **Photo by Robert McEwan, courtesy Lone Dragon Productions, Inc.:** p. 188; **Photo by Bachrach, courtesy of Ivy Books:** p. 191; **Courtesy of Greg Louganis,** p. 196; **International Swimming Hall of Fame:** p. 195; **Photo by J. Henry Fair, courtesy of ICM Artists, Ltd.:** p. 205; **Courtesy of Mako:**

p. 207; **Courtesy of Tom Matano:** p. 210; **Courtesy of Robert T. Matsui:** p. 213; **Courtesy of Nobu McCarthy:** p. 217; **Courtesy of Sonny Mehta:** p. 219; **Courtesy of Zubin Mehta:** p. 221; **Photo by Satoru Ishikawa, courtesy of The Midori Foundation:** p. 224; **Courtesy of Dale Minami:** p. 227; **Courtesy of Norman Mineta:** p. 230; **Courtesy of Patsy Mink:** p. 233; **Courtesy of the Academy of Motion Picture Arts and Sciences:** p. 237; **Courtesy of William Mow:** p. 239; **Photo by Christian Steiner, courtesy of Columbia Artists Management Inc.:** p. 244; **Courtesy of Perez Production Ltd.:** p. 247; **Photo by Michael Geissinger, courtesy of Irene Natividad:** p. 251; **Courtesy of Josie Natori:** p. 253; **Courtesy of Haing S. Ngor:** p. 257; **Courtesy of Gyo Obata:** p. 263; **Photo by Frank Wolfe, LBJ Library Collection:** p. 267; **Courtesy of NASA:** p. 270; **Photo by Christian Steiner, courtesy of Seiji Ozawa:** p. 275; **Courtesy of the Los Angeles Dodgers:** p. 278; **Photo by Ingbet Grüttner, courtesy of I. M. Pei:** p. 281; **Courtesy of Arati Prabhakar:** p. 285; **Courtesy of Beulah Quo:** p. 291; **Courtesy of AST Research:** p. 294; **Courtesy of Jhoon Rhee:** p. 297; **Courtesy of Patricia Saiki:** p. 300; **Courtesy of Richard Sakakida:** p. 302; **Courtesy of Allen Say:** p. 307; **Courtesy of San Diego Chargers:** p. 310; **Courtesy of The White House:** p. 313; **Photo by John Eddy, courtesy of Cathy Song:** p. 317; **Photo by Kevin Leong, courtesy of Anna Sui:** p. 322; **Photo by Carol Takaki, courtesy of Ronald Takaki:** p. 325; **Courtesy of Paramount Pictures:** p. 329; **Courtesy of G. P. Putnam's Sons:** p. 333; **Photo by John Blaustein, courtesy of Chang-Lin Tien:** p. 335; **Courtesy of NASA:** p. 342; **Photo by Deborah Storms, courtesy of the estate of Yoshiko Uchida:** p. 345; **Courtesy of Huynh Cong Ut:** p. 348; **Patsy Lynch:** p. 351; **Courtesy of John D. Waihee:** p. 354; **Courtesy of Wang Laboratories:** p. 356; **Courtesy of NASA:** p. 359; **Courtesy of Vera Wang:** p. 361; **Courtesy of Michiko Nishiura Weglyn:** p. 367; **Courtesy of the Academy of Motion Picture Arts and Sciences:** p. 370; **Courtesy of Touchstone Picture & Television:** p. 373; **Courtesy of Flossie Wong-Staal:** p. 376; **Courtesy of Bruce Yamashita:** p. 385; **Courtesy of Jeff Yang:** p. 389; **Photo by K. Yep, courtesy of Laurence Yep:** p. 391; **Courtesy of HarperCollins:** p. 392; **Courtesy of Shirley Young:** p. 395; **Photo by Danny Feld, courtesy of Teddy Zee:** p. 397.

ASIAN AMERICAN BIOGRAPHY

Yo-Yo Ma

Cellist
Born October 7, 1955, Paris, France

"I first heard Yo-Yo play in Paris when he was five or six years old. The cello was literally larger than he was. I could sense then, as has now been confirmed, that he was one of the most extraordinary talents of this generation."—Isaac Stern

Yo-Yo Ma is arguably the finest cellist in the world today. His performing career began at the age of five when he gave his first recital, at the University of Paris, playing both the piano and cello. After a rocky and rebellious adolescence, Ma developed into one of the most renowned musical performers in the world. He has played all over the world with virtually every major orchestra, has made well over 50 recordings, and has won eight Grammy awards.

Although he is best known for his interpretations of the works of Johann Sebastian Bach, Wolfgang Amadeus Mozart, and Ludwig von Beethoven, in recent years he has begun expanding his repertoire to include more contemporary composers. In 1992 he recorded an album called *Hush* with the popular jazz vocalist Bobby McFerrin, and he also gave a series of concerts in collaboration with the Massachusetts Institute of Technology in which he played on computer-generated "hyperinstruments."

Intensive early training

Ma is one of two children born to Hiao-Tsium Ma, a violinist and former professor at Nanjing University in China, and Marina Ma, a former student of Hiao-Tsium's. The elder Mas met in China and married in Paris, where Yo-Yo was born. Ma began studying the cello at age four, learning from his father in an incremental way that suited a young child's attention span. Ma described his early education by his father for the *Saturday Review,* relating, "It wasn't hard. My father didn't believe in long hours of practicing; he really believed in very concentrated work.... I used to only practice five to ten minutes a day."

In 1962, one year after Ma gave his first public performance at the University of Paris, his family moved to New York City. In New York, Ma began studying with Janos Scholz, the distinguished cellist. He also began performing with major orchestras around the world. Isaac Stern, the famous violinist, recalled in the *New Yorker* the first time he heard Ma play, stating, "I first heard Yo-Yo play in Paris when he was five or six years old. The cello was literally larger than he was. I could sense then, as has now been confirmed, that he was one of the most extraordinary talents of this generation."

A stormy adolescence

When Ma was nine he began to study with a new teacher, Leonard Rose, under whom his talent blossomed. But while Ma the musician excelled, Ma the child was having difficulty adjusting to the notoriety his playing ability had brought him. He struggled with his new life in the United States—as a person of Chinese descent whose first home had been France—in addition to handling the problems every young adolescent must face. Ma spoke of these conflicts in the *New Yorker:* "At home we spoke only Chinese; we were taken to Chinese movies to remind us of our traditional values. But I was also American, growing up with American values.... My home life was totally structured. Because I couldn't rebel there, I did so at school. In the fifth grade, I began to cut classes, and I continued to do so through high school. I spent a lot of time wandering through the streets, mainly because I just wanted to be alone."

Thus began a tumultuous period in Ma's life. After his parents discovered he was skipping classes, he was transferred to a different private school, where he was put in an accelerated program with the hope that if he were more challenged academically he would be more focused. He graduated from high school at the age of 15.

After graduation Ma spent a summer at Meadowmount, a camp for young musicians in the Adirondack Mountains of New York. It was Ma's first experience away from home. He told the *Saturday Review,* "I just went wild: Never showed up at rehearsals, left my cello out in the rain, beer bottles all over the room, midnight escapades to go swimming, and just about everything." In spite of this behavior, however, Ma's playing took on an added dimension. The personal freedom he was discovering was helping to establish artistic freedom as well.

In the fall, Ma enrolled in Columbia University in New York City. He quickly found himself just as bored at Columbia as he had been in high school and before long dropped out without telling his parents, with whom he was living, and began hanging out at the Juilliard School, the prestigious performing arts school in Manhattan. He got himself a fake ID and began drinking to excess. One

day he passed out in a practice room after throwing up and was taken to a hospital. "All I was trying to do was to be accepted as one of the guys," Ma told the *New Yorker,* "and not be considered a freak. But for the next five years everywhere I went people would look at me and think, 'This guy's trouble.'"

A career in music

In 1972 Ma transferred to Harvard, where he began to take his life and career more seriously. He carried a full academic load and maintained an active performing schedule. He made his London debut during this period, and as concert requests became more and more frequent, he realized for the first time that he could support himself as a musician. He considered dropping out of school at this point, but his father insisted he stick it out, which he did. In 1977 Ma married Jill Horner, whom he had met when he was 16. His father was originally anxious about his son marrying a Westerner, but he has since come to accept his daughter-in-law.

After graduating from Harvard, Ma was made artist-in-residence at the school's Leverett House, and Jill was offered a position teaching German. Ma's concert career was taking off in ways that neither of them knew how to handle; Ma was ending up with as many as 150 concerts a season, leaving him virtually no time to be with his wife. "I was always flirting with getting burned out from exhaustion," he told the *New Yorker.*

In 1980 the first of two life-altering events occurred: Ma underwent an operation to correct scoliosis, a curvature of the spine that could have rendered him unable to play the cello ever again. The operation was a

Yo-Yo Ma

success, though Ma had to spend six months in a body cast. The experience gave him a new sense of values. "I was prepared for the possibility that [the operation] might not turn out successfully," he told the *New Yorker*. "I had decided that there's more to life than the cello.... Perhaps I'd do social work, or become a teacher."

The other event that altered Ma's life was the birth of his first child, Nicholas, in 1983. Becoming a father made Ma establish boundaries to his career. He made vows to spend more time with his family and to remain aware of his level of enjoyment, deciding to quit performing if he ever lost his love for it. With his family as his first priority, Ma has learned well how to balance the professional and personal aspects of his fast-paced life.

Ma's philosophy of performance

Despite the fact that he is nearly universally lauded as one of the greatest living musicians, Ma described himself in the *New Yorker* as "just a performing musician." He gives all the credit to the music's composers, saying, "I feel that when a composer writes a piece of music he's translating a human experience into sound." As a performer Ma seeks to transfer those inspired ideas through his skill to the audience. "One must go out of oneself," he believes, "finding empathy for another's experience, forming another world."

Ma is especially renowned for his mastery of the works of Bach. About this great composer he told the *New Yorker*, "I know my greatest joy as a musician when I am playing a concert dedicated exclusively to Bach. Then for a whole evening I'm living in one man's mind—and a great man's mind. That's how I can justify being a performer. One is involved in a process that is larger than oneself."

Sources:

Blum, David, "Profiles: A Process Larger than Oneself," *New Yorker,* May 1, 1989, p. 41.

"The Courage to Go Forth: Yo-Yo Ma in Conversation," *Economist,* vol. 322, no. 7746, February 15, 1992, p. 107.

Eisler, Edith, "Yo-Yo Ma: Music from the Soul," *Strings,* May/June 1992, pp. 58-62.

ICM Artists, promotional material, New York, August 1993.

Thorne, Richard, "The Magic of Yo-Yo Ma," *Saturday Review.* July 1981, pp. 55-58.

Mako

Actor, director
Born December 10, 1933, Kobe, Japan

In 1965, Mako and a group of friends from the Asian American community decided to do something about their exclusion from Hollywood films; rather than beg for substantial, meaningful roles, they formed their own theater company, the East West Players.

Mako is the stage name of Makoto Iwamatsu. He is a well-respected actor and director who was nominated for an Academy Award as best supporting actor in *The Sand Pebbles,* a 1966 film starring Steve McQueen. He is also a respected stage actor and is best known as one of the founders and the artistic director of East West Players, the first Asian American theater group in the United States. The theater, which was founded in 1965 as a home for serious drama featuring Asian American writers and actors, has since become the premier showcase for such talent and has helped launch the careers of several prominent Asian American dramatists and actors, including playwright **Philip Kan Gotanda**.

The fat Americans

Mako was raised in Japan by his grandparents after his parents left the country for political reasons. He spent the duration of World War II in Japan and then was reunited with his family in 1949 when he arrived in New York. "It was a big adjustment coming from Kobe to New York," Mako recalled in an interview with *Asian American Biography (AAB)*. "I came from postwar Japan, where people had nothing to speak of, where they were just beginning to reconstruct Japan. When I arrived in New York, the first thing that came to mind was how fat, how obese these people were. In postwar Japan, there were very few fat people. In the U.S. there were so many."

Mako's family lived on New York's Lower East Side, an immigrant neighborhood remarkable for its concentration of the impoverished and homeless. Mako found it odd that a world superpower would have such a poor neighborhood in its biggest, most important city. "There were so many derelicts and winos on the sidewalks, I thought this was a very strange country that had come up victorious in World War II."

Mako

Introduction to theater

Mako was educated in the public school system and then enrolled in Pratt Institute in Brooklyn, one of the best design, graphic arts, and architecture schools in the country. He was originally interested in studying architecture but got derailed when a fellow student asked him to help with the design of a set for an upcoming production. Mako was intrigued by the work, and he found himself drawn further and further into theater. "It seemed more interesting than remaining in school," he told *AAB,* "and I became more involved in theater, artistically and emotionally." Over the next year or so Mako missed so many of his classes that he lost his draft deferment—the military could not draft men in college—and he was drafted into the army. At the time, there was an undeclared war being fought in Korea, and Mako spent most of his two years in the service there and in Japan.

After being discharged, Mako went to Los Angeles to stay with his parents, who had since moved there. He was still very interested in theater, so he used the G.I. Bill, a government scholarship program for veterans, to study at the Pasadena Playhouse. He initially wasn't at all certain if he wanted to study acting or not, but he thought it would be good to get his foot in the door and see which areas interested him. As he began his studies there, Mako felt slightly overwhelmed by what he perceived as the professionalism of the other students. "They seemed so seasoned, even though they were only in their late teens and early twenties," he told *AAB*. "I felt I had nothing and, in essence, I was in awe of these people." Despite his reticence, however, Mako stuck it out at the playhouse and, as the instructors weeded out the less promising students at the end of each quarter, Mako grew more confident.

After graduating from the playhouse, Mako went to New York to study at the Actors Studio, then a very fashionable acting school where some of Hollywood's most important actors had studied, including Paul Newman and Marlon Brando. Mako auditioned for the Actors Studio for two years but was never accepted. He did, however, study with a graduate of the school who taught the young actor the technique known as method acting (in which the actor seeks to gain complete identification with the inner personality of the character being portrayed).

Racism in Hollywood

When Mako returned to Los Angeles he found it virtually impossible for an Asian American actor to find a decent role. He was consistently offered roles as houseboys, gangsters, and other villains, while leading roles as Asians were being filled by European Americans in heavy makeup. In 1965, Mako and a group of friends from the Asian American community decided to do something about their exclusion; rather than beg for substantial, meaningful roles, they formed their own theater company, the East West Players. The original founders included Mako, James Hong, June Kim, Guy Lee, Yet Lock, and **Beulah Quo,** and their premier production was staged in a church basement—a popular venue for new theater companies—in 1966.

By 1968, East West Players had a permanent home on Santa Monica Boulevard in Los Angeles's Silverlake area, with Mako serving as artistic director. Initially, the company focused on producing adaptations of the works of Asian novelists, but at the same time, it produced Western (primarily European and North American) classics of the stage, providing some of the Asian actors with their first opportunity to play characters that had always been denied them because of their race. By the early 1970s, the company began to concentrate on a new genre, plays written by Asian Americans, premiering at least one original work every season.

During Mako's two-decade reign as artistic director, he not only directed and performed in plays, he wrote one as well. Titled

There's No Place for a Tired Ghost, the work was about Japanese Americans who died in internment camps during World War II (when Japanese Americans were held prisoner because the U.S. government feared they would be a security risk in the event of a Japanese invasion of the West Coast). In 1977, East West Players won three Los Angeles Drama Critics Awards for their debut production of Wakako Yamauchi's *And the Soul Shall Dance.* In 1989, Mako resigned his post as artistic director because of disagreements with the company's board of directors. Although he is no longer involved with the group he helped create, he remains an important figure in Asian American theater.

In February 1994, Mako was honored with a star on the Hollywood Walk of Fame. He was touched by the recognition and gratified that an Asian American had been included on the famous street, but he offered a realistic appraisal of the effect the gesture would have on his career to *AAB:* "In a way, it was anti-climactic.... The Stars event was sponsored by the Hollywood Chamber of Commerce as opposed to the [entertainment] industry and so it has little impact on one's career." Today Mako still struggles with taking less than ideal roles while working to maintain his idealism. "Compromise happens with almost every role, in any job," he told *AAB.* "One learns to compromise one's ideals, though not sacrifice them. A give-and-take situation happens every time."

Sources:

Fields, Sidney, "Only Human," *New York Daily News,* January 9, 1976, p. 81.

Haru, Sumi, "Mako," *Asian Week,* February 18, 1994.

Mako, telephone interview with Terry Hong, March 7, 1994.

Pacheco, Patrick, "When Worlds Collide," *Los Angeles Times Calendar,* April 19, 1992, p. 3.

Tom Matano

Automotive designer
Born October 7, 1947, Nagasaki, Japan

"When I was growing up, I read many success stories, and one of the common threads was that every one of them had made huge mistakes ... so I thought if I could organize my mistakes and my many unique and interesting experiences, then one day I may get to tell a story or two."

Tom Matano is the executive vice president of the design division of Mazda Research and Development of North America. Since he became vice president, his studio has produced the designs for such popular cars and trucks as the Navajo, MX-3, MX-6, 626, 929, and the B Series trucks Mazda introduced in 1994. He was also a contributor to the design of the Miata, which, when it was introduced in February 1989, became one of the most successful and sought-after cars in recent history; dealerships had long waiting lists for the cars and Mazda was swamped trying to keep up with demand. Because of the success of the Miata, many of the major international auto makers have introduced models similar to the sleek roadster.

Born just after the war

Matano was born just two years after the United States dropped nuclear bombs on Hiroshima and Nagasaki—Matano's birth-place—in the only uses of nuclear weapons on civilian populations in history. The Matano family was fortunate enough to live on the other side of a mountain from "ground zero" (where the bomb actually made contact) and thus was spared the most damaging effects of the bomb. Matano's father was a salesman with the industrial giant Mitsubishi Heavy Industry, working in the shipbuilding division. His mother was a traditional homemaker. The family left Nagasaki for Tokyo when Matano was still an infant, and for the remainder of his child-hood, they lived in and around Tokyo.

An early love

In the years immediately after the war, Japan was a devastated country. Tokyo espe-cially had suffered from incessant bombing and was in ruins. Yet Matano had friends, neighbors, and family members who had cars, some of the very few privately owned automobiles in the country. He had an uncle, a former kamikaze (suicidal crash bomber) pilot with Japan's Royal Air Force, who had built a car from spare parts and often took the family on trips. This uncle also owned a gas station, and Matano recalls, "I still remember the smell that filled the workshop when the station opened in the morning." When he was five, he "developed a fetish for leather seats ... when my grandfather bought a Moris Minor with red leather seats. At the same time, my neighbor across the street had a Lincoln with a large red tail light.

Tom Matano

Another neighbor had a Citroen 2CV." Matano's wealthy great-uncle owned a 1951 Cadillac. When he later traded that car in for a 1957 Cadillac, Matano recalled being "spellbound by this piece of art [especially] the tail fins."

In high school Matano was an above-average student. The Japanese educational system did not offer public school classes in automotive shop or design, so Matano would occasionally skip school to hang around car shops, which, like all his early experiences with cars, he remembers as fas-cinating. After graduation from high school,

Matano enrolled in Seiki University in Tokyo, where he studied analysis engineering. He had wanted to study design, but the Japanese system would have required him to take an additional two years of classes before even being allowed to take admittance exams. While attending Seiki, Matano worked part-time for a large Tokyo advertising agency that had hired him to drive cars—often in the middle of the night—to remote sites for photographic shoots. Soon he was working on the production team scouting locations for the shoots.

A taste for more

In 1969 Matano visited the United States for the first time. He arrived, via cargo ship, in Everett, Washington. "I then hopped on a Greyhound bus," he told *Asian American Biography (AAB),* "bound for Los Angeles. Not quite seeing enough, I then traveled on to New York and back to Los Angeles again. I had seen the States and this trip gave me the taste of long-distance driving." By the time Matano returned to Japan, he knew he wanted to work in the design field; he had been told by friends and business connections that he had the talent—all he needed was the degree. He went to the U.S. embassy in Tokyo to research American schools of design, and in 1971 he began classes at the Art Center College of Design in Los Angeles.

While in school, Matano observed that most of the Japanese students kept to themselves. He didn't want to isolate himself, however, so he spent his lunch hours sitting with the Americans, listening to how they talked, trying to learn the language more completely. For doing this, he remembers,

he was shunned by the Japanese students. His studies, however, went well in Los Angeles. Matano wanted to study environmental design, "however," he admitted, "I could not draw a perspective of a room containing furniture. So I drew cars and got into the transportation design class instead." In 1974 he earned a bachelor of science degree in transportation design.

After graduation, Matano was offered a job with General Motors working on their design staff in Warren, Michigan. He remained at this job for 18 months, at which point he was unable to renew his visa to stay in the United States. In 1976 he left the country for Australia to work for General Motors operations there. He stayed in Australia for six and a half years and then accepted a job in Germany working for BMW. He enjoyed the working environment at BMW but couldn't adjust to the Bavarian climate, and in 1983 he left to join Mazda's design team in California, where he continued to work through the 1990s.

Two of Matano's first jobs with Mazda were on the MPV, Mazda's entry into the lucrative minivan market, and the Miata, a classic roadster. A sporty two-seater convertible, the Miata became so popular that Mazda had difficulty keeping up on orders for it. Matano told *AAB* that when he was working on the Miata, he relied on his belief that one can literally "plan" to make history. With the correct attitude, he explained, one can, from the outset of an endeavor, plan to make it succeed in a history-making way.

In 1991 Matano was made vice president of the California design team. As such, he is responsible for taking the work of several designers and distilling from them a final vision for a car. This final design is then sent to Mazda's headquarters in Japan to be reviewed. Along with the designers' drawings and computer images of the final product, a full-scale handcrafted clay model is sent along as well.

Even as vice president of design, Matano still works on these clay models, trying to instill in them his philosophy of design, which he described for *Metropolitan Home* magazine: "Think of a raindrop when it falls on a curve. As long as the raindrop doesn't have to think twice about where it's going to go next, then the design is good. So, in my imagination, I become a raindrop and go all over the surface to find the stoppages. Then I go back and smooth them all out." This remarkably poetic philosophy of design helps explain the success Mazda has had in 1980s and 1990s, and the singularity of the look of its cars in an industry increasingly dominated by what many feel are formless, unimaginative vehicles.

Don't be afraid of mistakes

Matano considers himself an American and plans to apply for citizenship in the near future. He believes that the success stories of Asian Americans should serve as inspiration to *all* Americans and not just to those of Asian descent. He told *AAB* that his motto is: "Don't be afraid of mistakes, and never repeat the same mistake twice.... When I was growing up, I read many success stories, and one of the common threads was that every one of them had made huge mistakes ... so I thought if I could organize my mistakes and my many unique and interesting experiences, then one day I may get to tell a story or two."

Matano has received numerous awards for his work over the years. In 1992 he was one of six designers selected to attend then-President-Elect Bill Clinton's Roundtable discussion of design. The following year he was named one of the top 40 designers in the United States by *ID* magazine. Also in 1993 he was a featured speaker at the Automotive News World Congress. Matano is an active member of the board of trustees of the World Design Foundation.

Sources:

Matano, Tom, telephone interview with Jim Henry, April 13, 1994.

Mazda Corporation, Department of Research and Development, press releases and internal documents, April 1994.

"Thinkers," *Metropolitan Home,* vol. 26, no. 2, March/April 1994, p. 52.

Robert Matsui

U.S. congressman
Born 1941, Sacramento, California

"I'm a politician who happens to be Asian American.... I can go on the floor of the House and speak about discrimination; I can talk about this knowledgeably because of my values, my upbringing, and my heritage as an Asian American. My decision-making process is influenced by my unique ethnic background, and I'm very proud of it."

R obert Matsui serves in the U.S. House of Representatives, where he represents California's fifth district—the Sacramento area. He was first elected to this position in 1978 and has won reelection by wide margins every two years since. During his tenure in Congress, Matsui has become a powerful member of the House Ways and Means Committee, the body that appropriates federal money, making it probably the most powerful committee in the federal government. He has taken the lead on many public policy issues involving taxes, health care, welfare reform, and other social issues. In late 1993, the new administration of Bill Clinton entrusted Matsui with drumming up congressional support for the passage of the North American Free Trade Agreement (NAFTA), a hotly debated free trade agreement between Canada, the United States, and Mexico. The treaty seemed at times to be close to defeat, which would have been a major blow to the new president. Matsui's leadership on the issue put him in the national spotlight, and the treaty's ultimate approval was due in no small part to Matsui's efforts.

Robert Matsui

Sent to the internment camps

Matsui was born in Sacramento the year the Japanese bombed America's naval base at Pearl Harbor, the event that sparked U.S. involvement in World War II. This was a dark time in American history; it was during this period that the federal government began rounding up Japanese Americans living on the West Coast and sending them to so-called "internment camps," which were actually large prisons located in remote parts of the West—often in extreme environments. The government acted on the premise that Japanese Americans would be a security risk in the event of a Japanese invasion of the West Coast.

In April 1942, the Matsuis were taken into custody, relieved of their possessions, and sent to a camp where they would spend the next three years of their lives. Robert recalled this period for A. *Magazine,* revealing, "I have no memory of it, just flashbacks; we were released when I was about four. My parents rarely talked about it, since it was an issue of shame that our loyalty was put into question. They were citizens, born in this country. Yet because we were at war with a country that our ancestors happened to come from, we were considered a security risk."

This reaction of shame was common among those Americans imprisoned during the war; few spoke about it afterwards. That the government had even acted in such flagrant violation of the constitution went largely unquestioned for more than a generation, until activists began doing research in the 1960s and 1970s.

After the war, the Matsuis were released. They moved back to Sacramento, where they began the long process of trying to put their lives back together. As a young man, Matsui was interested in architecture and until his early teens thought he would like to become an architect. Then he read the autobiography of Clarence Darrow, the famous trial attorney. Darrow believed that the basis of the law was to protect the underdog and that idea appealed to Matsui. He saw himself assuming such a role in life, lending assistance to those on the fringes, those less fortunate. This sense of protecting the interests and rights of the underrepresented would stay with Matsui all of his life.

Inspired by Kennedy

After high school, Matsui enrolled in the University of California at Berkeley, one of America's finest public universities. When Matsui was a sophomore, John F. Kennedy was elected president and, like many of his generation, Matsui was inspired by the young president's agenda. For many people, Kennedy embodied the spirit of public service, which he articulated in his famous inauguration address when he said, "Ask not what your country can do for you; ask what you can do for your country." Matsui knew he wanted to follow the model Kennedy had

laid out for him, and after earning his bachelor's degree, he enrolled in law school.

In 1966, Matsui received his law degree and left Berkeley to return to Sacramento with his new wife, Doris (Okada), to begin a law practice. The early years of the practice were extremely difficult, as they invariably are for a new lawyer, but Matsui stuck it out. By 1970, he was an established part of the local community.

Public service

In 1971, Matsui saw his opportunity to run for public office when Sacramento's city council districts were redrawn, leaving the incumbent Republican in his district vulnerable. He ran an inexpensive campaign that relied heavily on volunteer work from the many contacts he had made, especially those in the Asian American community. Matsui won the race and served on the city council until 1978, when he ran for the U.S. Congress.

The idea to run came to Matsui when the incumbent congressman, whose previous three campaigns Matsui had managed, told Matsui he would retire after his next term. Three contenders immediately jumped into the primary campaign, with Matsui trailing in early polls. But as he had done in his first council race, Matsui ran a grass roots campaign, calling again on his extensive connections in the community. The *New York Times* wrote an article highlighting certain congressional races that year; it said of Matsui's, "National Democratic officials say he ran one of the best campaigns of the year, and he was able to attract campaign help from House Speaker Thomas O'Neill,

Vice President Mondale, and President Carter." Again the hard work of a largely volunteer staff paid off as Matsui was elected to Congress.

In Congress

In his first term in Congress, Matsui expressed interest in sitting on the House Judiciary Committee, but he was derailed by racial stereotyping when the Democratic leadership suggested he might be more interested in serving on the Immigration Committee. Matsui persisted and was given a seat. He was also given a seat on the Commerce Committee. During his first term, Matsui voted with the Democratic leadership 90 percent of the time. In his second term, he was granted a seat on the Ways and Means Committee. Over time he has shown himself to be a moderate Democrat who takes liberal stands on social legislation but is strictly pro-business in other areas.

In foreign policy and defense, Matsui has a record of supporting most weapons systems, many of which are built in California, home to a significant number of defense contractors. He was generally opposed to the U.S. involvement in international civil wars during the Reagan and Bush administrations, especially those in Central America. More recently, he voted against the use of force against Iraq in 1991, just prior to the massive U.S.-led assault on that country, which had occupied tiny, oil-rich Kuwait.

One of Matsui's most passionate areas of concern is international free trade. He has often voted against the Democratic party in this area, as many Democrats believe that opening the United States to products produced in other countries—where workers are paid nearly slave wages—is unfair to the American worker. Matsui's long-standing support of international free trade led him to assume a high-profile role in the passage of NAFTA. As a spokesperson for the trade pact, Matsui appeared on *Meet the Press, The CBS Evening News, The MacNeil/Lehrer NewsHour* and several other political talk shows.

Of all his distinguished work in the U. S. Congress, though, Matsui is probably most proud of his help in the passage of the Japanese American Reparations Act of 1987. This law offered a formal apology to the 120,000 Japanese Americans who had been imprisoned during World War II, as well as providing monetary compensation for the government's seizure of their property.

An Asian American

Matsui takes pride in his ethnic heritage and doesn't shy away from discussing it. He told *A. Magazine,* "I'm a politician who happens to be Asian American. I take my experience with me; I don't deny my past, and I *shouldn't* deny my past. I can go on the floor of the House and speak about discrimination; I can talk about this knowledgeably because of my values, my upbringing, and my heritage as an Asian American. My decision-making process is influenced by my unique ethnic background, and I'm very proud of it. It got me where I am today."

In addition to his legislative duties, Matsui is active in the Democratic party and was named its treasurer in 1991. He lives with his wife, a deputy assistant to President Bill Clinton, in Washington, D.C.

Sources:

Office of Congressman Robert Matsui, Sacramento, California, 1994.

Yang, Jeff, "Power Brokers," *A. Magazine,* vol. 2, no. 3, December 15, 1993.

Yang, Jeff, "The Power of Two: An Interview with Bob and Doris Matsui," *A. Magazine,* vol. 2, no. 3, December 15, 1993.

Nobu McCarthy

Actress
Born November 13, 1934, Ottawa, Canada

*"You have to keep [a] fire burning in your heart....
Just never, ever give up. That's the key to success."*

Nobu McCarthy has been a dancer, a singer, a model, an actress, a teacher, and the artistic director of the nation's first Asian American theater, the East West Players. She credits supportive parents, hard work, and a diverse cultural background with her success. Her physical appearance, described as "exquisite" and "glamorous" by the *New York Daily News*, coupled with her prodigious talent have brought distinctive character to the prominent roles she has played in such movies as *Pacific Heights* (with Michael Keaton), *Karate Kid II* (with Pat Morita and Ralph Macchio), *Walk Like a Dragon* (with Jack Lord), and *Two Loves* (with Shirley MacLaine). McCarthy also has made more than one hundred television appearances on shows such as *Batman, Quincy, Happy Days, T. J. Hooker, Hawaii Five-O, Magnum P.I.*, and *China Beach*.

"To be a success in anything I tried"

McCarthy was born Nobu Atsumi on November 13, 1934, in Ottawa, Canada, where her father was serving as a diplomatic aide to Prince Tokugawa of Japan. When she was a few months old, the family returned to Japan and settled in Tokyo.

"At the age of four ... my mother took me to see [the Shakespearean play] *A Midsummer Night's Dream* and from that time on, I wanted to be on the stage," McCarthy told *Asian American Biography (AAB)*. By the age of six, she was already studying the piano, modern dance, and voice. An appealing performer, she signed a contract with King Records in Japan and became a child singer, appearing onstage and on radio. At 11, McCarthy enrolled in the Pavlova School of Ballet in Tokyo, where she studied dance.

Growing up in Japan was difficult at times for McCarthy. "Because my father spoke English and I was born outside of the country, the children were very cruel," she explained. "I remember as a child being ashamed because I wasn't born in Japan. At school, my classmates often teased me and called me 'Mary,' an insult reserved for those who were pro-Western in their thinking and behavior.... [That] negative response from my peers ... only served to motivate me. In fact, if there was one single thing that I had to point out as the catalyst that moved me forward, it would be that. I vowed I would show everyone that I could be a success in anything I tried to do. Luckily, my father was my strongest supporter, and my mother was never far behind. They counseled me to finish whatever I started, and to do it with zest!"

This dedication to succeed helped McCarthy become one of the top professional models in Japan. Her father, who had resigned from his diplomatic career to pursue fashion design, created all of McCarthy's clothes. She told *AAB*, "A friend who was close to the editor of a teen fashion magazine suggested to the editor that he do a feature story about a teenaged ballerina who wore beautiful clothes designed by her father. The photos and the article so impressed the editor that he hired me to be his personal model for the magazine and my career began." Within a year, McCarthy was one of Japan's leading models. "Things were tough in early postwar Japan, but with the money I made as a model, I was able to put my four brothers through school."

Star of film, television, and stage

In 1955, Nobu married a young American soldier named David McCarthy and despite protests from Japan's fashion industry, she traveled to the United States and settled in Los Angeles, California. Six months later, she was "discovered" by a Hollywood film agent while eating dinner in a restaurant. The agent asked her to meet with comedian Jerry Lewis, who was casting his latest film, *Geisha Boy*, about a magician and his rabbit who are lured by a beautiful woman away from the United States to the theaters of Japan. McCarthy was dressed in a Japanese kimono at her first meeting with Lewis, and he turned her down. They met again, and this time McCarthy wore fashionable Western clothes. Lewis immediately cast her in her first starring role.

Nobu McCarthy

McCarthy's acting career was quickly established. Both film and television offers were abundant. Before long, she was working with some of the industry's best. "I had the chance to meet and be friends with many of the giant stars—Gary Cooper, Cary Grant, Fred Astaire, Sammy Davis, Jr., Marlon Brando, Anthony Quinn, and others," she said.

In spite of her fairy tale "discovery" and the many offers of parts, McCarthy quickly realized that roles for Asian Americans were limited and usually stereotypical. A turning point in McCarthy's career came when she was 37: she played the 53-year-old mother in the award-winning television film *Farewell to Manzanar.* Because of her excellent performance, she began to be typecast predominantly in, as she put it, "old mother, granny roles." Nonetheless, from then on, she was offered more honest and fully developed parts.

In the late 1960s and 1970s, McCarthy decided to try stage acting because good film and television roles had become hard to find. In 1971, she played opposite the respected actor **Mako**, who was the founder of East West Players. McCarthy eventually became actively involved with East West Players, perfecting her acting skills and discovering her directing talents.

During the 1970s and 1980s, McCarthy's stage credits grew steadily. Among her numerous performances, McCarthy originated the leading role in noted playwright **David Henry Hwang**'s *As the Crow Flies,* for which she won, among other honors, the Los Angeles *Drama-logue* Award. She also created the leading role of Masi in prominent dramatist **Philip Kan Gotanda**'s *The Wash,* making her New York debut at the Manhattan Theater Club and later reprising the role at the Mark Taper Forum in Los Angeles and other regional theaters. She won another *Drama-logue* Award and the San Francisco "Bernie" award for her performances.

From 1982 to 1987, McCarthy taught acting at California State University, Los Angeles, and was the director of the Asian American Theater Project. Since 1991, she has also taught acting at various other universities, including the University of California at Los Angeles. In 1989, she added a new element to her career when she became

artistic director of East West Players six months after Mako resigned. "When the board first asked me, I said no, but eventually I had to agree. My thought at the time was that I could feed my passion for helping Asian American actors. I would do the job for three years, put my life into it and then search for a successor," McCarthy said. Those three years grew to five as she expanded the East West Players from a theater group to a formal artist training facility. She developed and directed the theater's Professional Actors' Training Program and founded the David Henry Hwang Writers' Institute.

"Never give up"

McCarthy returned to acting full time after her work with East West Players ended. In 1994, she appeared once again as Masi in Gotanda's *The Wash* at the Studio Theater in Washington, D.C. Earning rave reviews, McCarthy proved that she was still a leading actress. The *Washington Post* called the play "graceful, subtle and moving ... more powerful than an evening of ... fireworks" and referred to McCarthy's performance as "truly remarkable."

"I've been very lucky in that I don't have to take roles to eat," McCarthy said. "But acting is really a blade with two sides. If you really do pick and choose your roles, then you end up never acting." In spite of the lack of satisfying roles for Asian Americans, McCarthy encourages young actors. "Yes, it's a very tough road, but you cannot give up your desires," she asserts. "You have to keep that fire burning in your heart. You just have to do it. It's quite a bit of suffering, but you can't count just the suffering. There's so much joy, too. Just never, ever give up. That's the key to success."

Sources:

Gardella, Kay, "Star of 'Manzanar' Film Gives Japanese View of U.S.," *New York Daily News,* March 5, 1976, p. 98.

McCarthy, Nobu, telephone interview with Terry Hong, May 28, 1994.

Rose, Lloyd, "'The Wash': Delicate Cycle," *Washington Post,* March 17, 1994, pp. D1, D5.

Sonny Mehta

Book publisher
Born 1942, India

When Mehta joined Alfred A. Knopf in 1987, he decided to make some changes. Knopf had developed a reputation for publishing books that received critical praise, but did not sell well. Mehta devoted himself to pursuing projects that would appeal more to the general public.

Sonny Mehta

Ajai Singh "Sonny" Mehta is the president and editor-in-chief of Alfred A. Knopf, a part of the Random House book publishing company. He is also the president of the Knopf Publishing Group, which includes Knopf, Pantheon Books, Schocken Books, Vintage Books, and Random House Large Print Publishing. Random House is the largest general trade book publisher in the United States and the English-speaking world. (The term *trade* indicates books that are marketed to the general public).

Mehta became head of Alfred A. Knopf in 1987. His division publishes the works of John Updike, John Hersey, André Gide, and Albert Camus, among others. In recent years Knopf has published the works of Toni Morrison, V. S. Naipaul, John le Carre, Gabriel García Márquez, Michael Crichton, and Cormac McCarthy. Alfred A. Knopf writers have won more Nobel Prizes than those of any other publisher. Knopf writers have also won numerous Pulitzer prizes and other literary awards.

Privileged roots

The son of a diplomat, Sonny Mehta was educated at the Lawrence School in Sanwar, India, and at Cambridge University in England. He began his publishing career in London at Rupert Hart-Davis. After founding Paladin Books, he became editorial director of Granada Paperbacks, where he supervised the operations of the Panther, Mayflower, and Paladin book lines. In 1972 he became publishing director of Pan Books and started the Picador trade paperback line.

When Mehta joined Alfred A. Knopf in 1987, he decided to make some changes. Knopf had developed a reputation for publishing books that received critical praise, but did not sell well. Mehta devoted himself to pursuing projects that would appeal more to the general public.

The making of a bestseller

His first hits in his role as publisher at Knopf were *American Psycho* by Bret Easton Ellis and *Damage* by Josephine Hart, both of which caused controversy over either explicitly sexual or violent imagery. Critics were not kind to these works, but millions of people bought them. Mehta marketed these novels so well, in fact, that they went to the top of the *New York Times* bestseller list shortly after they were released.

On a typical day, Mehta reads numerous manuscripts in search of new work worthy of publication by Knopf. He breaks only to change CDs—his musical tastes range from classical composers Beethoven and Mozart to Biber—and watch cricket matches on cable TV. At 4:00 in the afternoon he generally stops reading and catches up on phone calls until it is time for dinner.

Sources:

Alfred A. Knopf, "Ajai Singh Mehta," official biography, January 1, 1994.

Conant, Janet, "The Very Furry Feet of Sonny Mehta," *Esquire,* April 1993, pp. 106-9.

Streitfeld, David, "Life at Random: Reading Between the Lines at America's Hottest Publishing House," *New York,* August 5, 1991, pp. 30-44.

Yang, Jeff, "Power Brokers," *A. Magazine,* December 15, 1993, pp. 25-34.

Zubin Mehta

Conductor, music director
Born April 29, 1936, Bombay, India

"Mehta's career in this internationally minded age has possibly profited from the exotic value attached to being the only India-born conductor to attain prominence. But he does not trade on such externals.... He hasn't needed them. His musical abilities alone have been sufficient."—Albert Goldberg, Los Angeles Times

Zubin Mehta is one of the world's most renowned conductors of classical music. He has served as conductor and music director for the New York Philharmonic, the Los Angeles Philharmonic, the Montreal Symphony, and the Israel Philharmonic, for which Mehta is music director for life. He has recorded hundreds of albums and has appeared as a guest conductor with dozens of orchestras around the globe. Mehta has a reputation for flamboyance and frankness and for taking classical music into new areas. Albert Goldberg, music critic of the *Los Angeles Times* said, "Mehta's career in this internationally minded age has possibly profited from the exotic value attached to being the only India-born conductor to attain prominence. But he does not trade on such externals. Press agents and publicity play no part in his strategy. In fact, it is doubtful if he is ever conscious of the usual gimmicks to promote careers. He hasn't needed them. His musical abilities alone have been sufficient."

A musical family

Mehta's father was a violinist and the cofounder of India's Bombay Symphony. As a teenager, Mehta was very involved with the orchestra. When his father traveled, he would leave Mehta in charge, allowing him to conduct the orchestra. At 18, the young musician left India to study classical European music in Vienna, Austria, where he worked with the great master Hans Swarowsky. At the age of 22, he won his first major international prize when he took first place in the 1958 Liverpool International Conductor's Competition. Over the next three years he served as guest conductor with some of the world's great orchestras, including the Vienna Philharmonic, the Berlin Philharmonic, and the Montreal Symphony. In 1962 he appeared as conductor of the Los Angeles Philharmonic, standing in for Fritz Reiner. He was then appointed assistant music director, and, when the director resigned, he became one of the youngest conductors of a major U.S. orchestra at age 26.

In Los Angeles, Mehta became something of a cult figure, drawing attention for his youth, his Asian heritage, his style, and his tendency to speak his mind. *New York*

Zubin Mehta

magazine described the city's feelings about its internationally acclaimed conductor: "Los Angeles—well, most of Los Angeles—adores Zubin Mehta.... A much-bigger-than-life portrait of the resident hero, eyes ablaze and sensuous lips enigmatically agrin, is the only portrait on view in the Dorothy Chandler Pavilion [home of the Los Angeles Philharmonic].... The mayor proclaimed October 25, 1973, Zubin Mehta Day.... Audiences cheer his entrance, even though he eyes the public on his way to the podium with proud disdain. He does not milk applause. They love him for it. They even ignore his gum-chewing at the podium."

The New York Philharmonic

After 16 sometimes turbulent years at the helm of the Los Angeles Philharmonic, Mehta accepted the directorship of the New York Philharmonic. The move caused a stir in the music world. Mehta had often mocked the New York Philharmonic, saying that the Los Angeles ensemble was superior. He had even spoken ill of the city of New York, something New Yorkers rarely forgive. He also would be replacing Pierre Boulez, one of the great conductors of modern times. It was thought that one of the reasons Mehta made the move was to be involved in opera, which he enjoyed guest conducting. In making the highly publicized switch, he released a statement that said, "My association with the musicians of the Los Angeles Philharmonic has been of a very intense nature, and our growth together over the past 15 years has included both the joys and triumphs as well as those trials and tribulations that go into making the orchestra what it is today."

During Mehta's 13-year history with the New York Philharmonic, he conducted more than 1,000 concerts, holding the post longer than any music director in the organization's modern history. Still, the city's relationship with their maestro was stormy. It had been hoped—and Mehta had hinted—that he would introduce more modern works into the orchestra's repertory. By his third season, however, there was grumbling that the director was not moving fast enough. The *New York Times* wrote, "By now you might think that a Mehta plan for revitalizing the Philharmonic's repertory and broadening its

audience's tastes would be discernible, even if far from realization. But an examination of next season's programs ... simply confirms that in spite of a few flourishes the Philharmonic will go on playing pretty much the same old tune."

The Israel Philharmonic

Mehta first became associated with the Israel Philharmonic in 1961 when he traveled there to substitute for Eugene Ormandy. He was an immediate success with the Israelis and in 1969 was made an "official adviser" to the orchestra. In 1977 he was made its music director, and four years later he became music director for life. Mehta loves working in Israel and feels an affinity for the Jewish people, yet he is frustrated by his inability to diminish Israeli hostility toward two composers he adores, Richard Wagner and Johann Strauss, because of their German ancestry.

Mehta has also caused controversy in Israel. He described one instance in the *New York Times Magazine:* "I brought rock into Israel for the first time, too. I had a rock group play their version of Bach's *Concerto for Two Violins.* Old subscribers shouted, 'Shame, shame.' The deputy minister of defense said 'What are you doing with our orchestra?' I said, 'Welcome to the Philharmonic Discotheque!' Frankly, I thought it sounded awful ... [but] I got all those young people to hear [classical music]."

Indian heritage

Despite living most of the year in the West, Mehta remains deeply committed to his native country and still retains his Indian citizenship. He has taken the New York Philharmonic to Bombay, and when the Festival of India came to the United States, its opening was led by Mehta conducting the Philharmonic. Mehta is deeply committed to his religious roots as well. He belongs to the Zoroastrian faith, the world's oldest monotheistic (believing in one god) religion. There is a large community of Zoroastrians in Bombay and pockets in Pakistan and Iran as well. Mehta appeared in a feature-length docudrama about the life of Zoroaster, also known as Zarathustra, the religion's founder. The film, entitled *A Question for Zarathustra,* was meant to introduce the little-understood religion to the world. Mehta told the *New York Times,* "Parsis [followers of Zoroastrianism] don't convert, so this is not a way of getting into the world religious market. It's merely an attempt to tell people what the first monotheistic religion was about."

Mehta has received numerous awards and honors for his work over the years, including the Vienna Philharmonic Ring of Honor and the Hans von Bulow medal bestowed by the Berlin Philharmonic. He was awarded the Padma Bhusan (Order of the Lotus) by the Republic of India and the Defender of Jerusalem Award by Israel. He is the only non-Israeli ever to receive the Israel Prize.

Mehta continues to be a major force in the classical music world. In 1994 he conducted a much-publicized concert at Dodger Stadium in Los Angeles that brought together three of the world's finest tenors, Jose Carreras, Placido Domingo, and Luciano Pavarotti in a rock concert-like atmosphere preceding a match at the World Cup soccer tournament. He also led a performance by the Sarajevo Symphony in the war-ravaged Bosnian capital. The concert featured Mozart's *Requiem,* or mass for the dead. Many of the symphony's musicians had died in the long, bloody war, and still others were fighting the attacking Serbian army and returned to Sarajevo for the concert, performing in their military uniforms. The worldwide broadcast of the concert was expected to raise $5 million to aid the besieged citizens of Sarajevo.

Sources:

Bernheimer, Martin, "Don't Call Him Zubi-baby," *New York,* April 5, 1978, p. 67.

Henahan, Donal, "Ruffles and Flourishes on an Old Tune," *New York Times,* April 5, 1981.

Rockwell, John, "Zubin Mehta Will Appear in a Film About Zoroaster," *New York Times,* April 10, 1985.

Stereo Review, September 1978.

Sudetic, Chuck, "In the Very Ashes of War, a Requiem for 10,000," *New York Times,* June 20, 1994.

Midori

Violinist
Born October 25, 1971, Osaka, Japan

"Midori's playing had cast such a spell that the audience's rapt attention continued through the pause between movements."—Philadelphia Inquirer

Midori—who uses only her first name—is one of the world's most celebrated violinists. She trained at the Juilliard School of Music and performed at Carnegie Hall before she was 18. And she won the respect of even the most cynical critics at age 14, when a series of broken strings forced her to complete a difficult concerto on two borrowed violins. Now in her twenties, she commands performances with world-famous ensembles: the Philadelphia Orchestra; the Maggio Musicale in Florence, Italy; the NDR Symphony Orchestra in Hamburg, Germany; La Scala Philharmonic in Milan, Italy; Orchestre de Paris in France; and Germany's Frankfurt Radio Symphony, among others.

Midori has received numerous honors, including the Los Angeles Music Center's Dorothy B. Chandler Performing Arts Award, New York State's Asian-American Heritage Month Award, and Japan's Crystal Award for her contribution to the arts. In 1992, she founded the Midori Foundation, which seeks to expose children to the arts. Midori devotes her time to the foundation by giving special concerts in schools, hospitals, and institutions where children often do not have the opportunity to come into direct contact with the arts.

Midori

The beginning of "a miracle"

Midori was born October 25, 1971, in Osaka, Japan. Her father was an engineer, her mother a professional violinist. From the beginning, her mother was her trusted friend, her coach, and her first music teacher. But, because her mother was working, the young girl often practiced on her own. "When she came home, she was cooking and I would practice in the kitchen," Midori told Robert Schwarz of the *New York Times Magazine* in 1991. Along the way, she memorized works by composers Johann Sebastian Bach, Béla Bartók, and Niccoló Paganini. When Midori was eight, an American associate of her

mother's heard her perform and made a tape, a homemade recording that also included sounds of the family dog barking in the background. The tape found its way to Dorothy DeLay, a world-renowned music teacher at the highly prestigious Juilliard School in New York. DeLay was impressed enough to bring Midori to the 1981 Aspen Music Festival as a scholarship student. Midori made her U.S. debut and, with her mother, settled in New York City.

Pinchas Zukerman, a widely acclaimed violinist and one of Midori's early idols, heard the girl perform for the first time at

Aspen. "She tuned, she bowed to the audience, she bowed to me, she bowed to the pianist—and then she played the Bartók concerto and I went bananas," he told Schwarz in the *New York Times Magazine.* "I sat there and tears started coming down my cheeks." Later, Zukerman turned to the audience and said, 'Ladies and gentlemen, I don't know about you, but I've just witnessed a miracle.'"

Study in a new land

In 1982, Midori began studying with DeLay at Juilliard's pre-college division. She rapidly learned vast amounts of music, despite the shock of adjusting to a new culture and juggling academics with music lessons, practice, and a slowly growing concert schedule. Her parent's divorce in 1983 added to this pressure. But music was a stabilizing influence that helped her face the changes in her life. Playing the violin was always her choice, she insists. Her mother never forced her to learn; she taught Midori because Midori wanted to learn.

When Midori began working with an agent, her performance schedule was carefully limited; initially, she gave no more than eight to ten performances a year, each of which was chosen to help enhance her learning process. She made her Canadian debut in 1985 with the Toronto Symphony. Midori traveled to Japan later that year to perform with Leonard Bernstein and the European Youth Orchestra in a special concert commemorating the 40th anniversary of the devastating atomic bombing of Hiroshima, Japan, by the United States, which effectively ended World War II.

On a hot and humid night in July 1986, Midori, then 14, made a now-legendary appearance at the Tanglewood Music Festival in rural Massachusetts, one of classical music's most important festivals. While playing Bernstein's "Serenade," her E string broke. She put her violin down and borrowed the concertmaster's instrument. The E string broke again. She picked up the assistant concertmaster's violin and finished her performance without a flaw. The audience went wild.

Most teenagers go through a period of rebellion, and Midori was no exception. At age 15, she decided to leave Juilliard. She continued to work with her managers at ICM Artists, who kept strict control over her schedule and made sure she gave no major recitals until she was ready. In October 1989, Midori made her New York recital debut at Carnegie Hall before a sold-out audience. Her performance was later released on a Sony Classical laser disk. The violinist later confided that she was not nervous. "I feel so comfortable onstage; I feel safest," she told Schwarz. "The best part of giving concerts is just being out there and playing, nothing else."

Now, as a full-time professional performer, Midori gives about 80 recitals a year, traveling to 30 cities on both sides of the Atlantic. She records exclusively for the Sony Classical record label.

Mature artist

Barely five feet tall, with delicate features, Midori often looks fragile and vulnerable onstage. She was perhaps one of the most-watched child sensations of her time.

In fact, many wondered whether her extraordinary childhood talent would mature into a sophisticated level of artistry. Or, would she, like so many other child stars, stumble? She did not.

A 1993 recital tour and three separate performances of the Sibelius Violin Concerto drew rave reviews. The *Los Angeles Times* reported that Midori played "with all the passion, authority, ease and penetrating detail one has come to expect of all her performances." And the *Philadelphia Inquirer* remarked, "Midori's playing had cast such a spell that the audience's rapt attention continued through the pause between movements."

As she grows older, Midori's challenge will be to continue to let her sense of her music mature with her. Schwarz recalled one particularly vivid and revealing image of Midori: After a rehearsal, she stood on a stage, playing a difficult solo. Nearby, stage equipment was noisily being taken apart. Midori, lost in her music, didn't appear to notice the commotion. Swaying, bending into her violin, she played on.

Sources:

Cariaga, Daniel, "More Volume than Finesse at the Bowl," *Los Angeles Times,* August 27, 1993.

Goodman, Peter, "Midori: No Longer Just a Superstar," *New York Newsday,* September 27, 1993.

Schwarz, K. Robert, "Glissando," *New York Times Magazine,* March 24, 1991.

Valdes, Lesley, "Haydn with a Twinkle, Spellbinding Sibelius," *Philadelphia Inquirer,* September 23, 1993.

Dale Minami

Attorney, activist
Born October 13, 1946, Los Angeles, California

Minami founded the Asian Law Caucus, the Asian American Bar Association, and the Asian Pacific Bar of California.

Dale Minami is the founder of several civil rights and political advocacy organizations that work on behalf of the Asian American community in the San Francisco Bay Area in California and across the country. Among the organizations he has founded are the Asian Law Caucus, the Asian American Bar Association, and the Asian Pacific Bar of California. The Asian Law Caucus has represented the Asian American community in many prominent cases, including the landmark 1987 appeal of the **Fred Korematsu** case, in which a World War II internment resister's conviction for ignoring internment orders was overturned. In the political arena, Minami has served as co-chair of Northern California Asian Pacific Americans for the Clinton/Gore presidential campaign in 1992 and as a member of California senator Barbara Boxer's judicial screening committee.

Born after the internment

Minami's father, a second-generation Japanese American, was a gardener and owner of a small sporting goods store. During World War II, the family was "interned" with 120,000 other Americans of Japanese ancestry living on the West Coast on the government's premise that they would be security risks in the event of a Japanese invasion. The family home and business were taken away, and the family was sent to live in a horse stable at the Santa Anita raceway. From there they were shipped to their final destination, an internment camp in Rowher, Arkansas, where they stayed for the duration of the war.

After their release, the Minami family moved to Los Angeles, where Minami was born in 1946. He was educated in the public school system and graduated from high school in 1964. He then enrolled in the University of Southern California, where he received a bachelor's degree in 1968, graduating *magna cum laude* (with high honors) and as a member of the honor society, Phi Beta Kappa. Following his graduation he went on to the University of California at Berkeley's School of Law, one of the finest law schools in the country. He earned his law degree in 1971 and was admitted to the California Bar in January 1972.

During his time on the campus of Berkeley, the university was wracked by student unrest. There were protests against American involvement in the war in Vietnam, but there were also protests by minority students demanding a less European-dominated curriculum. These protests, known as the Third World Strikes, had a profound impact on higher education that is still being felt today in the debates over political correctness (the use of language and practices designed to eliminate offending others, particularly in terms of race, class, or gender) and multiculturalism (the recognition that diverse cultures—and their unique attributes and

Dale Minami

histories—make up the nation). They also had a major impact on Minami, who for the first time felt the power of concerted, organized dissent.

Following graduation from law school, Minami opened a private practice that specialized in personal injury, entertainment law, and civil litigation. He also began teaching and spent one year as an instructor at Mills College in the department of ethnic studies. He became a lecturer at the University of California at Berkeley in Asian American studies as well.

Asian Law Caucus

In the early 1970s Ken Kawaichi (now a superior court judge) and Minami began working toward establishing the Asian Law Caucus (ALC), a legal advocacy organization dedicated to helping the Asian American community in the areas of civil rights, employment and housing discrimination, and immigration. They co-founded the organization in 1972, and Minami became its first attorney. He handled all cases and wrote proposals for funding. Getting the money to start the ALC was fairly easy, but maintaining its operations proved problematic until it was granted a special tax status that allowed it to charge nominal fees—something nonprofit organizations are generally not allowed to do. Minami served as director of the ALC for three years, during which time he also taught at Berkeley and continued in his private practice.

One of the ALC's first prominent cases was *Chan* v. *City and County of California,* in which the ALC represented Barry Chan, a photography student at Berkeley. Chan had been in San Francisco's Chinatown one day when he noticed police engaged in what looked like a random round-up of Asian American men; the officers were handcuffing them and taking them in to the station to be fingerprinted and photographed. Chan began snapping pictures, and when an officer noticed him, he came over and broke Chan's camera and handcuffed him. The ALC was alerted to the case by Chan, and they brought suit against the city. The city defended these blatantly unconstitutional sweeps as necessary to fight Asian gang violence. The ALC publicized this practice and a huge public uproar ensued that caused the

city to settle the case before trial, with promises to end this discriminatory practice.

Another prominent ALC case was *Wong* v. *Younger,* in which the ALC sued the attorney general of California to halt distribution of a pamphlet that depicted Asians as criminals, suggesting, among other things, that the Chinese love to gamble and smoke opium. The case was lost on First Amendment grounds (the right to free speech), but the publicity generated by it caused the state to discontinue use of the pamphlets.

Private practice

Minami left the ALC in 1975 to devote more time to his private practice. In 1989 he formed the law firm of Minami, Lew, Takami and Lee, headquartered in San Francisco. He continues to specialize in employment discrimination and personal injury law. He also works as an entertainment lawyer, representing clients that include such noted Asian Americans as playwright **Philip Kan Gotanda,** the actor **Mako,** and **Kristi Yamaguchi,** the figure skater.

In addition to co-founding the Asian Law Caucus, Minami co-founded the Asian American Bar Association of the Greater Bay Area in 1976, the first Asian American bar association in the United States. In 1988 he co-founded the Asian Pacific Bar of California, a statewide consortium of Asian Pacific bar associations. And in 1989 he co-founded the Coalition of Asian Pacific Americans, the first Asian Pacific political action committee, which lobbies locally and nationally for issues of concern to the Asian community. Minami has lectured and published extensively and has received many awards for his career of service. Among these are the State Bar of California's President's Pro Bono Service Award (1984), the Coro Foundation Achievement Award (1986), the Harry Dow Memorial Fellowship "Justice in Action" Award (1988), and the Organization of Chinese Americans Leadership Award (1989).

Sources:

Minami, Dale, telephone interview with Jim Henry, August 4, 1994.

Minami, Lew, Takami and Lee, "Personal Resume of Dale Minami," August 1994.

Norman Y. Mineta

U.S. congressman
Born November 12, 1931, San Jose, California

"Injustice does not dim with time. We cannot wait it out. We cannot ignore it, and we cannot shrug our shoulders at our past. If we do not refute the shame of the indictment here and now, the specter of the tragedy will resurface ... and the injustice will recur."

Norman Yoshio Mineta represents one of the nation's most populous congressional districts—California's fifteenth—which includes the south San Francisco Bay, part of the city of San Jose, and a large chunk of Santa Clara and Santa Cruz counties. As chair of the House of Representatives' powerful Committee on Public Works and Transportation, Mineta wields considerable influence, for it is up to this committee to determine how the nation should deal with its four million miles of highways and bridges, and 438 mass-transit systems. And, as *A. Magazine* noted in December 1993, "with the nation's highways and railroads careening toward disaster, Mineta's role in the House is likely to balloon in the years to come."

Yet, of all his many achievements, one in particular stands out in most people's minds when they think of Norman Mineta. Hundreds of thousands of citizens know him for the role he played in 1987, when in the historic 100th Congress, he and another Japanese American congressman convinced their colleagues to approve a measure offering an official apology from the federal government and a $1.2 billion award, or redress, to the 120,000 Japanese Americans, who, like themselves, were forced to move from their homes during World War II into isolated relocation camps.

The dream is shattered

Born in 1931 in San Jose, Mineta was the son of Japanese immigrants. His father had emigrated from Japan in 1902, and his mother had come in 1912. Neither, however, could become U.S. citizens because of the Oriental Exclusion Law of 1924. Nevertheless, Mineta's father, believing in the American dream like many immigrants, established an insurance agency in 1920. The family's life was relatively stable until Japanese troops bombed Pearl Harbor in 1941, essentially forcing the United States to enter World War II.

In early 1942, the federal government, acting under an executive order, began to remove Americans of Japanese ancestry from their homes to relocation camps. Families

Norman Y. Mineta

often were given only a few hours to dispose of property and set their affairs in order before troops came. They were then allowed to carry only what possessions they could handle in their arms.

The internment begins

Mineta remembers one night in early 1942 when his father called the family together. "He said he did not know what the war would bring to my mother and to him, since they were resident aliens," Mineta said during the House of Representatives debate on the redress issue. "However, he was confident that his beloved country would guarantee and protect the rights of his children, American citizens, all. But his confidence, as it turned out, was misplaced."

On May 29, 1942, the Mineta family received word that it would be relocated. With armed guards watching, Mineta's father loaded his family onto a train. Mineta, age ten, was wearing a Cub Scout uniform as the train headed for a relocation camp in Wyoming.

Mineta's father described in a letter to friends in San Jose what happened as the train pulled out. In his remarks to Congress, Mineta quoted from the letter: "I looked at Santa Clara's streets from the train over the subway. I thought this might be the last look at my beloved home city. My heart almost broke, and suddenly hot tears came pouring out, and the whole family cried out, could not stop, until we were out of our loved county."

For three years Mineta's family remained in the camp. At the end of World War II, he and his family—like thousands of other Japanese Americans—returned to their homes and picked up the pieces of their previous lives.

From civic involvement to the mayor's chair

Mineta went to San Jose High School and later to the University of California, Berkeley, where he earned a bachelor's degree in business in 1953. He joined the army and served as a military intelligence officer during tours of duty in Japan and Korea. Meanwhile, his father reopened his insurance agency, and when Mineta left active army service in 1956, he went to work for his father.

Over time, as a business executive who believed in active community involvement, Mineta became involved with the Japanese American Citizens League, the Greater San Jose Chamber of Commerce, the Rotary Club, and other civic groups. Community involvement led to government involvement. In 1962, he became a member of San Jose's Human Relations Commission, then later served on the city's Housing Authority.

In 1967, he was appointed to fill a vacancy on the city council and became San Jose's first minority councilman. He was elected to the council seat in 1969 and decided to run for mayor of San Jose in 1971. When elected, he became the first Japanese American mayor of a major city. He quickly established himself as an aggressive spokesperson for the needs of urban areas. At the time, the San Jose area was growing considerably, and Mineta called for limits on the city's growth.

National politics

Mineta's rising in political ranks continued through the 1970s. He ran for Congress as a Democrat in 1974, drawing broad support from a small but close-knit Japanese American community in San Jose and winning a seat long held by Republicans. He became part of a new Democratic leadership—as one of seventy-five reform-minded Democrats elected to Congress that year.

In Congress, his influence continued to grow. He was deputy whip for the House Democratic Leadership and served on the Budget Committee, the Policy and Steering Committee, and the Post Office and Civil Service Committee. He also held several chairs on subcommittees under the Public

Works and Transportation Committee he now heads. When elected to chair the Public Works and Transportation Committee in 1992, he assumed a very powerful place in Congress.

Righting the wrongs

But even as Mineta climbed the ranks politically, a feeling of shame lived within him, as it did within many Japanese Americans who had tried for decades to forget World War II, the executive order, and living in the relocation camps. For Mineta, this sense of shame was channeled into a desire to right wrongs. He had wanted to obtain some form of compensation for Japanese Americans for more than a decade. In 1978, he won passage of a bill to grant previously denied retirement benefits to Japanese American civil servants who had been interned in the camps. But his fight for full justice continued.

In 1987, when the bill for redress for internment came to the floor of the House of Representatives, Mineta urged members of Congress to right the wrongs of the past: "We lost our homes, we lost our businesses, we lost our farms, but worst of all, we lost our most basic human rights," he said. "Our own government had branded us with the unwarranted stigma of disloyalty which clings to us still to this day."

"Injustice does not dim with time," he added. "We cannot wait it out. We cannot ignore it, and we cannot shrug our shoulders at our past. If we do not refute the shame of the indictment here and now, the specter of this tragedy will resurface just as surely as I am standing here before you, and the injustice will recur.... The bill's impact reaches much deeper into the very soul of our democracy. Those of us who support this bill want not just to close the books on the sad events of 1942; we want to make sure that such blatant constitutional violations never occur again."

Continuing the fight for all people's rights

After Congress passed the legislation, Mineta signed the bill on behalf of the House. In October 1990, the first government letters of apology and redress payments of $20,000 went out to victims of internment camps. About half of those who had been interned, however, did not live to see the redress, some 40 years after the injustice occurred. Apology letters and redress payments were directed to their heirs.

For Mineta, the chapter on discrimination had not completely closed. He later pushed for legislation authorizing a memorial honoring Japanese Americans who served in the military, and he helped pass the Americans with Disabilities Act, which requires businesses and public buildings to make their facilities more accessible to people with disabilities.

And when the Persian Gulf War began in 1991, Mineta urged federal law enforcement officials not to target Arab Americans—he didn't want the same discrimination that occurred during World War II to happen again.

Sources:

Kenworthy, Tom, "House Votes Apology, Reparations for Japanese Americans Held During War," *Washington Post*, February 18, 1991.

Mineta, Norman, "Nation's Transportation Moving into a Crossroads," *Nations Cities Weekly*, February 18, 1991.

"Power Brokers," *A. Magazine*, December 15, 1993, pp. 25-34.

Tumulty, Karen, "House Votes to Pay Japanese WWII Internees," *Los Angeles Times*, September 18, 1987.

Patsy Mink

Legislator, lawyer
Born 1927, Maui, Hawaii

Mink believes that every citizen has the obligation to think independently and challenge the power structure of American society if he or she believes this course is warranted.

Patsy Takemoto Mink was the first Asian American woman and the first Hawaiian woman elected to Congress. Her 30-year political career has included eight terms as Hawaii's delegate in the U.S. House of Representatives and numerous other terms as a lawmaker at the state and municipal levels. She was also one of the first Japanese American women to practice law in Hawaii.

Throughout her life and career, Mink has supported legislative reforms in health care, education, women's rights, environmental affairs, cancer research, and employment. She has often taken unpopular positions on these and other issues, believing that every citizen has the obligation to think independently and challenge the power structure of American society if he or she believes this course is warranted.

Comfortable beginnings

Mink's father was a civil engineer who was able to afford an upper-middle-class lifestyle for his family. The family lived in a comfortable cottage on two acres of land. This was quite different from the humble living conditions of many other Hawaiians. Mink demonstrated an independent streak early on. She insisted on starting school when she was four years old, a year earlier than is generally expected. In another break from custom, she later attended the all-European American Kaunoa English Standard School, which rarely admitted students of color. Because of the long travel time to the new school and the often unfriendly environment, Mink spent much of her time reading and listening to the radio. Learning about leaders like India's Mahatma Gandhi led her to dream about becoming a doctor, a career she had considered since undergoing surgery for appendicitis at the age of four.

Mink's experiences at school became even more unpleasant when the Japanese attacked Pearl Harbor and Japanese Americans throughout the United States were forced to report to internment camps. (The government said this unconstitutional act was a precautionary measure, because in the event of a Japanese invasion of the West Coast, Japanese Americans might be tempted to assist the Japanese). Though they were allowed to remain in their homes, Mink and others of Japanese descent in Hawaii were frequently reminded that they were considered the enemy of the United States. Eventually, Mink transferred to Maui High School, where her career interests turned to politics.

Patsy Mink

After graduating first in her class from high school, Mink enrolled at the University of Hawaii, where she was elected president of the Premedical Students Club and chosen as a member of the Varsity Debate Team. She left the University of Hawaii following her sophomore year and ultimately graduated from the University of Nebraska, with stops at two other colleges along the way. Her first year after graduation was frustrating; every medical school to which she applied rejected her. She worked at a clerk-typist job in a small museum in Honolulu while trying to decide what to do next.

Political interest grows

Then an adviser suggested that she go to law school. She was soon admitted at the University of Chicago, where she met John Mink, a graduate student in geophysics. Despite opposition from her parents, the two married six months later, in January 1951.

Although John found a job immediately after graduation, Mink was unable to find work. Not only was she a woman, but she was an Asian American woman in an interracial marriage, and no one would hire her. She was forced to return to her student job at the law school. She continued to receive employment rejections even after the couple had moved back to Hawaii and Mink had passed the Hawaii Bar Exam. Not one to accept defeat easily, however, Mink started her own law practice with some help from her father. She took divorce, criminal defense, adoption, and other cases that didn't interest established law firms. She also taught business classes at the University of Hawaii.

In 1954 Mink was elected president of the Young Democrats, a powerful political group that grew out of an organization that Mink had founded called Everyman's Organization. Mink had established this group to push for Democratic party participation among young Democrats.

Between 1957 and 1964 Mink held elected positions as a representative and a senator in the legislature of Hawaii, which until 1959 was a U.S. territory. There she developed a reputation for supporting the underdog. As a senator she authored the "Equal Pay for Equal Work" law, and, while serving as a representative, she sponsored a successful resolution protesting Great Britain's nuclear testing in the South Pacific.

Six-term congresswoman

Mink took the oath of office in January 1965 for the first of six consecutive terms as U.S. representative. While a member of the House, she supported the regulation of strip mining, sponsored the Women's Educational Equity Act, opposed the U.S. role in the Vietnam War when it was still politically risky to do so, and successfully sued the federal government in a Freedom of Information Act case. That case later helped prosecutors obtain secretly recorded tapes that contained key evidence relevant to prosecution of the Watergate conspirators. (The Watergate Scandal, which exposed criminal misdeeds in then-President Richard Nixon's reelection campaign, ultimately led to his forced resignation as president.) Mink was also involved in legislation regarding education and child care issues.

Mink became the first Asian American to run for the presidency in 1972. Both that campaign and a later run for the U.S. Senate were unsuccessful. Mink served for three years in the administration of President Jimmy Carter as Assistant Secretary of State for Ocean and International, Environmental and Scientific Affairs. She resigned in 1980 to serve for three straight terms as national president of the Americans for Democratic Action.

More lawmaking

Mink returned to Hawaiian politics in 1983, when she was elected to the Honolulu City Council. She served there for four years. And though she was defeated in races for governor of Hawaii in 1986 and mayor of Honolulu in 1988, Mink won an election in 1990 to serve the remainder of

Representative **Daniel Akaka**'s term in the U.S. House; Akaka had been appointed to the Senate seat left vacant after the sudden death of Senator Spark Matsunaga that year.

In 1991 Mink authored legislation that enabled more would-be students to qualify for federal aid to help pay for a college education. In 1992 she introduced legislation that provided full funding of the Headstart Program (a federal program for pre-schoolers created by President Lyndon B. Johnson in his "War on Poverty") and increased federal funding levels for secondary and elementary schools. Despite her belief that "women who have a brain and an idea" will face hostility in public life, Mink never shied away from such hostility during her highly successful career as a lawmaker.

Sources:

Mink, Patsy Takemoto, resume and press release provided by Mink, 1994.

Pat Morita

Actor
Born June 28, 1933, Isleton, California

"You always want to give up in this business, but something inside you says, 'You've gotta keep going.'"

Noriyuki "Pat" Morita is a film and television actor perhaps best known for his role as the karate master in the *Karate Kid* films. The first of the series,

The Karate Kid, an unexpected critical and commercial success, earned Morita an Academy Award nomination. He also appeared in the film's sequels, *The Karate Kid: Part II* and *The Karate Kid III.* Earlier in his career he was a regular on television programs including *Sanford and Son* and *Happy Days.*

Born in poverty

Morita's father was a migrant farmer in the fruit orchards of California—an extremely difficult, very low-paying type of work. Morita was a sickly child, suffering from spinal tuberculosis, at that time usually a fatal disease. He spent almost the entirety of his childhood, from age two to 11, in the hospital and did not learn to walk until he was 11 years old. It was during this long hospital stay that Morita acquired his American nickname. He told the *New York Daily News,* "There was this wonderful priest who used to visit me all the time.... At one point he wanted to baptize me, and he picked out my name. I was to be Patrick Aloysius Ignatius Xavier Morita.... But he'd always call me Pat when he stopped by, and the name kind of stuck."

From hospital to internment camp

Just as Morita was finally free from his many years of hospitalization, World War II broke out. In response to anti-Japanese hysteria brought about by Japan's bombing of the U.S. Naval base at Pearl Harbor, Hawaii, then a U.S. territory, the U.S. government issued a blatantly unconstitutional order to imprison Americans of Japanese descent in what were called internment camps. (It was believed that in the event of a Japanese invasion of the West Coast, Japanese Americans in the West might aid the Japanese.) The government seized what little the Morita family owned, and they were sent to a prison camp in Arizona. Morita recalled the years he spent as a prisoner in his own country in *People,* explaining, "I went from being an ailing child to a public enemy. I became 'Jap' overnight. These were enormously difficult years for our people. Suicides, people walking into the desert never to be seen again. Or hanging themselves. It was horrible. Horrible."

After internment

When the family was released, they moved to Fairfield, California, 40 miles from Sacramento, the state's capital, where Morita's father opened a Chinese restaurant in a predominantly black neighborhood. Morita attended public schools and tried college briefly before giving it up to work with his family at the restaurant. He got married and had a daughter.

When the family restaurant closed, Morita found a job at Aerojet-General Corporation near Sacramento. The job provided the young man with a steady income, but it was tedious. He told *Cable Guide,* "That job was just laborious for me. I didn't have a degree so I felt like a second-class citizen. And all the time there was this huge machinery talking back at me or people telling me that I've got to make sure the computer goes on at 6:55 in the morning.... It drove me nuts."

Morita's dissatisfaction with this job and the prospect of working in so lifeless an environment brought to the surface a

lifelong desire buried for many years: he wanted to go into show business. He had dreamed of being an actor most of his life but simply felt that it was out of his reach; his unhappiness, though, drove him to make the effort. Friends told him he was funny, so he decided to attempt a career in stand-up comedy.

The "Hip Nip"

Morita got his first break in 1964, when he was working as the emcee of a Japanese nightclub in San Francisco. As an emcee, Morita would introduce the night's acts and do a little stand-up between performances. The popular singer Sam Cooke had been shot, and the owner of the famed Copacabana in Los Angeles needed someone to fill the bill. Morita's agent, Sally Marr (comedian Lenny Bruce's mother), got Morita the show. He billed himself as the "Hip Nip" and went on that night. He continued performing for many years under that name. Today such a name may sound racist or self-denigrating, but at the time Morita was one of a number of minority comedians who drew attention to their ethnic heritage, using social stereotypes in their nicknames in an attempt to diffuse the negative power those names had.

Morita's act from this period was reviewed in the *Newark Evening News* in 1969. He told the paper: "The early part of my act is devoted to Oriental gags, exploding myths. For instance, I tell 'em I'm not going to give a demonstration in flower arrangement. I also say that I thought about a karate exhibition, but it smarts too much.... Then I tell them that being Japanese has its problems. The Negroes can't work much during the sit-ins, and the Jewish comedians

Pat Morita

also began working in television, landing small parts on shows like *Love American Style* and *Hawaii Five-0*. In 1973, Morita got his big television break when he was offered the role of Al, the local restaurant owner on the television show *Happy Days*.

Morita left *Happy Days* after just two seasons to star in his own series, *Mr. T. and Tina*. It was a risky move, leaving an established success for an unknown show, but Morita felt confident about it. The show did not last, however. This misfortune was followed by several others in the next few years, both personal and professional; Morita's home in Tarzana, California, was destroyed by a storm, his second wife's mother died, and then his youngest daughter, Tia, was diagnosed with kidney disease. In 1980, Morita left his second wife and moved to Hawaii, where he stayed for two years. When he returned to Los Angeles in 1982 for a role that never materialized, he and his wife reconciled.

The Karate Kid

In 1984, Morita was hired to play Miyagi, the martial arts master in the movie *The Karate Kid*. Getting the role had been difficult. The producer of the film, Jerry Weintraub, told *People,* "I didn't want him. I've known Pat for 20 years and used to book him into the Catskill hotels when I was a kid. But his audition made me cry." The film was made for the relatively modest sum of $10 million and nothing much was expected of it. Even Morita was skeptical about *The Karate Kid's* success, admitting, "I thought the film would be a summer in-and-outer like *Porky's* or *Police Academy*." *The Karate Kid* ended up taking in over

find things slow during Yom Kippur. Me, I don't get any work around December 7th," referring to the anniversary of the Japanese attack on Pearl Harbor. The *Evening News* went on to note that Morita, a native-born American, "bears no trace of a Japanese accent"!

Success

In the late 1960s and early 1970s, Morita was a much sought-after opening act for performers such as comedian Redd Foxx and singers Vic Damone and Connie Francis. He

$100 million, a 1,000 percent profit. It also earned Morita an Academy Award nomination. In 1986, *The Karate Kid: Part II* was released, and in 1989, *The Karate Kid III* hit the theaters.

In 1991, Morita continued his film career in *Do or Die.* The following year he made *Goodbye Paradise,* which was a critical success. His next two films, however, were not very well received; *Even Cowgirls Get the Blues,* based on the wildly popular Tom Robbins novel, was ridiculed on its release and quickly disappeared. And then, in 1994, Morita made *The Next Karate Kid.* This time Miyagi's student was a girl. The film was a commercial and critical flop. Also in 1994, Morita tried his luck with a television series, starring in a pilot called *Greyhounds* for CBS. The show featured Morita, Dennis Weaver, and Robert Guillaume as retired cops who team with a retired con man to solve crimes. It was not picked up for further broadcast.

Morita worked long and hard for many years as a character actor and bit player before receiving his Oscar nomination. He often considered giving up show business altogether. He told the *Cable Guide:* "You always want to give up in this business, but something inside you says, 'You've gotta keep going. This is it, bottom line, you can't get any lower than this. The valley's gone. But in order to get good, you've got to get to that spot. I know I had to get there a few times, and I'm sure that everyone I've worked with has had more than their share of the bottom line. Success, in whatever form, doesn't come to the undeserving. Those of us that hit a measure of it certainly have earned it."

Sources:

Brady, James, "In Step with: Pat Morita," *Parade Magazine,* February 21, 1988, p. 22.

Burden, Martin, "Money-Making Martial Art," *New York Post,* June 26, 1989, p. 23.

Livingston, David, "Close-Up: Pat Morita," *Cable Guide,* October 1985, pp. 39-40.

O'Haire, Patricia, "You Mean He Can't Even Do One Little Chop?," *New York Daily News,* June 19, 1986.

Stark, John, "After a Lifetime of Misfortune, *Karate Kid's* Noriyuki 'Pat' Morita Battles His Way to a Happy Ending," *People,* June 30, 1986, pp. 101-2.

William Mow

Entrepreneur
Born 1936, Hangchow, China

"I felt that anybody who could invent equipment with millions of wires and hundreds of thousands of components ... should be able to make a pair of pants.... How wrong I was."

William C. W. Mow is the chair and chief executive officer (CEO) of the clothing manufacturer Bugle Boy Industries. Mow started Bugle Boy in 1977 after losing control of Macrodata, a computer industry firm of which he was chairman and CEO, during a bruising legal battle. At the time, Mow knew nothing about the apparel industry—he holds a Ph.D. in electrical engineering—but he had a keen sense of business and marketing. In the mid-1990s, Bugle Boy had sales in excess of $500 million annually, and as 90 percent owner of the privately held company, Mow was personally worth several hundred million dollars.

William Mow

Son of a Chinese diplomat

Mow's father was an important United Nations' official in New York City; he was chief of the military committee representing Chiang Kai-shek's Nationalist Chinese government when Communist leader Mao Zedong's revolution defeated the Nationalist military in China. As a high-ranking member of the defeated government, the elder Mow chose wisely not to return to China and instead had his family join him in America, where they started over and built a new life.

Mow grew up in Great Neck, New York, and worked his way through Rensselaer Polytechnic Institute in New York, where he studied electrical engineering. In 1967 he earned his Ph.D. in electrical engineering from Purdue University. Mow credits much of his later success in life to the emphasis his family placed on education when he was a child. All but one of his four brothers have Ph.D.s; the fourth is an architect.

After graduating from Purdue, Mow moved to California and went to work for Litton Industries. In 1969 he left this job to start his own company, Macrodata, hoping to cash in on the then very young computer industry. Mow eventually sold control of his company to a conglomerate, hoping that with someone else handling management, he would be free to explore the science and technology of the industry. The relationship instead was characterized by mistrust, and Mow was sued by the conglomerate. Mow then countersued. (The case was finally settled out of court in 1988, with an $850,000 payment to Mow.)

The beginning of Bugle Boy

In the mid-1970s, Mow found himself with devastating legal bills and unable to work in the electronics industry because of a non-compete clause in his agreement with the conglomerate that had purchased Macrodata. He told *Nation's Business,* "I had to get myself into a financial position where I could defend myself." He then met some people in the apparel industry who told him of a niche he might want to explore—helping Asian manufacturers import into the United States. Mow had family living in Taiwan and felt that this, combined with his

Asian heritage and American upbringing, would position him perfectly for such a business. He began importing in 1976.

This taste of fashion whetted Mow's appetite, and he wanted to get involved further. In 1977 he formed Buckaroo International, with an executive of a designer jeans company as his partner. Buckaroo sold its creations under the Bugle Boy label. Mow described his apprenticeship years in *Nation's Business,* saying, "I felt confident I could do it. I felt that anybody who could invent equipment with millions of wires and hundreds of thousands of components, measuring accurately to a billionth of a second, should be able to make a pair of pants.... How wrong I was."

The beginnings of success

Bugle Boy suffered for a few years as Mow blindly made his way through the fashion world, about which, he readily admits, he knew almost nothing. In 1981 he promoted Vincent Nesi, who had considerable retail experience, to president and then began researching which countries produced what kind of apparel best and at the cheapest prices.

In 1983 Bugle Boy had its first big success with what were called parachute pants—baggy, casual pants made of woven nylon. They were an enormous fad with young people and Bugle Boy began to rely on their sales, not anticipating that, like all fads, the parachute pants craze would end. Since then, Bugle Boy has been wary of investing in fads, seeking instead to "create a label that consumers love. We deliver fresh product to the store virtually every month," Mow said. In subsequent years, Bugle Boy continued to diversify its lines; in 1984 it launched the boys and junior divisions, and in 1987 it launched products aimed at men and girls. The next year Bugle Boy premiered the jeans and misses divisions, signed their first foreign license (with Canada; a foreign license is an arrangement in which a company lends its name to a product made by another manufacturer in return for a share of resulting profits), and began one of the most successful and talked about advertising campaigns in recent fashion advertising.

The Bugle Boy ad

Bugle Boy began an advertising campaign featuring large bus shelter ads in 1984. The ads often did not display a specific product, just a striking picture and the name Bugle Boy. "In the beginning, people didn't know what Bugle Boy was," Mow said. "They thought it was toilet paper or cigarettes." The confusion got people talking, and with particular graphics, the ads began to portray an image, a crucial factor in the success of a fashion product. Over time, the advertising strategy has proven successful and has earned attention for its inventiveness. *Adweek's Marketing Week* ran a story specifically about the campaign in 1990 called "Bugle Boy's Guerrilla Tactics." In that story, Suzi Sheimann, advertising manager for Bugle Boy, said, "We liked the visual approach of that large logo. It met our objectives of getting the brand out to the marketplace. It gave us an on-street consistent awareness. And at the time it wasn't being done by others in the fashion industry."

Another popular ad campaign, this one made famous on television, depicted a male hitchhiker standing on the side of a deserted country road. A sleek sports car pulls up and the driver rolls down the window. Inside is a beautiful woman who asks the young man, "Are those Bugle Boy jeans you're wearing?" The man answers, "Why yes, they are Bugle Boy jeans." The woman responds, "I thought so," and drives off. The phrase "Are those Bugle Boy jeans you're wearing?" became very popular and variations of the ad followed.

Today Bugle Boy sells to more than 7,000 department and specialty stores. Products are mostly manufactured outside the United States, where labor is cheap. The line is sold all over the world, with licensing agreements with Japan and other East Asian countries, Australia, New Zealand, Mexico, Spain, and the Caribbean Basin. The company is headquartered in Simi Valley, California, in a 325,000-square-foot complex.

Mow and his wife have two small children. He also has two grown children from a previous marriage.

Sources:

Barrier, Michael, "From Riches to 'Rags'—and Riches," *Nation's Business,* January 1991, p. 32.

Bugle Boy Industries, "Dr. William C. W. Mow," biographical information, Simi Valley, California, March 1994.

Mow, William, interview with Helen Zia, June 1994.

Dhan Gopal Mukerji

Author
Born July 6, 1890, near Calcutta, India
Died July 14, 1936, New York City

"The work I consider the most valuable juvenile book I have written is Ghond, the Hunter. *In it, I have sought to render the inmost things of Hindu life into English."*

Dhan Gopal Mukerji was a prolific writer of poetry, plays, children's literature, and religious works. He was a former Hindu priest from India's Brahmin caste who gave up the religious life his family had been living for centuries to pursue an education and a Western lifestyle. He was active in the Indian independence movement, but he died, by suicide, before his country was able to throw off the colonial rule of Britain.

Of the dozens of volumes Mukerji published in his abbreviated lifetime, he is best known for his children's books. In 1927 his work *Gay-Neck: The Story of a Pigeon* was named one of the best 50 books of the year by the American Institute of Graphic Arts. He was named to that list again in 1928 for his book *Ghond, the Hunter.* Also in 1928 Mukerji received the highest honor given to writers of children's literature when he won that year's Newbery Medal from the American Library Association for *Gay-Neck.*

Brahmin by birth

India's traditional Hindu society is made up of a structured caste system that defines people's stations in life by the class into which they are born. Mukerji was born into the Brahmins, an aristocratic class in which priests are traditionally raised. His family had managed the Hindu temple in his native village, just outside of Calcutta, for generations.

As a teenager, Mukerji followed the dictates of the Brahmin caste and entered study for the priesthood. Before he would actually become a priest, however, Mukerji decided to spend some time traveling so he could see other ways of life. He set off on what would become a two-year journey around India and other countries of South and Southeast Asia, living as a beggar. These travels had a profound impact on the young man, and when he returned to his village he decided that the priesthood, which he actually did assume for a brief time, was not what he wanted. To go against the caste system in such a brazen way was a very difficult thing to do in a tradition-bound culture like turn-of-the-century India, but Mukerji was determined to pursue the life he wanted, no matter what tradition allowed.

The life he desired was the academic one. He first went to college in India at the University of Calcutta but then transferred to the University of Tokyo, where he earned an undergraduate degree in 1909. The following year, Mukerji immigrated to the United States and enrolled in Stanford University in California, where he studied comparative literature and earned a doctorate in 1914. After his graduation Mukerji stayed briefly at Stanford, where he was a lecturer in comparative literature.

The writing life

During this period, Mukerji began writing. In 1914 he collaborated on a play with Mary Carolyn Davies. *Chintamini: A Symbolic Play* was based on another play and was first published the year Mukerji graduated from Stanford. During the following three years, Mukerji published another play, *Layla-Majnu,* and two volumes of poetry, *Rajani: Songs of the Night* and *Sandhyu: Songs of Twilight.* In 1918 Mukerji married Ethel Ray Dugan, a teacher. The couple had one child, a son named Dhan Gopal II.

In 1922 Mukerji published his first children's book. Entitled *Kari, the Elephant,* the book established what would become Mukerji trademarks: animal characters in a jungle setting engaged in a spiritual journey. That year he also published another play, *The Judgment of India.* In 1923 Mukerji published his first work of nonfiction, an autobiography called *Caste and Outcast* that detailed the rigidity of India's caste system and his troubles as an Asian American early in the century. That same year, he completed his second children's book, *Jungle Beasts and Men,* a collection filled with exciting descriptions of the jungle life he had known as a young boy as told by its animal inhabitants. Margery Fisher, writing in the magazine *Growing Point,* said that in this book Mukerji created "a piercingly real picture of the jungle and those who are native to it." In 1924 Mukerji published two more books, as he had in each of the preceding two years: one a children's book and one a work of nonfiction. The children's book was called *Hari, the Jungle Lad* and the work of nonfiction was called *My Brother's Face.*

A tremendous output

Mukerji was producing books at a prolific rate, averaging about two a year for most of the 1920s. In 1926 he published his first novel, *The Secret Listeners of the East,* and in 1928 he produced what would become his most famous work, the children's book *Gay-Neck: The Story of a Pigeon.* The tale tells the story of a pigeon who accompanies his owner, Ghond, through a series of adventures as they make their way through a jungle engulfed in a conflict Mukerji calls the Great War. The book received excellent reviews and was awarded children's literature's highest honor, the Newberry Medal.

Soon after, Mukerji published a sequel to *Gay-Neck* called *Ghond, the Hunter.* Like its predecessor, *Ghond* was highly acclaimed and sold very well. Clyde Fisher, writing in the *Saturday Review of Literature,* called it a "truly a great story of the jungle and its inhabitants." Mukerji himself felt that *Ghond* was his finest effort; he wrote in the introduction to his *Bunny, Hound, and Clown,* "The work I consider the most valuable juvenile book I have written is *Ghond, the Hunter.* In it, I have sought to render the inmost things of Hindu life into English."

This was the essential quest in most of Mukerji's writing: to bring the West to understand Hinduism. In 1929 he edited an English translation of Hindu religious works called *Devotional Passages from the Hindu Bible.* In 1931 he was both editor and translator for the publication of *The Song of God: Translation of the Bagavadgita,* Hinduism's holy book. Two years later, he published *Daily Meditation: or, The Practice of Repose,* and in 1934, *The Practice of Prayer.*

Gay-Neck and *Ghond* proved to be Mukerji's most successful works, and after their publication he continued to produce children's literature to good reviews and a growing reputation. In 1936, however, eight days after his 46th birthday, Mukerji took his own life by hanging himself at his home in New York City.

Sources:

Contemporary Authors, volume 136, Detroit: Gale, 1992.

Dounce, Harry E., "In the Jungle," *Saturday Review of Literature,* November 8, 1924, p. 259.

Growing Point, vol. 5, no. 1, May 1966, p. 728.

Mukerji, Dhan Gopal, *Bunny, Hound, and Clown,* New York: Dutton, 1931.

Kent Nagano

Orchestra conductor
Born 1948, Morro Bay, California

"We live in an international world now and, if only through the media, we all have been exposed to those various sounds. Music has always been an international language, and there are no Berlin walls in culture any more."

Kent Nagano is a rising star in the classical music world. He is the music director of California's Berkeley Symphony Orchestra, the director of France's Opera de Lyon and the Halle Orchestra in Manchester, England, and he is the associate principal guest conductor of the London Symphony Orchestra. He also has moved into the international music recording scene; in 1993, Nagano signed a contract with Erato Records to deliver 15 compact discs over a five-year period.

A master of complex contemporary scores, Nagano is credited with transforming the Berkeley Symphony into a group much respected for its performances of twentieth-century music. In 1985, Nagano won a Seaver Conducting Award, a $75,000 prize intended to foster the development of "American conductors on the threshold of major international careers."

Strong Japanese influence

Kent Nagano was born a third-generation Japanese American in 1948. Raised on a farm in Morro Bay, California, he was brought up in a Japanese-speaking household. Still, Nagano had time for cheeseburgers, surfing, and Beethoven symphonies. His mother, an amateur cellist, introduced the family to music. "We did a lot of family entertainment sort of things," said Nagano in a 1986 *Image* magazine article. "We'd act out plays together or stand around the piano with my mother playing and we'd all sing."

Kent Nagano

Nagano has said that he did not experience racism while growing up, though he admitted sensing that he was in some ways made to feel different. He understood why after a 1985 trip to Japan with conductor **Seiji Ozawa** and the Boston Symphony; there, for the first time in his life, he felt what it was like to blend into a crowd.

Nagano studied at Oxford University in England and graduated from the University of California at Santa Cruz with a sociology/pre-law degree. A multitalented musician who plays the piano, viola, clarinet, and koto (a Japanese string instrument), he said he was drawn to music because it is among the most highly developed means of communication. Nagano observed, "We live in an international world now and, if only through the media, we all have been exposed to those various sounds. Music has always been an international language, and there are no Berlin walls in culture any more."

Nagano studied for his master's degree in music at San Francisco State University. While working toward his degree, he served as assistant to conductor Laszlo Varga at the San Francisco Opera. His interest soon turned mainly to conducting. "I'd always been dedicated to every aspect of music, including composition, and at one point I realized I was doing more conducting than anything else," he said during a June 1985 interview with *Ovation*. The conductor, as Nagano said, "has a very simple and direct function. He's supposed to keep an orchestra together, harness their ability into a unified statement."

Contemporary music advocate

In 1978, the young maestro took over the financially troubled Berkeley Symphony Orchestra. He decided to concentrate on the music of living composers to revive its fortunes rather than compete with the many orchestras that base their repertoires on past masters. Nagano has displayed much inventiveness at Berkeley; among the works he has programmed are a concerto featuring rock guitarist Ronnie Montrose, the acoustical premiere of Wendy Carlos's "Moonscapes" (originally written for synthesizer), and a Vivaldi violin concerto performed by 40 Suzuki students playing in unison. (Suzuki is a method of violin study that starts very young children on small-scale violins, the instrument increasing in size as the child grows.) He also premiered "Noosphere," an original composition by bass guitarist Phil Lesh of the popular San Francisco Bay Area rock band the Grateful Dead.

Aside from leading the Berkeley Symphony, Nagano has conducted other orchestras both at home and abroad. He has chosen a path of broad experience, which has included tackling such unusual projects as recording the late rock pioneer Frank Zappa's orchestral works with the London Symphony for Zappa's label, Barking Pumpkin Records.

One of Nagano's most ambitious undertakings came in 1983 at the invitation of Olivier Messiaen, a well-respected modern French composer. Messiaen invited Nagano to conduct the last of eight performances of the world premiere of his six-hour opera, *St. Francis of Assisi*. The first seven were to be conducted by **Seiji Ozawa**, music director of the Boston Symphony.

Career highlights

Assisting Ozawa in preparing the *St. Francis of Assisi* score proved memorable for Nagano. As a child he had considered Ozawa a role model. His parents also admired him and "were very proud that a Japanese person was having a career in the United States with no apologies," Nagano told *Image* magazine. "As a Japanese American, I had always looked up to Ozawa and paid a lot of attention to him," he commented in *Ovation*.

In December 1984, again as Ozawa's backup—this time with the Boston Symphony—Nagano stepped in without a rehearsal and led the orchestra in critically praised performances of Gustav Mahler's *Ninth Symphony*. In November 1989, Nagano led the Orchestre de Paris in the world premiere of Toru Takemitsu's *A String Around Autumn* as part of a massive international celebration of the French Revolution's bicentennial.

Sources:

Marum, Lisa, "Kent Nagano, Conductor," *Ovation,* June 1985.

Pfaff, Timothy, "Trans-bay Conductor," *San Francisco Examiner,* January 3, 1990.

Reynolds, Richard, "Remarkable Conduct," *Image,* December 21, 1986.

Mira Nair

Filmmaker
Born 1957, India

"I've always been drawn to stories of people who live on the margins of society, ... dealing with the question 'What, and where, is home?'"

Filmmaker Mira Nair has translated her passion for her native culture onto film, sharing with worldwide audiences the beauty and hardships of life in India and as an ethnic minority in the United States. Her first feature film, *Salaam Bombay!,* won the top awards in 1988 at France's prestigious Cannes Film Festival. *Salaam Bombay!* was also nominated for an Academy Award in the foreign film category that year. Nair's first English-language film, *Mississippi Masala,* tackled the thorny problem of racism in a southern American rural town. It featured top box-office draw Denzel Washington and attracted critical acclaim. *The Perez Family* (1995) is about recent immigrants to the United States and explores the tangle of emotions experienced by several characters involved in the Mariel boat lift from Cuba in 1980.

Nair has concentrated on society's outcasts in many of her works. "I've always been drawn to stories of people who live on the margins of society," she said in a 1992 interview with *Time,* "people who are on the edge, or outside, learning the language of being in between; dealing with the question 'What, and where, is home?'"

Affluent childhood

Unlike many of the characters she features in her films, Nair has a strong sense of her own roots. Born in 1957, she grew up in comfortable surroundings in Bhubaneswar, a small town in the delta region of eastern India. There Nair played among ancient stone temples and rice fields.

"I remember the emptiness. Playing hide-and-seek in the temples," Nair said in a 1992 *Vogue* interview. "How there was time to dream because nothing ever happened." Nair has vivid memories of seeing the 1965 film *Dr. Zhivago* on a hot summer day: "When the power broke down, the cinema manager just got on-stage and said, 'All the fans have stopped, ladies and gentlemen. Now think of Russian snow to become cool.'"

Nair's first passion was theater. After graduating from an Irish Catholic missionary school in Simia, she attended Delhi University for one year, during which she acted with an amateur theater group that performed the works of William Shakespeare. In 1976 Harvard University offered Nair a full scholarship. She grabbed the opportunity to travel to the United States. But at Harvard, she began to lose interest in theater, discovering instead a love of film, specifically documentaries. "Documentaries really grabbed me," she said in *Time.* "They were a way of entering people's lives—if they should choose to let you enter—and embracing them."

Film career begins

Nair's first documentary, *Jama Masjid Street Journal,* was made as a student project at Harvard in 1979. It explored the lives of a traditional Muslim community in

Old Delhi and was told from the perspective of an Indian woman—Nair herself—wearing a camera instead of the burkha (veil) worn by most Indian women.

Nair's later films tackled other difficult subjects. Her 1982 work, *So Far from India,* relates the story of an Indian subway newsstand worker in Manhattan who returns to his wife in India only to find that they have grown apart. In *India Cabaret,* made in 1985, Nair illustrated the hard lives of women dancers working in a Bombay nightclub. The film won best documentary prizes at the American Film Festival and the Global Village Film Festival. Nair's 1987 film, *Children of a Desired Sex,* caused an uproar; it confronted head-on the Indian cultural tendency to prefer boys over girls.

After completing four documentaries, Nair wanted more control over the filmmaking process and decided to branch out to feature films. Her first attempt was *Salaam Bombay!,* a 1988 film about a homeless child living on the streets of Bombay, trying to raise money through begging so that he can return to his mother in the country. *Salaam Bombay!* was filmed on location in Bombay and featured the actual homeless children of the city. Made on a $900,000 budget—small by Hollywood standards— the film was a commercial and critical success.

Several years later came *Mississippi Masala.* The word *masala* refers to the colorful mix of spices used in Indian cooking. The 1992 film was a humorous yet thought-provoking look at the lives of Indians who were forced to leave their native land of Uganda, in eastern Africa, when dictator Idi Amin expelled Asians from the country in 1972. Many moved to the United

Mira Nair with her son, Zohran.

States, settling in Mississippi and buying motels. Nair got the idea for the movie from a *New Yorker* magazine article about the subject. "I was so fascinated that I got in a car and started driving through Mississippi, staying in those motels," Nair said in *Vogue.*

While the film does contain some humor, *Mississippi Masala* concentrates on the problems of racism among people of color. The story centers on a young Indian woman named Mina who, against her family's wishes, begins a love affair with Demetrius, an African American man. The role of Demetrius is played by Denzel Washington.

"People think of racism as black versus white, but there's a different kind of consciousness of color within minority groups as we equate beauty with fairness and ugliness with darkness," Nair said in a 1992 interview with *Mother Jones*. Nair had trouble financing this film because of its mostly non-white cast. Even her casting of a big star like Washington and her successful track record would not convince financial backers. Eventually, though, she collected the $7 million she needed.

Nair directed another well-received movie, *The Perez Family,* released in 1995 and starring Anjelica Huston, Marisa Tomei, and Alfred Molina. Based on a novel of the same name by Christine Bell, *The Perez Family* is the story of several characters affected by the Mariel boat lift, in which more than a hundred thousand Cubans came to Miami, Florida, in 1980. The film was praised for countering the stereotypes of immigrants that have prevailed in the media, but it drew some criticism as well for casting non-Hispanic people in the leading roles.

Citizen of the world

Nair filmed on location in Uganda during the making of *Mississippi Masala*. While there, she met and fell in love with Mahmood Mamdani, a political scientist who was born in India but grew up in Uganda and earned his Ph.D. from Harvard. Mamdani moved to Tanzania, in eastern Africa, after Amin's expulsion order and returned to Uganda in 1979 when the restrictions against Asians were lifted. The couple eventually married and bought the Kampala, Uganda, home Nair used as a setting for

Mississippi Masala. In 1992, Nair gave birth to a son, Zohran.

Nair said the toughest challenge she faces as a filmmaker of color is revealing truths most communities prefer to hide. "You're expected to put the best foot forward, present the noble face," she said in *Mother Jones*. "But I'm not one for being the ambassador of a community. The challenge is in how to present the idea—if it's done well, it's not just 'airing dirty laundry.'"

Nair is truly a person of the world, having lived in India, England, the United States, and now Kampala. Yet her roots—and her strong identity—remain firmly planted in India. That sense of home inspires her and fuels her creativity. "Knowing where you come from gives one an incredible amount of self-confidence," she said in *Time*.

Sources:

Mehta, Gita, "Vogue Arts," *Vogue,* February 1992, pp. 114-18.

Nair, Mira, professional resume, 1994.

Orenstein, Paggy, "Salaam America!," *Mother Jones,* January/February 1992, pp. 60-61.

Outlaw, Marpessa, "The Mira Stage," *Village Voice,* February 18, 1992, p. 64.

Simpson, Janice C., "Focusing on the Margins," *Time,* March 2, 1992, p. 67.

Irene Natividad

Political activist, commission chair, educator
Born September 14, 1948, Manila, the Philippines

"It is satisfying knowing that for a brief point in time you made a difference."

When Irene Natividad was a child, her family moved often due to her father's job as a chemical engineer. During stays in the Philippines, Japan, Iran, Greece, and India, Natividad learned how to get along with people from other countries and cultures. She also realized that in many places, women have limited options compared to men when it comes to employment and political influence. Natividad would call on these experiences later in life as she became what *Ladies' Home Journal* in 1988 called one of the "100 Most Powerful Women in America."

Currently, Natividad is chair of the National Commission on Working Women, which works to improve the economic status of working women in the United States. She also serves as leader to other organizations: she is director of the Global Forum of Women, an international gathering of women leaders that meets periodically to explore leadership issues for women worldwide; executive director of the Philippine American Foundation, which works to eliminate poverty in the Philippines; and head of Natividad and Associates, which advises organizations that wish to influence certain blocs of voters.

A childhood of change

Born in Manila, the Philippines, on September 14, 1948, Irene Natividad is the oldest of four children. Her ability to quickly master new languages was key to her adjustment to the ever-changing schools and communities she encountered while growing up. Partly because of her family's frequent moves, Natividad speaks Spanish, French, Italian, Tagalog (spoken in the Philippines), Farsi (spoken in Iran), and Greek fluently.

In a 1985 interview with the *Bergen* (New Jersey) *Record,* Natividad described how her mother's experience during the family's frequent moves helped to shape her own perspective on women's roles. "My father had his job, we kids had our schools, and she had nothing," Natividad said. "In all those countries, a woman was not allowed to work.... I think I have a very intelligent, outspoken, articulate mother, and she had no outlet."

Her parents had high expectations for their three daughters and one son. In Greece, Natividad completed her high school education at the top of her class. A few years later, her mother expected nothing less from her at Long Island University; motivated by her mother's threat not to attend graduation if Natividad wasn't at the top of the class, she earned the number one spot in the class of 1971. In 1973, she received a master's degree in American literature and, in 1976, a master's in philosophy, both from Columbia University in New York. She was awarded honorary doctorates from Long Island University in 1989 and Marymount College in 1994.

Natividad's first jobs came during the 1970s. She was an English instructor at Lehman College of the City University of New

York in 1974, an English instructor at Columbia University from 1974 to 1976, and director of continuing education at both Long Island University and William Paterson College in New Jersey from 1978 until 1985. As she worked with students returning to college as adults, she found she particularly enjoyed supporting and guiding women who wanted to return to the work force or improve their skills.

Political activism

While working as a waitress, Natividad launched her career as an activist by organizing the other waiters and waitresses to demand higher pay. Although she was fired as a result, Natividad's calling as an activist—employing organizational and political means to achieve a goal—was born. In 1980, Natividad served as founder and president of Asian American Professional Women and as founding director of both the National Network of Asian-Pacific American Women and the Child Care Action Campaign.

It wasn't long before Natividad applied her leadership talents to the political arena. Her first taste of politics came in 1968, when she distributed campaign leaflets for Eugene J. McCarthy's presidential campaign. She went on to serve as chair of the New York State Asian Pacific Caucus from 1982 to 1984, and as deputy vice-chair of the Asian Pacific Caucus of the Democratic National Committee. In 1984, when Geraldine Ferraro made history by becoming the first woman from a major party to run for vice president of the United States, Natividad served as Asian American representative for Ferraro's campaign. Ferraro joined Walter Mondale on the Democratic ticket. Although the Mondale/Ferraro team lost the election to Republicans Ronald Reagan and George Bush, Natividad viewed the campaign as a significant turning point for women in politics.

National Women's Political Caucus

By 1985, Natividad's career as a political activist was in full swing. She was elected to chair the National Women's Political Caucus, becoming the first Asian American woman to head a national women's organization. The National Women's Political Caucus, headquartered in Washington, D.C., was founded in 1971 by a small group of feminists—including former congresswomen Bella Abzug, Shirley Chisolm, and **Patsy Mink**—to focus on putting women in public office. The caucus is neither Republican nor Democratic; as a registered Democrat, Natividad succeeded a Republican as leader of the group.

Throughout her career, Natividad has utilized the collective power of organizations to achieve her goals. Her election to head the 77,000-member caucus was a logical step in her mission to help women gain power and influence through the political system. In a 1985 interview with the *New York Times,* Natividad laid out her goals for the caucus: "One of our missions is to transfer the political experience we have developed on a national level to the state and local level. We want to train women to run for local offices because if we don't feed that pipeline we won't have state winners. We have to insure that we have more wins at the local level, for that is where it all starts."

Irene Natividad

During her term as chair, the caucus trained candidates and their staffs throughout the United States on how to campaign for office. The group also ran workshops on polling, fund-raising, organization, and strategies for handling the news media.

Under Natividad's leadership, the caucus analyzed how well women were represented in state governments. It also established the first-ever Minority Women Candidates' Training Program and created the Good Guy Award honoring men who support the cause of women's rights. As a result of their activities, the caucus gained real clout. And through the work of the caucus's Coalition for Women's Appointments, in 1988 Natividad was invited to meet with President George Bush to promote women candidates for administration posts. An estimated one-third of all women appointed to high-level positions in the Bush administration had been recommended by the coalition led by Natividad.

In 1989, Natividad stepped down as chair of the National Women's Political Caucus to pursue other interests and to make way for fresh leadership. Her interest in and commitment to women's issues since has not declined; it has, in fact, taken on an international dimension.

International focus of the 1990s

Natividad's interests are truly global in scope. She has frequently written and spoken on topics ranging from the struggles for democracy in Czechoslovakia and her native Philippines, to proposals for changes in the workplace that will benefit both women and men. Natividad is also editor of a 1995 reference book for public and school libraries, the *Asian American Almanac*.

In 1992, Natividad served as a director of the Global Forum of Women, a gathering in Dublin, Ireland, of 400 women leaders from 58 countries who met to intensively discuss women's issues. This international summit was followed in 1994 by a forum in Taiwan (attended by representatives from 80 countries). Through the Global Forum, Natividad maintained her efforts to train women to become effective political leaders. She continues to develop and lead political training workshops at locations around the world, from Barcelona, Spain, to Bangkok, Thailand.

Awards

Natividad's accomplishments have been recognized frequently. The Women's Congressional Caucus presented her with the Women Making History Award in 1985. Americans by Choice presented the 1986 Honored American Award to Natividad, and the following year, she received the Innovator for Women$hare Award from the Women's Funding Coalition. In 1988, *Ladies' Home Journal* included her in its list of the "100 Most Powerful Women in America." The National Conference for College Women Student Leaders awarded Natividad its Woman of Distinction Award in 1989, the year in which she also received an honorary doctorate in humane letters from Long Island University. In 1993, she was named one of the "Seventy-four Women Who Are Changing American Politics" by *Campaigns and Elections* magazine. And in 1994, *A. Magazine* named Natividad to its list of "Power Brokers: The Twenty-five Most Influential People in Asian America."

Sources:

"America's 100 Most Important Women," *Ladies' Home Journal,* November 1988.

Benedetto, Richard, "Women's Caucus Loses Cornerstone," *USA Today,* August 2, 1989, p. 2A.

Berger, Leslie, "Feminist Showing That Professionals Can Be Moms, Too," *Bergen* (New Jersey) *Record,* July 15, 1985.

Gamarekian, Barbara, "National Women's Political Caucus: Carrying Word of a Women's Agenda," *New York Times.*

Manuel, Susan, "Leading the Fight to Give Women Political Might, *Honolulu Star-Bulletin,* July 9, 1985.

Philippine American Foundation, "Irene Natividad Profile," Washington, D.C., June 1993.

Phillips, Leslie, and Sam Meddis, "Asian-American Leads National Group," *USA Today,* July 1, 1985.

Josie Natori

Entrepreneur, fashion designer
Born May 9, 1947, Manila, the Philippines

"My intent was to start a business with products from the Philippines. I never thought ... of starting a designer business or being called a designer."

Josie Natori is one of the top fashion designers in America. As the chair of The Natori Company, she oversees the operations of a $40 million concern that *Cosmopolitan* described as "the hottest name in the lingerie business." She started her company after leaving a very successful career as an investment banker with the Wall Street brokerage firm of Merrill Lynch. Her first designs were in lingerie, where she is regarded as having revolutionized the industry. She rejected the traditional notion that relegated lingerie to sleepwear, or as something to be worn only at home or under layers of clothes, and created a line of high fashion outerwear based on the look of lingerie.

Natori's soft, body-conscious designs are made of velvet, Lycra, and lace and are distinguished by their embellishments—the signature of her line. "My collection is based on my taste level," Natori told *Asian*

American Biography (AAB). "It's more of an attitude of dressing. Whatever I do, whether it's clothes or jewelry, there's always a feeling of luxury, a lot of detail ... and evidence of craftsmanship." Natori went on to say that her clothes are designed for the woman "who believes in pampering herself, in feeling good about herself."

Born in the Philippines

Josie Natori was born Josefina Cruz, the eldest daughter in a family of six children. Her father, Felipe F. Cruz, was an affluent entrepreneur, and her mother, Angelita A. Cruz, was a pharmacist who worked as his business partner. As a child, Natori wanted to be both a pianist and a stockbroker. She began studying piano at the age of four and performed as a soloist with a full orchestra at nine. Her family was Catholic and very strict. In an interview with *Cosmopolitan,* Natori said, "I couldn't even look at a man, much less date. When I was thirteen, my parents saw me dancing with the neighbor's son and I was grounded for two months." She added, "In the Philippines, people never showed affection. We didn't hug each other; we greeted by putting our palm to our forehead. We didn't even say 'I love you.' It's hard to believe."

After an extensive trip around the world with her mother at the age of 17, Natori decided she wanted to study in the West. She had loved Paris during her stay there but ultimately decided to go to New York. She enrolled in Manhattanville College, a small private school in New York City. Graduating in 1968, she joined Bache Securities as a stockbroker. In 1971, Natori left Bache to join Merrill Lynch, where she switched to

Josie Natori

investment banking. She was very successful in this lucrative field and soon became vice president of the investment banking division. She met her husband, Kenneth Natori, during this period. He was an investment banker for Shearson Lehman, a rival brokerage firm. They married in 1972. In 1976 the couple had a child, Kenneth, Jr. Two months after her son's birth, Natori returned to work but began feeling dissatisfied with her profession. "There's no aesthetic sense on Wall Street," she told *Cosmopolitan.* "We made creative deals, but there was nothing to look at."

Starting a business

Natori and her husband had for some time been considering starting their own business. She told *Cosmopolitan,* "We would wake up in the middle of the night and talk about all the options. We even parked outside carwashes to compute the possibilities." Finally, Natori decided to do something with which she was familiar and began importing handicrafts from the Philippines. It was an area in which she felt confident because she knew the culture and had connections in her home country.

Shortly after Natori began her business, a buyer at Bloomingdale's, the giant New York retailer, suggested that she lengthen a hand-embroidered blouse she was importing into a nightshirt. Not even sure what a nightshirt was, Natori took the buyer's suggestion and in less than three months had more than $150,000 in orders. The success came as a shock to Natori, who told *AAB,* "My intent was to start a business with products from the Philippines. I never thought in a million years of starting a designer business or being called a designer."

Natori's rise in the highly competitive world of fashion design was difficult and full of the kinds of problems that plague any new business. The peculiarities of the fashion trade also took their toll. "I was accustomed to Wall Street ethics—when they existed," she told *Cosmopolitan.* "I was unprepared for the rag trade. We got a twenty-five-hundred-dollar order from one major New York store, and after everything was made, they canceled it. On Wall Street, you cement a deal over the phone, but in fashion, you can sign in blood and it doesn't mean a thing."

In 1980 Natori opened a factory in the Philippines, financed and built by her father, which gave her full control over the production of her line. In 1985 Kenneth Natori joined the company full time, taking the title of president, with Josie remaining as chairperson.

Natori expands

By the mid-1990s, The Natori Company was a thriving $40 million business with operations in 40 countries. In 1991 Natori launched Josie Natori Couture, a collection of elegant eveningwear. In the fall of 1993, Natori expanded into accessories with the introduction of a fashion jewelry collection that she sells under a worldwide licensing agreement (lending her name to items produced by another manufacturer in return for a share of that producer's profits). The next year she introduced a day and evening footwear collection. Her next venture, a collection of fragrance and bath products to be sold through Avon, is slated to debut in 1995.

Natori credits her family, particularly the women who raised her, for her self-confidence and business savvy. Her maternal grandmother, Josefa M. Almeda, was especially influential as a role model. A businesswoman and workaholic, Natori's grandmother was a feminist in her day. "She believed in women running their own lives and not having to depend on anybody," Natori told *AAB* proudly. Natori says she also inherited much of her drive and business knowledge from her father, a "classic entrepreneur." Her artistic side, on the other had, she attributes to her mother. "The philosophy of The Natori Company is really very much the product of the influence of my mother,"

Natori added. Her mother was a pianist like Natori herself, and she loved to surround herself with luxurious clothes, antiques, and art.

Having grown up around such strong female role models, Natori never "questioned the power of a woman" and always felt that being female was a strength, not a liability, in the competitive world of business. "My business is about women," she told *AAB,* "and I use what I feel as a woman to determine what women want."

Sources:

"Josie Natori: Queen of the Night (gown)," *Cosmopolitan,* vol. 211, no. 6, December 1991, p. 74.

Loving and Weintraub, Inc., Public Relations, "Josie Natori," New York, March 1994.

Mall, Elyse, "The Power of Women," *Working Women,* vol. 16, no. 11, November 1991, p. 87.

Natori, Josie, telephone interview with Valerie Chow Bush, April 18, 1994.

Haing S. Ngor

Physician, actor, activist
Born 1947, Samrong Yong, Cambodia

"If I could be in this film [The Killing Fields] in any capacity, I could help tell the story of Cambodia. And that was important because it was a story nobody knew."

Haing S. Ngor is a Cambodian physician who survived and then educated the world about the genocide the Khmer Rouge inflicted on the people of Cambodia from 1975 until 1979. The Khmer Rouge was a Communist guerrilla revolutionary group that toppled the government of Cambodia in 1975. An extremely brutal and violent group, it instituted a policy of anti-Western, anti-intellectual reform meant to return Cambodia to the agricultural country it was before colonial domination by Europe and America.

Ngor was a practicing physician in the Cambodian capital of Phnom Penh when the Khmer Rouge marched into the city. During their brutal reign, Ngor was repeatedly tortured in prison camps, and he lost both his parents and all of his brothers to execution squads. He was able to flee the country in 1980 and eventually came to the United States. He achieved national prominence in 1985 for his portrayal of **Dith Pran** in the very successful film *The Killing Fields.* Ngor had never acted before, but his work in that film, which opened many people's eyes to the insanity that had engulfed Cambodia, earned him an Academy Award for best supporting actor. Since then, Ngor has continued to act, appearing in several films and television shows. He has also used his celebrity to publicize the plight of his people and to educate the world about the holocaust they endured.

Shattered tranquility

Samrong Yong, where Ngor was born, is a tiny farming village south of Phnom Penh. The son of a Khmer—a Cambodian ethnic group—mother and a Chinese father, Ngor remembers the Cambodia of his early years as a place of beauty and tranquillity. Writing in his autobiography, *A Cambodian Odyssey,* he described his memories of childhood: "Those are my first memories, the rice fields changing with the seasons and the monks coming to our house each morning. And that is how I would like to remember Cambodia, quiet and beautiful and at peace."

This peace did not last long, however. Southeast Asia had long been under the colonial domination of the French, and after World War II, struggles for independence began throughout this area. The French were eager to hold on to their colonies, however, and fought long and hard to keep them in line. It was during this period of warfare that Ngor decided to become a doctor, a bold decision for the son of a farmer, considering that his labor was needed and expected to help the family feed itself. Ngor was driven to this decision one day when he was trying to take his mother to a doctor and was thwarted by army guards. Shortly after this event, Ngor left home to live in a Buddhist temple where he could study with the monks in preparation for his medical education.

City doctor

Ngor specialized in obstetrics and gynecology. After medical school he set up his own practice in Phnom Penh and served as a medical officer in the Cambodian army. By this time, the political situation in Cambodia was deteriorating into near-chaos as the United States let its war against the Communist forces of North Vietnam slip over the border into the neighboring country. Heavy U.S. bombing raids on the countryside—illegal missions designed to root out the Communist Viet Cong—seriously destabilized the country and contributed to the anti-Western sentiments of the growing guerrilla insurgency known as the Khmer Rouge. The guerrilla fighters, who relied on

harassment and sabotage rather than traditional warfare, were led by Pol Pot, a disciple of China's Mao Zedong, who, like his mentor, believed that the countries of the West were evil. In order to save Cambodia, the guerrillas reasoned, all Western influence had to be eradicated and the people had to be returned to the countryside, by force if need be.

In 1975, when the insurgency occupied Phnom Penh, effectively sealing its control of Cambodia, Ngor was working in the city as a doctor. It was evident that he was highly educated, and thus he was a prime target for the Khmer Rouge, who would often kill someone for wearing glasses, which they took as evidence of being able to read—an unforgivable sin in their eyes. As the Khmer Rouge occupied the city they began forcefully evacuating its entire population, sending millions of people into the country to perform manual labor at huge camps.

Ngor bravely continued to practice medicine in secrecy but was eventually sent to the camps like everybody else. In one of these camps Ngor met and fell in love with Chang My Houy. He wrote about her in *A Cambodian Odyssey:* "[She] represented the best of womankind. She never caused pain. She was a healer. She was also much smarter than me. She was not the most beautiful woman in the world, but she was beautiful to me." Houy and Ngor lived together, but due to circumstances, were unable to marry. They decided to have a baby despite the terrible conditions of their lives in the camps. Disaster struck, however, when both mother and baby died during labor. Ngor was unable to help them without the proper equipment, medicine, and surgical tools.

Haing S. Ngor (left) receiving the Academy Award; (right) in his role in *The Killing Fields.*

The nightmare abates

Houy died in 1978 as signs began to appear that the madness that had gripped Cambodia was finally nearing an end. Vietnam invaded its neighbor in 1979 in an effort to overthrow the Khmer Rouge. In May of that year, Ngor rescued his niece, one of his few surviving relatives, and fled to Thailand. He worked as a doctor in the teeming refugee camps on the Thai-Cambodia border for 18 months while he tried to arrange immigration to the West. He was denied entry to Australia and America because he did not have close family already living there. These initial refusals did not deter him, however, and eventually he was granted permission to enter the United States. On October 1, 1980, Ngor left Thailand for Los Angeles, California.

Ngor could not practice medicine in the United States because his credentials, from a French colony, were not valid in America. His first job was as a night security guard for a company outside Chinatown. In November 1980, Ngor found a job as a caseworker for the Chinatown Service Center, where he helped Cambodian refugees find employment. Ngor was satisfied with this work because he was finally able to do what he had wanted to do since leaving his country—help refugees.

The Killing Fields

In March 1982, Ngor auditioned for a part in the film *The Killing Fields*. When friends first approached Ngor suggesting that he try out for a part, he refused. He was happy with his work, and it left him fulfilled. Finally, though, to satisfy his friends' nagging, he relented. After six interviews, Ngor's attitude about appearing in the film changed. He had promised Houy on her deathbed that he would work to tell the world about what had happened in Cambodia. He remembered in his book, "I had changed my mind. If I could be in this film, I decided, in any capacity, I could help tell the story of Cambodia. And that was important because it was a story nobody knew."

The film was based on a book written by Sydney Schanberg, a *New York Times* correspondent in Cambodia just prior to the Khmer Rouge takeover. The story centered on the relationship between Schanberg and his Cambodian assistant, translator, photographer, and close friend, Dith Pran. Ngor was hired to work on the film, though he was not told he would portray Pran until the company was on location in Thailand. Despite having never acted before, Ngor portrayed Pran so convincingly and with such feeling that he was awarded an Academy Award for best supporting actor. The film was hugely successful and did, in fact, educate millions about what had happened in Cambodia.

Since that first film, Ngor has appeared in several others, including *Heaven and Earth* (1993), directed by Oliver Stone, and *My Life* (1993), directed by Bruce Joel Rubin. He has also appeared on dozens of television shows in small parts. In 1987, he published his autobiography, written with Roger Warner and entitled *Haing Ngor: A Cambodian Odyssey*. The book was warmly reviewed.

The activist

Ngor has used his fame to further help the people of Cambodia. He now heads six separate organizations devoted to caring for Southeast Asian refugees and resettling them in the West. As of late 1994, he was at work on a second book, entitled *The Healing Fields*. He regularly visits Cambodia to deliver medical, educational, and other essential supplies. In his autobiography Ngor wrote, "I have been many things in my life: trader walking barefoot on paths through jungles; medical doctor, driving to his clinic in a shiny Mercedes. In the past few years, to the surprise of many people and, above all, myself, I have been a Hollywood actor. But nothing has shaped my life as much as surviving the Pol Pot regime. I am a survivor of the Cambodian Holocaust. That's who I am."

Sources:

Marion Rosenberg Office, biographical information, Los Angeles, California.

Ngor, Haing S., and Roger Warner, *Haing Ngor: A Cambodian Odyssey,* New York: Macmillan, 1987.

Ngor, Haing S., telephone interview with Visi R. Tilak, May 6, 1994.

Isamu Noguchi

Sculptor, architect
Born November 17, 1904, Los Angeles, California
Died December 30, 1988, New York City

"Though I am a mixture of extreme differences in heritage ... do not forget I am a real product of the Midwest."

I samu Noguchi was one of the most acclaimed sculptors, architects, and set designers of the twentieth century. His career in the arts spanned five decades, during which he worked with such legends as the choreographers George Balanchine and Martha Graham, the composer Igor Stravinsky, and the poets William Butler Yeats and Ezra Pound. His major sculptural works include *Red Cube* (1968), located in the plaza of the Marine Midland Building in New York City; the Billy Rose Sculpture Garden in Jerusalem, Israel; *2 Peace Bridges* in Hiroshima, Japan; and the sculpture garden he created for the Yale Beinecke Rare Book and Manuscript Library in New Haven, Connecticut.

Many of these large, outdoor works are comprised of large, primitive-looking stones, a medium Noguchi relished. "Stone is the fundament of the earth, the universe," the *New York Times* quotes him as saying. "It is not old or new but a primordial element. Stone is the primary medium, and nature is where it is, and nature is where we have to go to experience life."

Born to an eminent father

Noguchi's father, Yone Noguchi, was a respected writer who was well known in Britain and the United States for his many books of poetry and fiction and his eloquent interpretations of traditional Japanese poetry, just then being discovered by the West. While in the United States, the elder Noguchi married an American. Isamu Noguchi was born in Los Angeles. As a child, Noguchi had virtually no relationship with his father, however, as the elder Noguchi left the United States for Japan before his son was born and did not see him until he was two, when he and his mother moved to Japan. When he was 13 Isamu Noguchi was sent to the United States to attend a boarding school in Indiana. He left Japan in 1918; the young boy would not see his mother again for six years.

Interlacken, the boarding school to which Noguchi was sent, had permanently closed by the time he arrived there at the end of a month-long journey. He found himself stranded and penniless in the middle of Indiana. Fortunately, there were two caretakers from the school still in the area, and Noguchi was able to stay with them for a year. Then, the founder of Interlacken, Dr. Rumley, heard about the young boy's circumstances and found him a place to live in the nearby town of La Porte with the local minister and his family. There Noguchi finished high school while supporting himself with a variety of jobs.

Apprentice to a master

After graduating from high school, Noguchi, who had decided to become a sculptor,

Isamu Noguchi

was sent to apprentice with Gutzon Borglum, who was then sculpting the presidential monument on Mount Rushmore in South Dakota. Noguchi thus spent much of his childhood and early adulthood deep in the American Midwest. He told the *Journal of Modern Literature* that his early life was mainly influenced by "the Middle West and the idealism that flourished in the twenties and thirties.... Though I am a mixture of extreme differences in heritage ... do not forget I am a real product of the Midwest."

Noguchi's apprenticeship did not go well, and Borglum ultimately told him that he would never succeed as a sculptor. Thus, in the mid-1920s, he moved to New York City and enrolled as a pre-med student at Columbia University. Noguchi, however, did not want to give up so easily on his dream, so he also enrolled part time in the Leonardo da Vinci Art School, where he continued to study sculpture. There Noguchi was greatly encouraged in his talent. The director of the school was especially enthralled with his work and was moved to say that a new da Vinci had appeared (a reference to the Italian Renaissance painter and sculptor). This encouragement was just what Noguchi needed, and he dropped out of Columbia to pursue sculpture full time.

A sculptor emerges

Noguchi became interested in the modernist art scene as it was then developing in New York. He went to dozens of galleries and was especially influenced by the famous Romanian-born sculptor Constantin Brancusi, whose pure, simple works were a major influence on modern sculpture. Noguchi also exhibited his own work at this time. At one exhibit his work was seen by Harry Guggenheim, the wealthy patron of modern art, who suggested to the young artist that he apply for a Guggenheim Fellowship, which his family had recently established to help fund the arts. Noguchi won the award and spent the money traveling through Europe, where, in Paris, he spent time under the tutelage of Brancusi.

Back in New York in 1929, Noguchi continued his work and supported himself making portrait busts. In 1930 he again went to Paris and then on to Asia via the Trans-Siberian Railroad, the legendary rail line connecting Eastern Europe with northern Asia via Russia. He studied calligraphy and brush drawing while staying in Beijing, China, and then went on to Japan. He stayed in Japan for six months, studying clay and classical Japanese gardens.

A new kind of sculpture

By the mid-1930s, Noguchi had attained a limited success exhibiting drawings and terra-cotta pieces in Europe and America. However, he wanted to take sculpture beyond its traditional forms, to create a concept of design that incorporated architecture, sculpture, and landscape. In 1933 he proposed a design for a city park in New York, which he called *Play Mountain.* The plan was rejected by the parks department, however, and Noguchi became greatly disillusioned. He left the United States for Mexico, thinking that country would be more sympathetic to his new ideas about sculpture. There Noguchi completed what is considered his first major work, a high-relief mural in colored cement called *History Mexico* (1936).

Following the outbreak of World War II, Noguchi, who by this time had returned to America, founded an organization called Nisei Writers and Artists for Democracy in an attempt to counter the anti-Japanese hysteria that gripped the United States following the Japanese attack on Pearl Harbor. (A *nisei* is the child of Japanese immigrants who is born in America.) Noguchi, like many others, was outraged by the internment of Japanese Americans during the war, and although he was a resident of the East Coast, and therefore not subject to the internment order (which deemed Japanese Americans a security risk in the event of a Japanese invasion of the West Coast), he voluntarily entered a prison camp in Arizona, where he was held for seven months.

International reputation

By the early 1950s, Noguchi had achieved worldwide recognition as one of the most important living sculptors. In 1956 he was given the commission for the gardens of the UNESCO building in Paris. Other major projects of this prolific period include the Sunken Gardens for the Beinecke Rare Book and Manuscript Library at Yale, *2 Peace Bridges* in Hiroshima, and the Billy Rose Sculpture Garden for the Israeli Museum. The garden was built on a hill called Neve Shaanan, which means "place of tranquility." In 1985 Noguchi wrote that manifesting this quality in his design was his proudest achievement.

Noguchi was given a retrospective (a comprehensive exhibition of the work an artist produced over the span of his or her career) in 1968 at the Whitney Museum in New York and in 1978 at the Walker Art Center in Minneapolis. About the latter, Hilton Kramer of the *New York Times* wrote, "Noguchi is ... the purest of living sculptors."

Honors and awards

In 1982 Noguchi received the prestigious Edward MacDowell Medal for outstanding lifetime contribution to the arts. In 1984 his *Bolt of Lightning,* a 102-foot-tall stainless steel sculpture designed as a memorial to Benjamin Franklin, was installed near the Benjamin Franklin Bridge in Philadelphia, Pennsylvania, 50 years after the artist first conceived it. The next year, Noguchi financed and opened the Isamu Noguchi Garden Museum in an abandoned factory in Long Island City, New York. In 1986 he was selected to represent the United States at the Venice (Italy) Bienale. The next year, President Ronald Reagan awarded Noguchi the National Medal of Arts.

Anne d'Harnincourt, director of the Philadelphia Museum of Art, said of the sculptor, as quoted in the *New York Times* on the occasion of Noguchi's death in 1988, "He never lost his extraordinary youthful sense of invention and enthusiasm.... He was interested in the quality of everything, from the very simple Akari lamps to very elaborate stone sculpture in architectural surroundings. There was a pervasive sense of the individual object as a part of the whole. He was a wonderful free spirit." Martha Graham, the choreographer with whom Noguchi had worked repeatedly, remarked, "I feel like the world has lost an artist who, like a shaman, has translated the myths of all our lives into reality."

Sources:

Brenson, Michael, "Isamu Noguchi, the Sculptor, Dies at 84," *New York Times,* December 31, 1988, pp. 1, 9.

Hakutani, Yoshinobu, "Father and Son: A Conversation with Isamu Noguchi," *Journal of Modern Literature,* summer 1990, pp. 13-33.

Noguchi, Isamu, *A Sculptor's World,* New York: Harper & Row, 1968.

Gyo Obata

Architect
Born February 28, 1923, San Francisco, California

"I knew I wanted to be an architect by the time I was in sixth grade."

G yo Obata is one of the finest architects working today. He has designed some of the most discussed contemporary buildings in the world, including the National Air and Space Museum in Washington, D.C. (the world's most visited museum), the King Khalid International Airport in Saudi Arabia (the world's largest airport), the city of Baltimore's beloved new ballpark, Camden Yards, and the Living World Zoo in St. Louis, Missouri. In 1992, *Engineering News Record,* an architectural and engineering trade journal, ranked Obata's firm—Hellmuth, Obata, and Kassebaum—the top general building designer in the country. The firm, the second-largest in the world, has offices in eight U.S. cities and four overseas and had fees in excess of $82 million in 1991.

Through all of his success, Obata has been guided by the same principle: "Never lose sight of the complete picture," he told *Profile* magazine, "of the people who will spend time inside the building, who will be affected by the use of the space. I really believe in understanding people's needs, their intuitive and emotional goals as well as their functional needs."

A long line of artists

Obata's father, grandfather, and great-grandfather, were all painters from Japan, and his mother taught the traditional Japanese art of flower arrangement. When he was five years old, the family moved from San Francisco, California, to Sendai, Japan, their ancestral home. It was there that Obata attended kindergarten. The family returned to San Francisco a year later, eventually settling in Berkeley, where Obata's father, Chiura Obata, began teaching at the University of California. Obata decided on his career at a young age. He told *Asian American Biography (AAB),* "I knew I wanted to be an architect by the time I was in sixth grade. My mother, father, and many other members of

Gyo Obata

my family were artists. I became interested in a combination of science and art, so architecture was a natural choice."

After graduating from high school, Obata enrolled in the University of California at Berkeley, where he quickly distinguished himself. During his freshman year his class was assigned to produce five drawings to solve problems involving historical architectural landmarks. His success at this assignment was very encouraging, as he told *AAB:* "Three of my solutions were awarded first place! This was a very encouraging beginning for my study of architecture."

The internment

Obata had begun college in 1941. Much of the world was already embroiled in World War II, fighting the Germans in Europe and the Japanese in Asia, although America was not yet involved. Then, in December 1941, the Japanese bombed the American naval base at Pearl Harbor, Hawaii, setting off a wave of anti-Japanese hysteria throughout the country. Obata's father had foreseen trouble and, at his insistence, Obata had applied to Washington University in St. Louis, Missouri, as a way of fleeing the West Coast. In 1942, President Franklin D. Roosevelt issued an order calling for the internment of all Japanese Americans on the West Coast, maintaining that they would be a security risk in the event of a Japanese invasion of the coast. Obata left for school the night before his parents, brother, and sister were imprisoned in a camp in the Utah desert.

Obata found the relative normalcy of his life in St. Louis disturbing in relation to what his family was suffering. He recalled visiting his family in the camp at Christmas: "There I was studying in St. Louis, not really experiencing anything at all, and my family was being kept there in the desert. Looking back, it was all so absolutely stupid—all prejudice is crazy. But at the time, we all just kept looking ahead to what we would do later." After the war, his family joined him in St. Louis.

The birth of HOK

After graduating from Washington University in 1945, Obata studied for a year at Cranbrook Academy outside Detroit, Michigan. In 1946, he went to work for Skidmore, Owings, and Merril, one of the largest firms in the country. Two years later, after a brief stint in the army, he was hired by Minoru Yamasaki, a famous Asian American architect in Detroit, and assigned to design a new airport terminal in St. Louis. In 1955, Yamasaki became ill and decided to close his St. Louis office. Three of the principals there decided to form their own firm—thus Hellmuth, Obata, and Kassebaum, or HOK, was born.

In 1961, the firm won its first major private project when IBM hired them to design a research center in Los Gatos, California. Obata designed a unique structure, one that he initially had difficulty selling to the giant computermaker. "IBM was shocked at first when I clustered redwood buildings, not concrete structures," he told COMPASS Readings magazine. "It gave a humanizing touch to all the science work there."

In order to continue attracting private projects, HOK adopted a business strategy that called for maintaining a list of projects of different building types that suited different geographic regions. During recessionary times in the early 1970s, when many large architectural firms foundered, HOK turned to projects in Saudi Arabia, an oil-rich sheikdom. Its $3.5 billion King Khalid International Airport, the world's largest, in the capital city of Riyadh, has a mosque that can accommodate 5,000 worshippers. The firm also worked on a $3 billion national university on a 2,400-acre site outside Riyadh.

A niche for ballparks

Other high-profile projects Obata has undertaken include Mobil Oil's headquarters; the 1980 Winter Olympics facilities in

Lake Placid, New York; Taiwan's Taipei World Trade Center; and the acclaimed renovations to St. Louis's Union Station. HOK also designed Houston's Galleria, a mini-city that includes offices, hotels, an Olympic-sized skating rink, and a 12-story shopping mall. The firm's focus continues to be abroad, with a third of its new projects in 1992 originating overseas. There will be an airport in Hong Kong, a resort hotel in Indonesia, and a one-million-square-foot telecommunications center in Tokyo, Japan.

In recent years, HOK has gained a reputation as the designer behind an exciting new trend in both baseball and urban renewal. HOK designed a ballpark in downtown Baltimore, Maryland, that became a national sensation. When Camden Yards opened it was an instant hit, both with the fans in Baltimore and the urban planners of the city council. Other cities took note. In 1994, Jacobs Field in Cleveland and the new Comiskey Park in Chicago opened, both to considerable fanfare.

Environmental concerns

Obata and the entire design team at HOK are very concerned about the environment and strive to create designs that are friendly to it. Obata told *AAB*, "Environmental concerns must be a priority in all our actions.... Through humanistic design and thoughtful site planning, and by encouraging an awareness of our impact on the global ecosystem, we can help make the world a better place to live." Obata is a member of the Presidio Council, a citizen's group established by the Golden Gate National Park Association. The council is working to secure the transfer of the administration of San Francisco Presidio,

a complex of historic buildings, from the military to the National Park Service. By preserving its park, land, and seashores, he hopes to create a model for a sustainable environment. Obata told *CED News,* "I think architects have to become more vocal—I don't think [concern about the environment] is coming from politicians—or the world is not going to be a very nice place to live."

Sources:

Biemesderfer, S. C., "From the Ground Up," *Profile,* February 1993.

Montgomery, Roger, "A Conversation with Gyo Obata," *CED News,* University of California, Berkeley, spring 1992.

Obata, Gyo, interview with Ferdinand M. deLeon, March 18, 1994.

Weiss, Julian M., "Forging the Shape of Tomorrow," *COMPASS Readings,* May 1990.

Yoichi R. Okamoto

Photojournalist
Born July 3, 1915, Yonkers, New York
Died 1985

"Okamoto made one of the most significant contributions to government photography, particularly White House photography, of anyone in our time."—Frank Wolfe, Lyndon Baines Johnson Library

Yoichi R. Okamoto was head of the White House Photo Office and served as the principal presidential photographer from 1964 through 1968, during the presidency of Lyndon Baines Johnson. In a long career as a distinguished photojournalist, Okamoto's subjects included J. Edgar Hoover, head of the Federal Bureau of Investigation; Warren Burger, chief justice of the U.S. Supreme Court; and President Johnson. His work has been featured on the covers of *Smithsonian* and *Time* magazines. As head of the White House Photo Office, Okamoto made significant contributions to the body of photographic work documenting government in operation.

Okamoto was born on July 3, 1915, the oldest of two boys. His parents, both *nisei* (first-generation Japanese Americans), divorced when Okamoto was young, and he was raised by his mother in Yonkers, New York. He attended Colgate University in New York. It was while he was a student at Colgate that Okamoto developed a serious interest in photography.

World War II

After graduating from Colgate, Okamoto enlisted in the army. He served with the 442nd Regimental Combat Team, a legendary infantry regiment comprised solely of Japanese American soldiers that accrued one of the most distinguished records of service and bravery in the history of the U.S. Army while fighting in Europe from 1942 until 1945. Okamoto's son, Philip, told *Asian American Biography (AAB)* that Okamoto experienced one of the major disappointments in his life when he was dismissed from Officer Candidate School because of his Japanese descent. And, while he was serving in the war, Okamoto's mother and younger brother were sent to an internment camp in Kansas. (The forced imprisonment of Japanese Americans on the West Coast was a dark chapter in American history during which loyal citizens were taken from their homes and businesses because they were viewed as a potential security threat in the event of a Japanese invasion of the coast.) These events served to make him critically conscious of being Japanese. According to Philip Okamoto, "My father was always very self-conscious of being Japanese. He was also very proud of his heritage ... [and] felt that he had an obligation to show the world that being Japanese was something to be proud of and not to be ashamed of."

After the war, Okamoto transferred to the foreign service and was stationed in Vienna, Austria, with the United States Information Agency (USIA) until 1954. While in Vienna, he worked for General Mark Clark as a photographer. In September of 1947, he married Paula Schmuck-Wachter. In 1950, the U.S. government moved all dependents of personnel working in Vienna out of the city, fearing the threat of military activity by the Soviet Union. The Okamotos were moved to a village outside of Salzburg.

In 1954, Okamoto was transferred back to the United States to USIA headquarters, where he continued his work as a photographer. The Okamoto family settled in Bethesda, Maryland. An auspicious meeting occurred when Lyndon Johnson, then vice president, requested that the USIA provide a photographer to accompany him on a trip to West Germany. Okamoto was given the assignment, and the two got along well—so well, in fact, that Johnson requested that Okamoto accompany him on subsequent foreign trips.

Yoichi R. Okamoto

The White House Photo Office

In 1964, Okamoto became head of the White House Photo Office under President Johnson. In addition to managing a team of five photographers, he also served as the primary White House photographer. In that capacity, his main responsibility was to photograph President Johnson's activities on a daily basis. Frank Wolfe, chief of technical services at the LBJ Library in Austin, Texas, and a member of Okamoto's team of White House photographers, told *AAB*, "Yoichi's management style was to let the office run as it did as long as events were covered and the photography was good."

According to Wolfe, "Okamoto made one of the most significant contributions to government photography, particularly White House photography, of anyone in our time. He set the standards of an up-to-date, in-depth look at the give-and-take of government and politics as it happened. This type of photography never existed before

Okamoto." Until then, most photography consisted of ceremonial poses and other planned photographs. Wolfe continued (using the staff nickname for Okamoto), "Oki's candid look at government through his photographic lens set new standards. Many later presidential photographers modeled their work on [his] style."

In describing a 1991 Austin exhibition of Okamoto photos entitled "LBJ: The White House Years," the *Dallas Morning News* wrote, "Granted unprecedented and almost unlimited access to the president, his family and staff, Mr. Okamoto and his team of White House photographers captured President Johnson as he forged civil-rights legislation, sought to create 'The Great Society,' and, in the decade of Vietnam, decided in 1968 not to seek reelection."

After the White House

On his retirement from the White House in 1968, Okamoto cofounded Image, a professional photo lab in Washington, D.C. Okamoto continued his work as a freelance photographer, assembling a long list of photo credits, including the stage bills for Washington's Kennedy Center of the Performing Arts for a 12-year period beginning in 1968.

Okamoto also received frequent assignments from such Washington institutions as the Smithsonian and the U.S. Chamber of Commerce. Many Okamoto photographs have been published in *Smithsonian* magazine, including the first informal photos of Justice Warren Burger of the U.S. Supreme Court. Okamoto, on another assignment from the *Smithsonian,* photographed all the judges of the Supreme Court, both at the court and at home. Another Okamoto photograph of note was the last formal portrait of J. Edgar Hoover for the cover of *Time.*

Books

One hundred twenty of Okamoto's dramatic photographs of Johnson and the White House years are included in a book edited by Harry Middleton, the former Johnson speech writer who directs the LBJ Library and Museum. The book, *LBJ: The White House Years,* was published in 1990 to coincide with the silver anniversary of Johnson's inauguration as the 36th president in 1965. (Johnson was sworn in as president after John F. Kennedy's assassination on November 22, 1963. He was elected to his own term in 1964 and inaugurated in January of the following year.)

Okamoto had been working on a book of photographs of Vienna and the surrounding Austrian countryside for seven years prior to his death in 1985. He made one or two trips to Austria each year and shot over 500 rolls of film in the process. In 1987, Okamoto's widow, Paula, completed and published *Okamoto Sieht Wien: Die Stadt Seit Den Funfziger Jahren,* or *Okamoto's Vienna,* featuring Okamoto's photographs. The book was published in two versions, English and German.

Philip Okamoto summed up his father's basic philosophy, stating, "Whatever you choose to do, either professionally or as a hobby, learn all you can learn and do it as well as you can. In short, do it right or don't do it at all." Philip described his father as an avid reader, involved and interested in virtually all the arts, especially painting and sculpture. In addition, he had an intense love and appreciation for classical music.

In his business, professional, and personal life, Okamoto felt that he represented much more than himself—he represented Japanese Americans. Okamoto's legacy is the wealth of stunning, dramatic photographs that set the standard for White House photography.

Sources:

Feeney, Susan, "Johnson Legacy Saluted," *Dallas Morning News,* April 7, 1990, p. 4A.

Okamoto, Philip, telephone interview with Margaret Simon, July 7, 1994.

"Texas Travels: LBJ Exhibition," *Dallas Morning News,* January 20, 1991, p. 8G.

Wolfe, Frank, telephone interview with Margaret Simon, June 13, 1994.

Ellison Onizuka

Astronaut
Born June 24, 1946, Kealakekua, Hawaii
Died January 28, 1986

"When he was growing up, there were no Asian astronauts, no black astronauts, just white ones. His dream seemed too big."—Mitsue Onizuka

As a young boy, Ellison Shoji Onizuka was enchanted by the burgeoning U.S. space program, then in its infancy. He dreamed of one day becoming an astronaut. Though some deemed it unrealistic, Onizuka held onto his dream. Over

the years he worked steadily toward his goal, and in 1985, as part of the crew of the space shuttle *Discovery,* he became the first Asian American to fly in space. Later that year he was chosen to join the crew of another shuttle mission: the fateful January 1986 flight of the space shuttle *Challenger.* That flight ended in tragedy when, 73 seconds after takeoff, the craft exploded, killing all seven crew members, including Onizuka, in the worst accident in the history of the space program.

Born in Hawaii

Onizuka was born in a beautiful coastal town in Hawaii, the third of four children born to Masimutu and Mitsue Onizuka. His grandparents had immigrated to the islands from Japan around the turn of the century to work the sugar plantations as indentured servants, meaning that, in return for the expense of their travel and their maintenance, they became basically enslaved for a period of time. Onizuka, however, had an idyllic and in many ways ordinary childhood. He spent his free time exploring mountains and caves with friends and he played sports, especially basketball. He also helped out in the general store run by his mother in the small coffee-growing community of Keopu. He was an average student, but from a young age he displayed an intense curiosity about the way things worked. "When he was a young child," his mother said in an interview in the *New York Times,* "we would tease him because he would break things apart and not be able to put them back together again."

Onizuka also showed an early interest in space. He loved to explore the universe with

Ellison Onizuka

a telescope at Honolulu's Bishop Museum and daydreamed about one day exploring space in rockets. Later, as a teenager in the 1960s, he watched with fascination as America began exploring space—first in the Mercury and then the Apollo program. "He had it inside him, like a dream," his mother told the *Times*. "We didn't understand it, but he knew what he would do." She went on to say that he faced obstacles beyond his control in pursuing his dream: "When he was growing up, there were no Asian astronauts, no black astronauts, just white ones. His dream seemed too big."

While in high school, Onizuka was very active in extracurricular activities. He became interested in Buddhism, later becoming a Buddhist, and was also involved in the Boy Scouts and the 4-H Federation. He reached the rank of Eagle Scout during his senior year.

College on the mainland

In 1964 Onizuka left Hawaii to study aerospace engineering at the University of Colorado as a member of the Air Force Reserve Officer Training Corps (ROTC). He was an excellent student in this field that had fascinated him for so long. He graduated in 1969 with a bachelor's degree. That year he married Loran Leiko Yoshida, a fellow Hawaiian who was studying at a nearby college. The couple would later have two children.

In 1970 Onizuka entered active duty with the air force and became an aerospace flight test engineer with the Air Logistics Center at McClellan Air Force Base near Sacramento, California. In 1974 he enrolled in the Air Force Test Pilot School at Edwards Air Force Base. Here Onizuka gained a reputation as a spirited and inspiring student. Four years later, he began his training as an astronaut at the Johnson Space Center near Houston, Texas, becoming one of 35 people selected for training for the developing shuttle program. In 1979 he completed his training, making him eligible for assignment.

Flight

Onizuka's turn to fly came in 1985. He was assigned to crew a flight for the first Department of Defense shuttle project. During the mission, Onizuka was responsible for primary payload activities. Despite his extensive training, including simulations of takeoffs, he was stunned by the incredible force needed to lift a rocket out of the pull of the earth's gravity. The *New York Times* quoted a friend as saying that Onizuka told him, "You're really aware that you're on top of a monster, you're totally at the mercy of the vehicle." The *Discovery* circled the earth 48 times and successfully launched its secret payload before returning safely to the ground.

With the completion of the flight, Onizuka achieved several firsts: he was the first Asian American, the first Hawaiian, and the first Buddhist to travel in space, and he became a symbol of pride to all these communities. He became a popular public speaker and often participated in festivals and parades. Yet he always remained humble. "Around us he was just El," his brother Claude said in the *Times*. "When he'd come home, he'd drink beer and tell stories and just be another guy."

The Challenger disaster

After the *Discovery* flight, Onizuka began training for his next mission, slated for early 1986. On the *Challenger,* one of his jobs would be to film Halley's Comet with a hand-held camera. He was very excited at the prospect of having the best view in the world of this rare event. But this was not to be. All of America, and indeed, the world, was shocked and horrified when the *Challenger* exploded on ascent, killing Onizuka and his fellow astronauts.

After Onizuka's death, Bishop Seigen Yamaoka, head of the Buddhist Churches of America, told the *New York Times,* "As a test

pilot and an astronaut, he had to deal with life and death. As long as death is seen as the enemy, you fight it, and become more attached to life. In time, he came to the realization that death is not an enemy to defeat, but a compassionate friend."

In 1991 the Ellison S. Onizuka Space Center, a $2 million museum built in the astronaut's memory, was opened at Keahole Airport in Kona, Hawaii, not far from where Onizuka was born.

Sources:

Cohen, Daniel, and Susan Cohen, *Heroes of the Challenger,* New York: Pocket Books, 1986.

"Ellison Onizuka: 1946-1986," *Time,* February 10, 1986.

NASA, biographical data sheet.

Yoshihashi, Pauline, "Three Boys' Dreams of Space, Three Deaths in the Sky," *New York Times,* February 11, 1986.

Yoko Ono

Artist, filmmaker, musician
Born February 18, 1933, Tokyo, Japan

In 1961 Ono gave her first public concert. It featured a taped background of mumbling and laughter and a performer talking at the same time about peeling grapefruit and squeezing lemons.

Yoko Ono is an artist, filmmaker, and musician who became internationally famous when she married singer-songwriter-guitarist John Lennon in 1969. Lennon was one of the Beatles, probably the most popular and best-known rock and roll band in history. During the early 1960s, Ono was a member of a group of experimental New York artists known as Fluxus. She made several films, contributed art and sculpture to shows, and worked on many staged productions. With Lennon, she organized much of the couple's peace activist performances, including the famous "bed-in" of 1969, patterned after the civil rights era "sit-ins." She and Lennon also recorded with the Plastic Ono Band and worked together on many of Lennon's solo compositions, including "Imagine."

In the years following the breakup of the Beatles, Ono managed Lennon's finances. Her investments and financial decisions earned the couple one of the largest personal fortunes in the country. Since Lennon's murder in 1980, Ono has recorded two albums and has displayed her art and films at the Whitney Museum in New York City. She has also written and produced a rock opera for an Off-Broadway theater in New York.

Privileged childhood

Yoko Ono was born in Tokyo, Japan, into one of Japan's most prominent and wealthy families. Her mother, Isoko, is from the Yasuda family, one of the richest and most powerful clans in the country; her father, Eisuke, was descended from a samurai (one of the warrior aristocracy of Japan) and became the head of the Bank of Japan. As a young child, Ono attended the Gakushuin School, which usually enrolls only members of the royal family.

When she was seven, Ono's family moved to Long Island, New York. They returned to Japan just before the outbreak of World War II. During the war, when the U.S. Air Force began bombing Tokyo, the Ono children were sent to live in a country house their mother had specially built to protect them. Ono later said it was not a pleasant experience; the house was poorly constructed and the children didn't have enough food.

Return to America

For a short time after the war, Ono attended Gakushuin University in Tokyo. Then she moved again with her family to the United States. This time they settled in Scarsdale, a wealthy suburb of New York City. There Ono continued her studies, at Sarah Lawrence College, where she wrote poetry and short stories but neglected her academic responsibilities. She remained at Sarah Lawrence for three years and then dropped out without a degree.

In 1957 Ono met and married Toshi Ichiyanagi, a Japanese musician who was living in New York in order to study at the Juilliard School of Music. Ono has said that she married Ichiyanagi to escape her family, not because she loved him. But her husband knew many New York artists and, through him, Ono began to make contacts with artists such as John Cage and Merce Cunningham. These artists, all of them forward-thinking, rejected traditional art and music; instead, they used unusual—and often controversial—methods to communicate their ideas. In 1958 Ono began showing her own artwork in galleries.

Her reputation grows

In 1960 Ono started hosting concerts at her home. Performers at these events were part of the "Fluxus" movement. Fluxus art was in part inspired by composer John Cage's use of everyday noises in his compositions.

In 1961 Ono gave her first public concert. It featured a taped background of mumbling and laughter and a performer talking at the same time about peeling grapefruit and squeezing lemons. That same year, Ono began a series of events at Carnegie Recital Hall that she would continue to stage periodically until 1968. Her first program included *A Piece for Strawberries and Violin,* in which a performer repeatedly stood up and sat down in front of a table stacked with dishes. This went on for ten minutes. At the end of the piece, the performer would smash the dishes accompanied by what one reviewer called "a rhythmic background of repeated syllables, a tape recording of moans and words spoken backwards, and an aria of high-pitched wails sung by Ms. Ono."

In 1964 Ono left Ichiyanagi and married a film producer named Tony Lake. Also that year, she published *Grapefruit*, a collection of poems and meditations. Ono's work of this period was very much based on audience participation. When she began exhibiting at London's Indica Gallery, one of her works, *Apple*, featured an apple on a pedestal; viewers were invited to take a bite. Another such piece was *Painting to Hammer Nail In*, which was a wood panel with an attached hammer into which viewers were encouraged to pound nails. *Cleaning Piece* consisted of a white cloth, a dark glass box, and the instructions "clean it."

From its beginnings, the Fluxus movement had centered on filmmaking, and Ono had made several films. In 1966 she produced what is perhaps her best known, *Bottoms*. It is 80 minutes of bare rear-end

Yoko Ono

views of people walking on a treadmill. The film's soundtrack consisted of what the subjects were saying as they were being filmed.

Meeting John Lennon

In 1968 Ono met Lennon, who attended one of her shows. They were married a year later, on March 20, 1969, after they both had obtained divorces. By marrying Lennon, Ono instantly became an international celebrity. In the spring of 1969, the couple went to Toronto for the now-legendary "bed-in": Lennon and Ono sat in bed for a set period of time to promote world peace, especially an end to America's war in Southeast Asia, which by that time had spread beyond Vietnam into Cambodia and Laos. The bed-in was attended by many celebrities and media representatives, and Lennon's song "Give Peace a Chance," recorded there, became a hit.

Ono found it difficult to continue working in light of the intense publicity she and Lennon received wherever they went. In 1971 she gave her last show of this period. She began recording and performing with Lennon after the breakup of the Beatles. Partly because Lennon's work was more traditional than Ono's still largely experimental offerings, collaborations between the two artists were often perceived as failures. Critics blamed Ono for hurting Lennon's music. Indeed, she was vilified throughout the world for breaking up the Beatles.

In 1975 after the birth of their son Sean, Ono began managing the fortune Lennon had accumulated over the years. She became a skilled investor in art, real estate, and cattle, and she single-handedly transformed Lennon's sizeable portfolio into one of the country's largest personal fortunes. Its value is estimated today at between $500 million and $1 billion.

Lennon's murder

Lennon and Ono avoided the public eye for the remainder of the 1970s. Then, in 1980, they returned to the recording studio for the first time in five years to work on an album featuring seven compositions by Lennon and seven by Ono. The album was called *Double Fantasy.* Shortly after its release, the couple was returning home from a recording session when Lennon was shot to death in front of Ono on the sidewalk outside their New York apartment building.

In the years following Lennon's murder, Ono has kept a low profile. In 1981 she released an album called *Season of Glass.* She contributed little to the areas of art and performance throughout most of the 1980s. She made videos and some films, and collaborated on several John Lennon memorial concerts and albums. In 1989 the Whitney Museum of American Art in New York staged a show of her work from the 1960s, and the Museum of Modern Art screened several of her films, along with those by other Fluxus artists.

In March of 1994, Ono unveiled a rock opera at New York City's WPA Theater called *New York Rock.*

Sources:

Haskell, Barbara, "Yoko Ono: Objects," essay published in conjunction with the show "Yoko Ono: Objects, Films," New York: The Whitney Museum of American Art, 1989.

Palmer, Robert, "Yoko Ono Asks: 'Was I Supposed to Avoid the Subject?'," *New York Times,* August 5, 1981, p. C17.

Perreault, John, "Yoko Ono at the Whitney: Age of Bronze," *Village Voice,* February 7, 1989, p. 29.

Sessums, Kevin, "Yoko: Life After Lennon," *Interview,* February 1989, pp. 77–80.

Seiji Ozawa

Conductor
Born 1935, Shenyang, China

In 1949 the young Seiji Ozawa heard his first live symphonic performance, Beethoven's Emperor Concerto, and was so inspired by the music that he decided he wanted to conduct.

When Seiji Ozawa was named music director and conductor of the Boston Symphony Orchestra (BSO) in 1973, he became the first Asian—and the youngest person of any ethnicity—to direct one of America's major orchestras. Ozawa has helped to strengthen the world- renowned orchestra's distinguished reputation both at home and abroad with performances in some of America's finest concert halls and on tours of Europe and Asia. He has also championed the BSO's commitment to new music. Ozawa commissioned a series of compositions to mark the orchestra's 100th anniversary season in 1981 and a series of works celebrating the 50th anniversary of the Tanglewood Music Center, the orchestra's prestigious summer training school in western Massachusetts for young musicians. Under his direction, the BSO has recorded more than 130 works by 50 different composers on ten separate recording labels.

Seiji Ozawa

Religion introduces music

Seiji Ozawa was the third of four sons. His father was a Japanese dentist who had gone to China to find work. Ozawa's mother was a Christian who sent her sons to a Sunday school in Beijing where they sang hymns in the choir. As Ozawa recalled in *Opera News,* "Because we didn't have a piano, my older brother started playing the music at home on the accordion and harmonica." Soon, however, the family got an old piano for the boys to play.

When Ozawa was young, Japan invaded the Chinese region of Manchuria, and the family moved back to Japan to escape the invasion. Although life during the war was uncomfortable, music remained an important part of Ozawa's life. In 1949 he heard his first live symphonic performance,

Beethoven's *Emperor Concerto*. He was so inspired by the music that Ozawa decided he wanted to conduct. Many people discouraged him from pursuing this dream. At the time, it seemed unlikely that an Asian would ever conduct Western music with a Western orchestra. Fortunately, there was someone to encourage him. Hideo Saito, Ozawa's teacher at the Toho Gakuen School of Music in Tokyo, was working at the time to make Western music more popular in Japan. Under Saito's guidance, Ozawa was soon conducting concerts with the NHK Symphony and the Japan Philharmonic.

Travel and inspiration

At Saito's urging, the 24-year-old Ozawa left Japan for Europe. There he won first prize at the 1959 International Competition of Orchestra Conductors in Besançon, France. The music director of the Boston Symphony Orchestra, Charles Munch, was a judge at the competition and was extremely impressed by the young conductor. He invited him to Tanglewood, where Ozawa won the Koussevitzky Prize for outstanding student conductor in 1960. Later, Ozawa studied in Berlin with the legendary Herbert von Karajan, who emphasized the importance of opera in the development of the conductor. Ozawa recalled in *Opera News* that Karajan said, "There are two sides to conducting, symphony *and* opera.... So I did *Cosi* [*Fan Tutti*, a Mozart opera] for the first time, at Salzburg [Austria], with the Vienna Philharmonic."

Conducting opera has been a passion of Ozawa's ever since. He modestly attributes much of his success to the singers with whom he has had the good fortune to work.

"When I conducted my first *Tosca* at La Scala, you know who my first tenor was? [Luciano] Pavarotti! And when I conducted the same opera in Paris for the first time, my Tosca was Kiri Te Kanewa!"

Coming to America

Meanwhile, Ozawa came to the attention of Leonard Bernstein, the world-famous American conductor. Bernstein appointed him assistant conductor of the New York Philharmonic for the 1961–62 season. Ozawa made his first professional concert appearance in North America in January 1962, with the San Francisco Symphony. He went on to become music director of the Chicago Symphony Orchestra's Ravinia Festival for five summers, beginning in 1964, holding that post with the Toronto Symphony from 1965 to 1969 and the San Francisco Symphony from 1970 to 1976, followed by a year as the latter's music adviser.

Ozawa first conducted the Boston Symphony Orchestra at Tanglewood in 1964 and made his first Symphony Hall appearance four years later. In 1970 he was made artistic director of Tanglewood, and in 1973 he was asked to become the director of the Boston Symphony Orchestra. He remained as music director at San Francisco for three years, until the travel between the two cities became too tiring.

Ozawa's outstanding career

Ozawa has led the Boston Symphony Orchestra on seven European tours. They have appeared in Japan four times. One such trip, in 1989, included a performance in Hong Kong. The orchestra made its premiere tour of South America under Ozawa in 1992. In addition to his work with the BSO, Ozawa regularly appears with such prominent orchestras as the Berlin Philharmonic, the London Symphony, the Orchestre National de France, the Philharmonia of London, and the Vienna Philharmonic. He made his Metropolitan Opera debut—a longtime dream—in 1992, and appears regularly at Milan, Italy's La Scala and the Vienna Staatsoper.

Ozawa holds honorary doctor of music degrees from the University of Massachusetts, the New England Conservatory of Music, and Wheaton College in Norton, Massachusetts. He won an Emmy Award for the Boston Symphony Orchestra's PBS television series *Evening at Symphony.* In 1992, in honor of his teacher Hideo Saito, he cofounded the Saito Kinen Festival in Matsumoto, Japan.

Sources:

Livingstone, William, "Japan Meets the West," *Stereo Review,* February, 1990.

Office of Maestro Seiji Ozawa, biographical materials, Boston, February 1994.

Scherr, Barrymore Laurence, "Seiji: The Boston Symphony Music Director Attains a Longtime Dream with His Debut This Month in Eugene Onegin," *Opera News,* December 19, 1992.

Chan Ho Park

Baseball player
Born June 30, 1973, Kong Ju, South Korea

"I hope [Chan Ho Park] continues to pitch this way, I hope he continues to bow, and I hope he continues to do all the things unique to his culture.... He's unique, naive, and unspoiled."—Orel Hershiser

I n the spring of 1994, Chan Ho Park became the first Korean national to play for an American major league baseball team. The Los Angeles Dodgers signed the right-handed pitcher to a six-year contract with a signing bonus of $1.2 million, the second-highest bonus given a rookie in Dodger history. The 21-year-old first caught the attention of the Dodgers in 1991, when he pitched in Los Angeles during the Annual Friendship Series, a tournament between the United States, Japan, and South Korea. He played again in the United States as the starting pitcher on the Korean National Team at the World University Games in Buffalo, New York, in 1993.

Early interest in athletics

As a young boy Park began participating in track and field events at the Jung Dong elementary school in Kong Ju, South Korea. In high school, however, he switched to baseball because of his unusually large hands and feet. Kong Ju High School, where Park was a student, won the Korean National Championships during the National Sports Festival in 1992 and came in second in the

Chan Ho Park

Blue Dragon Flag Tournament, during which he was responsible for two saves. He graduated from Kong Ju High in 1992.

The first team to recruit Park was the Atlanta Braves, who offered him $200,000 on the condition that he join the team immediately after military service in Korea, which is mandatory for all males except university students. Officials of the Dodger organization, however, went one better by actually visiting high government officials in Seoul to persuade them to let Park out of this obligation. They agreed and Park signed with the Dodgers.

In 1994 spring training Park showed excellent promise. His fastball had been clocked in Korea at 99 miles per hour, though the fastest the Dodgers have seen it is 94—still quite formidable. In his first start against a major league team on April 7, 1994, Park threw three scoreless innings against the New York Mets, giving up one hit and walking one. Of the 11 batters he faced, he retired six in order and at one point threw 13 consecutive strikes.

Asked about the young pitcher, Dodger general manager Frank Claire told the *Christian Science Monitor,* "If Chan Ho Park were an American and had been eligible for last June's college draft, he probably would have been among the top five players picked. We think he is going to help us for a long time."

A controversial wind-up

Park has run into some trouble due to his habit of pausing in the middle of his wind-up. He was famous for it in Korea, where it is a perfectly legal trick to distract the hitter. In the United States, however, it is considered a balk, which is against the rules, and is cause for giving the batter first base. Park uses the move only occasionally, and league officials are still deciding what to do about it. Players are strongly against it. New York Mets manager Dallas Green was upset by the windup pause during the Mets' preseason game with the Dodgers and told the umpire crew chief that during the regular season his players would step out of the batter's box every time Park hesitated in his windup. Umpire Bruce Froeming was quoted in *Sports Illustrated* as saying, "The Dodgers think it's legal. I'm of the other opinion, as are the clubs. If the batter steps out, I'm going to give him time even if he doesn't ask for it. [The rules committee] puts us in the middle of the lake on this. While they can't make up their minds, the batters are going to keep stepping out, and we'll go have a pizza."

The rules committee, for their part, feels it is not up to them to make a ruling on the moves of an individual player and has left it up to the umpires to call it as they see it. Park himself said in *Sports Illustrated,* "I do it whenever it comes to me. I can't say no other pitcher in Korea does it, but I am noted for doing it. In Korea what I did isn't a problem. If I have to change, I don't see any problem with that. I'm very flexible."

The Park charm

Park is a favorite with crowds, who see in his demure and humble attitudes an innocence and reverence for the game that has long been missing from the American sporting scene. As he approached the plate during the Dodgers' preseason game against the Mets, Park removed his helmet and bowed to the umpire, who minutes before had been in a heated argument with Met Darryl Strawberry. The umpire told *Sports Illustrated,* "I was in a bad mood, and here comes this kid, tipping his helmet and bowing. I had to smile. I wish all the players would get in that habit." After charming the umpire and the attendant fans, Park hit a single and, while standing on first, bowed to the cheering crowd.

Dodger pitcher Orel Hershiser had this to say about Park: "This is what I hope. I hope he continues to pitch this way, I hope he continues to bow, and I hope he continues to do all the things unique to his culture. That's why this is so great. He's unique, naive, and unspoiled. Let's enjoy it. He'll be mixed in with the tossed salad soon enough."

Park spent the 1994 season pitching with the San Antonio Missions, a Dodgers farm team, until a players' strike aborted the season in August. The prospects for this young, endearing, very talented pitcher look excellent, however. His uncle, a Los Angeles architect who negotiated Park's contract, told the *Christian Science Monitor,* "For Park, I think it is only a matter of time before he makes the big leagues. But I wouldn't want to see him rushed before he is ready. One thing I think will help him here immediately is that the strike zone in the United States is larger than it is in Korea."

Sources:

Kurkjian, Tim, "Far East Update," *Sports Illustrated,* July 25, 1994.

Tuber, Keith, "Flamethrower from the Far East," *Transpacific,* June 1994.

Verducci, Tom, "Orient Express," *Sports Illustrated,* March 28, 1994.

I. M. Pei

Architect
Born April 26, 1917, Canton, China

"More than 50 years ago, my wife and I came to this wonderful country from China. For 40 of these years we dreamed that one day it would be possible to work in our native land.... Today, these dreams are dashed by the horrible events of Tiananmen Square.... China will never be the same."

Ieoh Ming Pei is one of the great architects of the modern era. He has designed some of the world's most prominent buildings, including the addition to the Louvre museum in Paris; the East Wing of the National Gallery of Art in Washington, D.C.; the John F. Kennedy Library in Boston; the Jacob Javits Center in New York City; the Guggenheim Pavilion, also in New York; the Fragrant Hill Hotel in Beijing, China; and the Dallas, Texas, City Hall. Pei is considered the dean of the modernist school of architecture. His style is sometimes controversial but always striking in its use of natural light, occasionally unsettling angles, and lots of steel and glass. In his long career, Pei has designed several dozen major buildings, 50 of them in the United States. Of these 50, more than half have won major awards.

Growing up in China

Pei's father, Tsuyee Pei, was a prosperous banker with the Bank of China, and in 1918, when Pei was barely a year old, the bank transferred the elder Pei to Hong Kong. There the family was safe from the civil war then being fought in China. The Peis remained in Hong Kong, a British colony, for nine years, returning to the mainland in 1927. Pei was educated in private schools, attending Saint John's Middle School, which was run by Protestant missionaries. The instruction at Saint John's was in Chinese, but Pei, along with other top students, read the Bible and the novels of British writer Charles Dickens in English.

In addition to private schooling, Pei knew other privileges during his childhood; the family had a country retreat called the Garden of the Lion Forest. The design of the garden there was inspiring to the young man, especially the harmonious way in which the buildings were situated in the natural environment and the way in which light and shadow figured in the design. He would return to the Garden of the Lion Forest 50 years later seeking inspiration for his design of the Fragrant Hill Hotel in Beijing.

I. M. Pei

Coming to America

Pei left China in 1935, hoping to study architecture at the University of Pennsylvania, one of America's top architecture schools. After only two weeks in the program, though, he became discouraged by the heavy emphasis on drawing, and he transferred to the Massachusetts Institute of Technology (MIT), where he took up engineering. His teachers at MIT recognized his talent for design, however, and convinced him to return to his original vocation. He graduated in 1940 with a bachelor's degree in architecture. He also began accumulating awards; he won

the American Institute of Architects Gold Medal, the Alpha Rho Chi (the national professional fraternity of architects) Medal, and an MIT traveling fellowship.

In 1942 Pei married Elaine Woo. During World War II he worked briefly for the National Defense Research Committee in Princeton, New Jersey, before enrolling in Harvard's Graduate School of Design in 1944. He graduated in 1946 and was awarded a Wheelwright Traveling Fellowship by Harvard in 1951, which enabled him to travel throughout Europe, something he had wanted to do for some time.

Life as a professional architect

Pei's first job as an architect was with Webb & Knapp, the architectural division of powerful real estate developer William Zeckendorf's empire. There Pei worked on large-scale urban projects that kept him busy but did not challenge him creatively. He remained with Webb & Knapp, however, and in 1955 he established I. M. Pei & Associates as a sideline to his daily work. In 1959 Pei received his first outside design job when MIT hired him to design a building for its Earth Sciences Center. In 1960 I. M. Pei & Associates amicably separated from Webb & Knapp and began the always daunting task of developing its own business in the highly competitive world of architecture.

In 1961 Pei's firm received its first major commission when Walter Orr Roberts, the astronomer who headed the National Center for Atmospheric Research (NCAR), presented Pei with the opportunity to create a research complex in Colorado. This commission allowed Pei to express himself creatively, employing the ideas he had been keeping inside for many years. Pei's personal style blossomed, resulting in a complex that rises over the slopes of a mesa (a flat, elevated piece of land) outside of Boulder, Colorado. (Few non-astronomers have visited this complex, but many remember it as the setting for the Woody Allen film *Sleeper.*) Pei would later describe this project, completed between 1961 and 1967, as his breakout building, the first design he was free to create as he wanted and one that was well received enough to confirm that his ideas would be popular.

As the firm's reputation grew during the 1960s, Pei took on a broad, conceptual role within I. M. Pei & Associates; he would envision the overall design of a project and then assign the nuts and bolts of the actual drawing to an associate. In 1966 the name of the firm was changed to I. M. Pei & Partners.

Some famous projects: The Kennedy Library

Pei's first project of national significance was the John F. Kennedy Library in Boston, Massachusetts. He was selected from among the top architects in the world in 1964 for this highly coveted honor. The process of building the library was long and somewhat tortured, involving three designs and three different sites, and the building wasn't dedicated until October 20, 1979. The final product was widely acclaimed, however, and the experience ultimately helped to refine Pei's method, teaching him to remain true to his course.

The East Wing of the National Gallery of Art

Paul Mellon, the wealthy philanthropist, and J. Carter Brown, then director of the National Gallery of Art in Washington, D. C., hired Pei to design a new wing for the museum in the mid-1970s. They wanted a gallery that was modern and challenging in design, as it would house some of the finest modernist art in the world. Pei was selected for his growing reputation as an innovator. He produced a striking design that managed to preserve the stately, classical feel of the existing building—something that was very important to conservative critics of the modernist style—while infusing it with energy and light and allowing for the flow of thousands of visitors.

The Louvre

Pei's design for an addition to Paris's Louvre, the most famous museum in the world, has been perhaps his most controversial. After he was contacted about undertaking the project, he began months of secretive research and then proceeded to make his plans in secret as well. The French official overseeing Pei's early plans was very enthusiastic about what was being developed, but when the plans—displaying a crystalline pyramid form that would create a new entrance to the existing seventeenth-century structure—were presented to an influential French commission, criticism was immediate and heated.

The Louvre curatorial staff—the art historians charged with maintaining the collection and the artistic integrity of the museum—refused to withdraw its support for Pei's design. The staff began a campaign to convince the opposition that while the design was indeed radical in many ways, it was one that would be admired by the people of France and the world at large. A media battle began in which leading French intellectuals joined Pei and the Louvre. Finally, it was agreed that a full-scale model of the pyramid would be erected on the site to give the public an accurate idea of the impact it would have. Pei's design eventually won approval, and the addition to the Louvre was completed to great praise all over the world.

Awards and honors

The awards accumulated by Pei during his distinguished career would fill a large trophy room. He is easily the most recognized architect in the world. Notable among these awards are: the Arnold Brunner Award for the National Institute of Arts and Letters (1963); the Thomas Jefferson Memorial Medal for distinguished contribution to the field of architecture (1976); the Gold Medal for Architecture from the American Academy of Arts and Letters (1979); the American Institute of Architects Gold Medal, the highest architectural honor in the United States (1979); the Grande Medaille d'Or from the French Academie d'Architecture (1982); the $100,000 Pritzker Architecture Prize (1983); and the Medal of Freedom, presented by former President George Bush in 1990. On July 4, 1986, at a ceremony celebrating the 100-year anniversary of the Statue of Liberty, Pei was presented with the Medal of Liberty by former President Ronald Reagan. Pei is a naturalized citizen of the United States.

Beyond architecture

Throughout his professional career, Pei has dreamed of one day returning to live and work in his native China. Political events have, however, forced him to stay away, despite working on various projects there. After the Tiananmen Square massacre on Saturday, June 3, 1989—in which government troops attacked pro-democracy demonstrators, many of whom were students, killing some 3,000—a devastated Pei spoke out in an editorial published in the *New York Times:* "More than 50 years ago, my wife and I came to this wonderful country from China. For 40 of these years we dreamed that one day it would be possible to work in our native land.... Today, these dreams are dashed by the horrible events of Tiananmen Square.... China will never be the same."

Sources:

Dell, Pamela, *I. M. Pei, Designer of Dreams,* Chicago: Children's Press, 1993.

Pei, I. M., "China Won't Ever Be the Same," *New York Times,* June 22, 1989, p. A11.

Pei Cobb Freed & Partners, "I. M. Pei," resume and biographical information, 1994.

Wiseman, Carter, *I. M. Pei: A Profile in American Architecture,* New York: H. N. Abrams, 1990.

Arati Prabhakar

Scientist, government administrator
Born February 2, 1959, New Delhi, India

"It never entered my mind that there were things you couldn't do."

Arati Prabhakar is a nationally prominent physicist who has worked most of her career in public service. She currently serves as the director of the National Institute of Standards and Technology (NIST), a federal agency responsible for establishing industrial and technological standards. The NIST is also responsible for funneling government research money into high-risk, high-technology enterprises that would not be sufficiently cost-effective or practical for private corporations to develop without taxpayer assistance. This broadening of the NIST's mandate took place partly in response to competition from countries like Germany and Japan, which have a high degree of cooperation between government and industry, something that, outside of the defense industry, has not been the case in the United States.

In this position, Prabhakar is on the cutting edge of fascinating new technologies, perhaps the most famous of which is the much-publicized "information superhighway," the network of computers, phone lines, and cable television systems that will one day allow ordinary citizens to do their banking, shopping, and studying and meet many of their entertainment needs without leaving their homes. The NIST will also be investing in many other areas; recent funding has contributed to the creation of an erasable optical disk drive for digital video recording, the development of a microfabricated chip incorporating synthetic DNA probes to help in the design of a low-cost DNA sequencer (DNA is the genetic material that determines which traits we will inherit from our ancestors), and improvements in cellular communications.

"Warped" from an early age

When Prabhakar was two years old, her mother immigrated to the United States from India to pursue an education in the field of social work. Within a year, Arati and her father joined her. Her father, an electrical engineer, worked on his doctorate in Illinois and then joined the faculty of Texas Tech University in Lubbock. Science has always played an important role in Prabhakar's family, and Prabhakar herself has always been fascinated by it. In an interview with the industry journal *IEEE Spectrum,* Prabhakar said that as a child she would pretend to be Madame Marie Curie, the Nobel Prize-winning physical chemist, when playing dress-up with friends, adding jokingly, "I was warped from an early age."

Prabhakar eventually chose to pursue a profession more akin to her father's, but she says her mother was her true inspiration. "It never entered my mind that there were things you couldn't do," Prabhakar told *IEEE Spectrum.* "That way of thinking really came from my mother."

Even though Prabhakar grew up in Texas at a time when the Asian Indian community was virtually nonexistent there, she feels she did not miss the security of the familiar. Not having a community to fall back on meant an opportunity to interact closely with the local population. "Actually, it made me learn more about Americans. I didn't feel isolated at all. I was part of the whole community," Prabhakar told *Asian American Biography (AAB)* in an interview.

Arati Prabhakar

A groundbreaking education

After graduating from high school in 1976, Prabhakar entered Texas Tech University, where she enrolled in the electrical engineering department, a field of study very few women chose at the time. She graduated in three years and then applied to Bell Laboratories Graduate Research Program for Women, which funded study towards her master's degree at the California Institute of Technology (Cal Tech). Prabhakar went on to earn a Ph.D. in applied

physics at Cal Tech, a program of study she found immensely difficult. She was able to persevere however, again with inspiration from her mother, and in 1984 she became the first woman to earn a Ph.D. in that field from Cal Tech.

Prabhakar's first job was as a congressional fellow at the U.S. Office of Technology Assessment. Prabhakar's outstanding work soon brought her attention and led to her appointment to the directorship of the Microelectronics Technology Office in the Defense Department's Advanced Research Projects Agency. There she managed a budget of $300 million and oversaw contracts and collaborations with hundreds of defense contractors. The purpose of the office she headed was to transfer public funds into private industry—especially the semiconductor industry—to help domestic firms that couldn't afford large-scale investment in research and development without public assistance. Prabhakar's expertise was used to help distinguish which companies should receive this "corporate welfare."

The NIST

In 1993 Prabhakar was chosen to head the NIST. Her appointment broke the long-standing tradition within the agency of selecting directors internally and by seniority. The NIST under President Bill Clinton is expected to grow from its current budget of $520 million to $1.4 billion by 1997. Prabhakar plans to bring technology development to a higher prominence among lawmakers and the general public. Aside from the Advanced Technology Program, the program that directly funds private research, the NIST also directs the Manufacturing Extension Partnership, which helps small and medium-sized companies adapt to new technologies.

Prabhakar has promised to run the NIST in a "pork free" manner, meaning that she will not make grants based on the political clout they will afford certain congressional representatives into whose districts the money flows. Instead, she will direct money to the most helpful and promising industries doing the most important work. If she is able to do only that, it will be a remarkable feat in Washington.

Reflections on ethnicity

In an interview with *AAB,* Prabhakar acknowledged the importance of her Indian heritage, remarking, "Being an Indian is a permanent part of me. I am extremely fortunate to have been born [as one]." She also said that she has noticed changes in the Asian Indian community since her early days in the United States. "When I went to study engineering, it was a novelty," she explained. "The other day a young Indian high school girl told me that her elder sister was going to college to study electrical engineering, and she didn't even bat an eyelid. It is no longer an exception to the rule."

Since her appointment as NIST's director, Prabhakar has become a role model for the Asian Indian community. "I have had Indian parents come up to me and say that now they truly believe that their kids can do anything they want," she reported. Prabhakar is flattered, but, she pointed out, "We tend to believe that one's role model has to be of the same sex and ethnicity. However, I believe that choosing a role model of a different sex and race may actually have a liberating effect."

Sources:

Adam, J. A., "Arati Prabhakar," *IEEE Spectrum,* December 1993, pp. 48-51.

Prabhakar, Arati, telephone interview with Shamita Das Dasgupta, June 22, 1994.

Dith Pran

Journalist
Born September 27, 1942, Siem Riep, Cambodia

"There is no doctor who can heal me. But I know a man like Pol Pot, he is even sicker than I am.... We both have the horror in our heads. In Cambodia, the killer and the victim have the same disease."

Dith Pran is a Cambodian photo-journalist who was hired by *New York Times* correspondent Sydney Schanberg as his photographer and assistant in covering the widening American war in Southeast Asia during the early 1970s. Schanberg and Pran developed a close relationship during their time together—as chronicled in the 1984 film *The Killing Fields*—but when the Americans withdrew from the former French colony of Cambodia in 1975, Schanberg was unable to help his friend escape as the murderous Khmer Rouge, the communist guerrilla insurgency, descended on the Cambodian capital of Phnom Penh. Pran was stranded in Cambodia as the guerrillas took power and initiated one of the holocausts of modern times.

From 1974 until 1979, Pran lived in almost daily fear of death. He lost more than 50 family members to the Khmer Rouge. His father died of malnutrition, his mother from the prolonged strain of living in famine and under wartorn conditions, and his three brothers and sister and their families perished as well. One brother, with his wife and five children, was rumored to have been thrown alive to hungry crocodiles. Such stories were common under the government of Communist leader Pol Pot, as he and his troops destroyed Cambodia in the name of ridding it of all Western influence.

Pran's tale of survival is miraculous, as are the stories of all of Cambodia's refugees. He attributes his survival to luck, resourcefulness, and constant prayer. As a Buddhist, Pran prayed daily to be saved from the madness consuming his country. After five years, when he was finally able to reach the border with Thailand and make contact with Schanberg, he felt his prayers had been answered. Schanberg, who had spent a great deal of time looking for his good friend, was able to help Pran immigrate to the United States. Today Pran lives outside of New York City with his family and works as a photographer for the *New York Times*. With the attention he has drawn to the horror of the Cambodian holocaust, Pran has emerged as an internationally respected advocate for peace in Cambodia. He has devoted his life to raising awareness of the situation in his homeland. "I'm a one-person crusade," he told *Asian American Biography*. "I must speak for those who did not survive and for those who still suffer. I don't consider myself a politician or a hero; I'm a messenger. If Cambodia is to survive, she needs many voices."

Born in the middle class

Pran's hometown is in the northeastern part of Cambodia near Angkor Wat, a spectacular cluster of ancient Buddhist temples in the thick Cambodian jungle. His father was a senior public works officer who supervised road building in the area. Pran had a comfortable childhood and was educated in colonial schools, where he learned French. (He taught himself English.) He finished high school in 1960 and went to work as an interpreter for a U.S. military assistance group then stationed in Cambodia as a part of America's long involvement in the war in Vietnam.

In 1965, Cambodia severed relations with the United States, charging that U.S. troops had violated international law when they launched attacks on Cambodian villages from their bases in South Vietnam. After the American military presence was forced out of Cambodia, Pran went to work as an interpreter for a British film crew and later as a receptionist at a tourist hotel near Angkor Wat, a popular destination for travelers.

In 1970, the Khmer Rouge escalated their guerrilla campaign against the U.S.-backed puppet government of Cambodia headed by Lon Nol. The Khmer Rouge were a guerrilla army that practiced sabotage and harassment instead of traditional warfare. They believed in the teachings of Chinese Communist leader Mao Zedong and sought to overthrow the government and install an agricultural, anti-Western regime. After an attack on Siem Riep, Pran's hometown, a group of Western journalists converged in the area. Pran helped them as an interpreter and guide. He was alarmed at the level of human suffering his people were enduring and he wanted to help spread the word to the West about what was happening. He soon moved with his wife and children to the capital of Phnom Penh.

The *New York Times*

In Phnom Penh, Pran was able to work with several news-gathering organizations, both in television and print. His first association with the *New York Times* was with Saigon bureau chief Craig Whitney. In 1972, Sydney Schanberg, who had been stationed in Singapore, was transferred to Cambodia as its civil war increased in intensity. America had become increasingly involved in the country as well, launching a secret war in which bombs were illegally dropped on Cambodia in order to root out Vietnamese Communist guerrillas, the Viet Cong. Pran began working with Schanberg exclusively and in 1973 he was officially hired by the *Times* as a stringer.

Pran and Schanberg became great friends as they worked at a hectic pace to cover the chaos that was sweeping across Cambodia. Their collaboration became almost constant as they traversed the city and the jungle surrounding it, the bond between them growing every day. In *The Death and Life of Dith Pran,* Schanberg's book about his experiences in Cambodia, he wrote, "It is difficult to describe how a friendship grows, for it often grows from seemingly contradictory roots—mutual needs, overlapping dependencies, intense shared experiences, and even the inequality of service, one serving the other. Our bond grew in all of these ways."

By 1975, it was clear that the Khmer Rouge would soon take control of Cambodia. On April 12 of that year, American officials announced their decision to leave the country. Pran was able to get his family out of Cambodia with the help of Schanberg, and they were evacuated on military planes. Six days later, the Khmer Rouge occupied Phnom Penh. Pran and Schanberg stayed behind to cover events, hoping the takeover would be peaceful. It was not. After taking control of the city, the Khmer Rouge began

Dith Pran

to force the populace out of the capital and into the countryside; those who refused were killed.

Split by war

Pran and Schanberg took refuge at the French Embassy with other Westerners and their Cambodian friends, but soon the Cambodians, including Pran, were ordered to leave the grounds. The French were in a politically difficult situation—if they wanted to get the Westerners out of the country, they could not defy Cambodia's demand that all its citizens be evacuated. Schanberg and others tried to forge a passport for Pran, but the scheme failed; Pran was forced to leave the compound, armed with food, cigarettes, and bribe money.

Pran understood the anti-Westernism of the Khmer Rouge and soon abandoned the money and cigarettes, fearing they would mark him as someone who had had contact with the West. The new government wanted to return Cambodia to a pre-colonial society, engaged solely in agriculture, with no ties to the outside world, which they blamed for the hellish war that had practically destroyed their country. Pran donned the clothes of a Cambodian peasant and made his way back to his hometown where he was put to work in the rice fields. He stayed in Siem Riep for the next two and half years, nearly dying of starvation as a famine set in and rations were reduced to one spoonful of rice a day. Villagers began eating whatever they could get their hands on to survive as the condition of the country deteriorated. Pran heard rumors of dead bodies being dug up for their flesh. The suffering of the people of Cambodia during this period was tremendous and extreme in a way few in the West will ever be able to fully understand.

Pran eventually left the village and went to work as a houseboy for a Khmer Rouge commune chief. Then, in 1979, Vietnam invaded Cambodia, and Pran decided to escape from the commune and return to Siem Riep. On his way he discovered "the killing fields"—acres of bones and skulls lying across the ground, the remains of the millions of Cambodians killed by the Khmer Rouge.

"We both have horror in our heads"

Under Vietnamese occupation, Pran worked as Siem Riep's administrative chief. When his superiors found out that he had once worked as a journalist, he feared he would be killed and made his escape. With a group of 12 men, he made the 60-mile journey to the border with Thailand, all the while in fear of Khmer Rouge guerrillas, Vietnamese patrols, unmarked mines, and other hidden traps. After four days, they reached the border and then hid for another two weeks waiting for an opportunity to slip across into the refugee camps. When he finally arrived, Pran found an American officer of the camp and asked her to contact Schanberg at the *New York Times.* Their joyous reunion is the emotional highlight of the highly acclaimed 1984 film *The Killing Fields,* which is based on Schanberg's account of his friendship with Pran.

Pran now lives in the United States, but his journey is far from over. He spends much of his time traveling to lecture about conditions in Cambodia. In recent years, as the country has begun to achieve a relative degree of peacefulness with the help of the United Nations, Pran has returned to Cambodia to deliver school materials, blankets, and other supplies to orphaned children. He hopes to bring the leaders of the Khmer Rouge to justice for war crimes at the World Court. He considers Elie Wiesel, a concentration-camp survivor who speaks out about the Jewish holocaust in Nazi Germany, his hero and role model.

Pran is still terrorized by memories of what he endured. In a 1991 interview with the *Los Angeles Times,* he said, "There is no doctor who can heal me. But I know a man like Pol Pot, he is even sicker than I am.... We both have the horror in our heads. In Cambodia, the killer and the victim have the same disease."

Sources:

Getlin, Josh, "Speaking for the Innocents: As Cambodia Undergoes a Painful Rebirth, Dith Pran Remembers—and Cannot Forgive," *Los Angeles Times,* October 25, 1991.

Grogan, David W., "When Newsman Sydney Schanberg Was Expelled from Cambodia, His Best Friend Was Left Behind in the Killing Fields," *People,* December 10, 1984, p. 65.

Pran, Dith, personal biography supplied by Pran, March 1994.

Pran, Dith, interview with Helen Zia, 1994.

Schanberg, Sidney, *The Death and Life of Dith Pran,* New York: Viking and Penguin Books, 1980.

Beulah Quo

Actress
Born in Stockton, California

"I would like to get to the point where theater and art know no boundaries. But first we've got to give people of color a chance to play their own color, and then give them a chance to play roles that were forbidden to them."

Actress Beulah Quo has appeared in many well-known films and television series. Now in her seventies, and devoting much of her time to volunteer community activities, Quo spent 40 years working in Hollywood. She can be seen in the films *Chinatown, Love Is a Many Splendored Thing,* and *Girls, Girls, Girls.* Her television credits include parts in *Starsky and Hutch, Hawaii Five-O, Magnum P.I.,* and *Trapper John, M.D.*

Quo speaks frankly about the lack of roles available to Asian American actors. She believes Asian and Asian American artists do not get the recognition in Hollywood that they deserve, acknowledging that suitable roles often go to Caucasian actors who are made up to look Asian. "I would like to get to the point where theater and art know no boundaries," Quo said. "But first we've got to give people of color a chance to play roles that were forbidden to them." Quo has dedicated her life in recent years to trying to change these casting policies—not for herself, but for future generations of Asian American actors.

Teacher training came first

Quo was born in the quiet, central California community of Stockton. Her parents did not have much money, but they wanted their daughter to have a good education. Quo graduated with honors from Stockton High School and from the University of California at Berkeley and earned a master's degree from the University of Chicago. She was trained to be a teacher and taught college in both the United States and China.

She and her husband, Edwin, were teaching at Ginling College in Nanjin, China, in the 1940s when the Communist Revolution engulfed the country. Quo and her husband fled with their two-month-old baby. Years later, Quo would remember this experience when she acted in *The Children of An Lac,* a

Beulah Quo

television drama about the founder of an orphanage in Vietnam who helped save hundred of orphans in Saigon.

Career change

Quo's acting career began by accident. In 1954 she applied for a job as a dialect coach to actress Jennifer Jones for the movie *Love Is a Many Splendored Thing.* Jones's part required that she speak with a British-Chinese accent. While Quo did not, in fact, get the job, director Henry King asked her to play the part of Jones's aunt.

One role led to another, and soon Quo was working full time as an actress. Quickly, she began to realize that acting was a lot like teaching; both were effective ways to reach an audience. She tried to combine careers for a while, but each eventually proved to be so time-consuming that she needed to make a choice between one or the other. She decided to pursue acting. "I felt I could influence people more," she told an interviewer. "I'm a social worker at heart, you see, and I tried to change the general public's concept of a person of color."

Throughout the 1960s and 1970s, Quo acted in films and dozens of popular weekly television dramas. Her film roles included parts in *Flower Drum Song, The Sand Pebbles,* and *Chinatown.* One of her favorite roles came in *The Sand Pebbles,* when her petite, five-foot, three-inch frame was built up with stuffing so she could play a "fat mama." She also remembers *Girls, Girls, Girls* and working with superstar singer Elvis Presley as a career highlight. "He was such a gentleman," she recalled. "He always had time to say hello and give a kind word to everyone."

On the stage, she was seen in *The World of Suzie Wong* and *Martyrs Can't Go Home.* From 1985 to 1991, Quo played Olin, a fast-talking, hip housekeeper on the television soap opera *General Hospital.* She was the only Asian American actor in soaps whose story line reappeared over several years. More recently, Quo played the role of the empress of Chinese dynasty founder Kublai Khan in the NBC-TV production of *Marco Polo,* one of the first major American film projects to be made in China.

Still committed to education

Because Quo believes the media is an ideal starting place for exposing the diversity of the Asian American community, she began working in public affairs programming. She ran a talk show for five years, frequently spotlighting Asian Americans and issues important to the Asian American community. She also began producing documentaries about well-known Asian Americans, including one about Oscar-winning filmmaker James Wong Howe. This documentary, *James Wong Howe: The Man and His Movies,* aired shortly before Howe died, and won a local Emmy Award.

Quo's list of volunteer activities stretches almost as long as her acting credits. She has contributed her time to the United Way, El Nido Social Services, the China Society, and the Asian Pacific American Friends of the Los Angeles Center Theater Group. She was also a founder of the East West Players (the first Asian American theater company in the United States) and has done work for the Association of Asian Pacific Artists, which honored her with its lifetime achievement award in 1990.

Sources:

Quo, Beulah, biographical materials and press releases provided by Quo.

Timmerman, Sonia, "A Classy Lady, Beulah Quo," *Port Charles Gazette,* January/February 1991.

Safi U. Qureshey

Entrepreneur, engineer
Born 1951, Pakistan

Qureshey's philosophy for succeeding in the current computer market is to increase market share. He hopes to expand market share by capturing international markets.

Safi U. Qureshey is one of three cofounders of AST Research, a business established in 1979, when Qureshey and two friends amassed $2,000 to start a small electronic design company. The firm moved into the field of computers in 1981, when the computer giant IBM began manufacturing personal computers. Qureshey and his partners, Thomas Yuen and Albert Wong, saw that the market for PCs (personal computers) would be huge and began manufacturing inexpensive add-ons, such as additional memory, to complement store-bought models. From this inspired market targeting, AST has grown at a phenomenal rate. The company went public in 1983, meaning Qureshey and his partners began selling shares of ownership in AST on the stock exchange, and it has continued its unprecedented growth rate. In 1990, AST's share price grew by 259 percent, the highest growth rate of any stock traded on a major exchange.

In 1988, Wong left the company; Yuen followed in 1992. Today AST is headed by Qureshey alone. The company is based in Irvine, California, and its products are manufactured in Fountain Valley, California, London, England, Hong Kong, Taiwan, and Ireland and are sold in 89 countries. AST employs 6,700 people worldwide, ranks 431st on the *Fortune 500* list of leading U.S. companies, and, since its acquisition of Tandy in 1993, has become the fourth-largest computer manufacturer in the country, after IBM, Apple, and Compaq.

Born in Pakistan

Qureshey, a devout Muslim, is a native of Karachi, Pakistan. He was educated at the University of Karachi, where he received a bachelor's degree in physics in 1970. He went to the United States shortly thereafter and enrolled in the University of Texas at Austin, where he studied electrical engineering. He earned his master's degree in 1975. After finishing his education, Qureshey held a variety of jobs in electronics and computer manufacturing and design. At one of these, as a test engineer with Computer Automation, he met Yuen, his future partner.

The birth of AST

Yuen persuaded Qureshey and another friend, Albert Wong, to pool their resources and begin an electronics consulting firm in 1979. Together they had only $2,000, but with that, the company was born. They used the initials of their first names as the company's name and drew straws for the positions of president, secretary, and treasurer. Qureshey became president—a position in name only as the friends worked as equals.

AST began selling PC enhancers, but, like most new companies, its beginnings were slow. Qureshey told *Contemporary Entrepreneurs* about their first sale, reporting, "We sold our first board to a customer in

Safi U. Qureshey

Orange County. They sent us a check for $82, and the check bounced. It was not a good feeling." By 1981, however, the company was beginning to do well, selling 64K to 256K expansion memory boards, multi-protocol communications boards, and an asynchronous communication card. In 1982, the company found itself in need of an influx of cash to help it expand. As it was a new venture, however, banks were reluctant to invest, so the three partners refinanced the mortgages on their houses to raise the $50,000 they needed. By the next year, sales had reached $13 million.

Innovation in a booming market

In the mid-1980s, the personal computer market skyrocketed as schools, businesses, and consumers began demanding faster, smaller, more efficient machines. Companies experienced dramatic ups and downs in sales as the market took shape. In 1985, IBM started producing its own enhancement products, which made a considerable dent in AST's profits. The trio adapted, though, as they always had, putting their energies into developing their own line of personal computers, which they introduced in 1986. The following two years saw further expansion when AST introduced 12 new PC systems and three new enhancement board products. In 1991, the company produced its one millionth computer, which was presented to President George Bush. In ten years AST sales had gone from $71,000 in 1981 to $688.5 million in 1991.

The rise of AST has not been without setbacks, however. In 1989, the company reported an $8.9 million loss and was forced to lay off 120 employees. It was during this crisis that Albert Wong left the business over a dispute about the company's future. Qureshey and Yuen took this opportunity to evaluate past errors and goals. They replaced Wong with a five-member executive committee, sold off their Apple and DEC divisions to pay off debt, and began a massive restructuring.

The key to AST's success

Observers attribute AST's success to a number of factors, including its humane working environment and an enterprising spirit. Until 1988, the company sponsored pancake breakfasts with employees to discuss company successes and problems. Another often-cited factor in the company's advances is the spirit of frugality and hard work of its three Asian immigrant founders. Although AST's bonus program includes all its employees, the company is conservative with stock options.

Employees describe the company's work ethic as challenging, fun, and fast-paced. Others say the challenges lie primarily in long hours and high stress levels. Indeed, such an environment can have a downside—AST has a high employee turnover rate, with burnout frequently cited as the reason. According to one former manager quoted in the *Orange County Business Journal,* workers have to tolerate frequent reorganizations and a variety of reporting relationships.

The future

In 1993, AST acquired Tandy's personal computer business for $117 million. This purchase surprised some and led, indirectly, to a temporary drop of 18 percent in AST stock. Qureshey believed the purchase was sound, however, and in the second quarter of 1994, revenues soared by 95 percent. Qureshey's philosophy for succeeding in the current computer market is to increase market share. "What you're going to see is a lot of people exiting the business," he told *U.S. News & World Report.* "Only the companies with enough market share are going to survive the shakeout."

One way in which AST hopes to expand its market share is by capturing international markets. Already, one in four computers sold in China are ASTs, and this is in a market where computer demand is expected to grow by 20 percent a year for the remainder of the decade. Sales in China account for about 10 percent of overall sales. Qureshey is also interested in pursuing the African market. "We're going to do the same thing in Africa [that we did in China] because we saw that they are not getting much attention there," he told *U.S. News and World Report.*

Besides his success as an entrepreneur, Qureshey is also a prominent citizen of Southern California. He is a member of the Southern California Technology Executives Network and holds a position on its board of directors. In 1992, he accompanied Congressman Christopher Cox on his visit to meet with Mexico's President Carlos Salinas regarding the North American Free Trade Agreement (NAFTA).

Sources:

Armstrong, Larry, "This 12-Year-Old Has Come of Age," *Business Week,* May 6, 1991, pp. 122-23.

Gillin, Paul, "AST Bids for the Big Time as Market Leaders Suffer," *Computerworld,* December 16, 1991, pp. 97-99.

Impoco, Jim, "A Smile of Recognition: AST Finally Gets Its Due as One of America's Top Computer Makers," *U.S. News & World Report,* March 21, 1994, pp. 54-55.

Longwell, John, "Corporate Challenge," *Orange County Business Journal,* August 12, 1991, p. 1.

McGuire, Mark, "AST Mounts Push for Big League Status," *PC Week,* August 30, 1993, p. 106.

"Safi U. Qureshey and Thomas C. K. Yuen," *Contemporary Entrepreneurs,* Detroit: Omnigraphics, 1992, pp. 402-7.

Jhoon Rhee

Martial artist
Born January 7, 1932, Sanyangri, Korea

Rhee has vowed to live until the age of 136. In his 1992 appearance before Congress, he did 100 push-ups in less than one minute and vowed he would be back to repeat the feat in 2032 at the age of 100.

Jhoon Rhee is a master of the Korean martial art of Tae Kwon Do, one of hundreds of variations of the martial art known as karate. Because he was the leading figure in introducing his art to the United States, he has often been called "the father of American Tae Kwon Do." Rhee is a tireless promoter of the inner strength and happiness that can be achieved through all forms of exercise, especially Tae Kwon Do. To this end, he created the Jhoon Rhee Foundation to teach inner-city elementary school children the "Joy of Discipline," an exercise program he hopes will stay with them throughout their lives.

In 1992, Rhee testified before the U.S. House of Representatives' Select Committee on Aging, telling lawmakers of his belief in the power of inner happiness as it can be attained through Tae Kwon Do and the importance of starting young. "It takes a year to harvest a crop, 10 years to see the full beauty of a tree, and 50 years to make a man," he testified. "So let us begin for our young children's education, motivating them to exercise and study."

Reverence for life

From his earliest years, Rhee was taught a reverence for life that began with a reverence for the body. His grandfather on his father's side was a scholar with a doctorate in Confucian literature (the study of the great Chinese philosopher Confucius), and Rhee admired him for his character, wisdom, and loving personality. His grandfather lived to be 92 years old, a feat Rhee attributes to the fact that he did 30 minutes of stretching exercises every morning. Such routines are common in Asia, and Rhee incorporated them into a regimen he promotes today called the "Jhoon Rhee Daily Dozen."

Rhee also learned from his esteemed grandfather the importance of honesty. In a story he tells often, his grandfather once bought him a kindergarten book that Rhee thoughtlessly left at his school's playground. When he came home, his grandfather asked him to read him a passage from the book; rather than admit his carelessness, Rhee lied and said he had lent the book to a friend. His grandfather then produced the book, spanked the young man, and told him that God watches closely over everything we do. The lesson was one he would never forget.

Discovering Tae Kwon Do

As a child, Rhee was not very physically active. In school he was always the slowest runner, the smallest child. In high school, he was tormented by bullies. In 1947, at the age of 15, he enrolled in the Chung Do Kwan School of Tae Kwon Do. At first he kept his lessons a secret from his father, who had a low opinion of the martial arts, thinking they were not very different from street fighting.

Jhoon Rhee

In the 11th grade, Rhee had his first opportunity to use his new skills when he was finally pushed over the edge by one of the school's most notorious bullies. After he refused to give back a pencil he took from Rhee, Rhee challenged the student to a fight after school. Rhee beat him easily and badly. The victory earned Rhee respect among his classmates and taught him a lesson about strength.

The American dream

After World War II, Korea was liberated from a long and brutal occupation by the Japanese. Having been set free primarily by the Americans, many people in Korea got an idealized sense of the United States. Rhee was also fascinated by the way American culture was portrayed in Hollywood movies, which were immensely popular at the time. He began studying English, hoping that some day he would be able to move to the United States.

After graduating from high school, Rhee made plans to attend Dong Kook University, but in 1950 the army of North Korea invaded the South, starting what would become a long and bloody civil war, eventually involving a large international force led by the United States fighting on the side of the South. Rhee and his nine-year-old brother fled south from their parents' home in Sunan province to their grandfather's house in Asan, far from the fighting. Within a couple of months, however, Rhee began to worry when his parents didn't join them, and he returned to his home to look for them. In Sunan, he braved repeated bombings and heavy fighting to look for his parents. He found his mother but never was able to locate his father. Rhee remained in the area, in hiding, until the American-led forces had pushed back the invaders, liberating Sunan. In 1951 Rhee was drafted into the Korean army.

Coming to America

Rhee served in the Korean army until the end of the war in 1954. In 1956, he was finally able to fulfill his dream and immigrate to America. He went to work at an aircraft maintenance program at Gary Air Force Base in Texas. He then enrolled in college to study engineering.

Throughout this time, Rhee had continued his study and practice of Tae Kwon Do, and in the summer of 1962, he moved to Washington, D.C., to teach at a karate school. The school, however, had very few students and before long they were unable to pay the teachers. Rhee was not dissuaded, sensing that, given enough exposure, Americans would flock to the martial arts. He boldly opened his own school and within months he had 100 students. Within three years, he was operating schools throughout the country.

As an engineering student in Texas, Rhee had applied the theories of static, mechanics, speed, and power he was learning in the classroom to the karate he was practicing in the gym. He developed a style that is now known as the "Jhoon Rhee fighting method" with the principles he learned as a student. Traditional Tae Kwon Do fighters essentially try to disable an opponent by knocking him off balance, using less contact than do practitioners of Rhee's method.

Rhee's form centers on learning a series of combinations of moves rather than relying simply on balance. Not surprisingly, traditional masters of Tae Kwon Do criticize Rhee's method. Rhee counters critics with the words of his longtime friend, the late martial artist and actor **Bruce Lee**: "When you are tied by tradition, there can be no improvement."

Prior to the explosion of interest in the martial arts in the late 1960s and early 1970s, Rhee often had a difficult time promoting his sport in America. Since then, though, Tae Kwon Do has become one of the most popular martial arts in the country. Rhee has increased this popularity with the help of celebrities who swear by his teachings. Former heavyweight champion of the world Muhammad Ali, for instance, credits Rhee with teaching him a special "accu-punch" that he says helped him win his famous "Thriller in Manila" fight. In 1975, Rhee brought his method to the halls of government when he sponsored a "Capital Hill Grudge Bout" featuring U.S. congressmen fighting. Democrats went up against Republicans in a semi-contact match.

Now in his early sixties, Rhee has vowed to live until the age of 136. In his 1992 appearance before Congress, he did 100 push-ups in less than one minute and vowed he would be back to repeat the feat in 2032 at the age of 100.

Sources:

Segerdal, Alasair, "Jhoon Rhee," *Combat,* February 1978.

Simpkins, Alex, and Annellen Simpkins, "Jhoon Rhee: Born to Be Happy," *Tae Kwon Do Times,* January 1994.

Testimony of Jhoon Rhee, presented before the U.S. House of Representatives' Select Committee on Aging, February 25, 1992.

Patricia Saiki

Politician
Born May 28, 1930, Hilo, Hawaii

"I've always been the kind of person who, when faced with something wrong, has to correct it."

Patricia Saiki has lived a life of public service. She is the first Republican to have represented Hawaii— from 1987 to 1991—in the U.S. House of

Representatives since it became a state in 1959. She was appointed in 1991 by President George Bush to head the U.S. Small Business Administration, an agency with 4,000 employees and a budget of $382 million. She taught at the Kennedy School of Government at Harvard University and was a candidate for governor of Hawaii in 1994.

From her early career as a teacher through her various political positions, Saiki has championed the rights of women and children. She says a strong early family life and a supportive husband and children have played a critical role in her success in all phases of her life.

Father inspires confidence

Saiki was the oldest of three girls born to Kazuo and Shizue (Inoue) Fukuda. Saiki's father's parents had come to Hawaii from Japan and labored in the sugar cane fields, earning a dollar a day to support their five sons. Saiki's father worked as a clerk, and her mother worked at home as a seamstress. There was no money for extras, not even a car. Education, however, was not considered an extra. The family devoted themselves to saving every dollar to pay for college for all three girls. Pat was the first to go off to school, and she lived in a dormitory where everyone shared chores. She sold stockings and babysat and graduated with a double major in education and history from the University of Hawaii in 1952. All three Fukuda girls eventually graduated and became teachers.

In an interview with Cobey Black, Saiki said her father was responsible for building her self-esteem: "Dad was the first feminist. But what Dad did that is more important is

inspire in me the confidence of my own worth. To believe in myself—that was a wonderful gift." Saiki managed to save enough money from her first teaching job to buy her father a used car and she taught him to drive it, helping complete the circle of family support.

On June 19, 1954, she married Stanley Mitsuo Saiki, a doctor 12 years her senior. Shortly after their marriage, he enrolled at the University of Pennsylvania to specialize in the area of obstetrics and gynecology, and the couple left Hawaii. Their first child, Stanley, Jr., was born soon after, and the growing family then moved to Toledo, Ohio, for Stanley Saiki's residency. There, two more Saiki children, Sandra and Margaret, were born. Saiki decided to return to teaching to help support her family. "Grading papers between three loads of laundry was a nightly ritual," she told Black.

Political beginning

The Saikis returned to Hawaii in the late 1950s, around the time Hawaii became a state. There they welcomed their fourth and fifth children, Stuart and Laura. Saiki got her first political job as a precinct officer in St. Louis Heights. She became angry when older, more established politicians, "old war-horses," pushed their candidates through without opposition. That was why she decided to speak up: "It didn't seem right, even to a busy homemaker, so I helped work up a slate and the next thing I knew, they'd made me a precinct officer—just to keep me quiet," she quipped.

In the 1960s, while teaching at Kaimuki Intermediate School, Saiki helped to organize a teachers' union. At that time teachers

Patricia Saiki

had no say in educational decisions and worked long hours under poor conditions. Saiki questioned whether "tracking" children—directing certain children toward college and others toward careers that didn't require college—was wise. She also felt that teachers should help set educational goals and design challenging curricula. She spoke up, and the head of the Hawaii Government Employees Association (HGEA) listened. Saiki helped to organize, and teachers joined, the Teacher's Chapter of HGEA.

Saiki soon became more active in politics and served in a number of different posi-

tions for the Republican party in Hawaii. In 1968, at the urging of her fellow teachers, Saiki ran for public office and was elected a delegate to the Hawaii State Constitutional Convention.

The following year President Richard Nixon appointed Saiki to the Presidential Advisory Council on the Status of Women. She served on the committee for eight years and was reappointed by Nixon's successor, President Gerald Ford. During that time, Saiki supervised the funding of the Hawaii State Commission on the Status of Women and served as a watchdog for women's rights. She was then elected to the Hawaii House of Representatives, where she served from 1968 to 1974, and the Hawaii State Senate, where she served from 1974 to 1982. She wrote 25 bills addressing equal rights for women, including the Equal Rights Amendment. In 1987, she was elected to the U.S. Congress and was afforded the opportunity to work on a national level to address her concerns about women's and children's issues. "I've always been the kind of person who, when faced with something wrong, has to correct it," Saiki observed.

After a successful term as congress-woman, Saiki decided to run for the U.S. Senate. When she lost, she was so disappointed she told her family she didn't want to talk to anyone on the phone. However, she did accept one call—from President George Bush. He consoled her on her loss and asked her to come back to Washington as part of the Small Business Administration (SBA).

Two weeks after she was sworn in as the administrator of the SBA, Saiki's husband died. The couple had been married for 37 years and, together, had watched as their children grew up; Stanley and Sandra became doctors, Margaret a veterinarian, Stuart a computer engineer, and Laura a businesswoman. "I've been blessed with two marvelous, encouraging men in my life, my father and my husband," commented Saiki.

Home to Hawaii

Saiki continued at the SBA until November 1992, when she decided to return to Hawaii to be near family. She wasn't home long, however, before she was called by the John F. Kennedy School of Government at Harvard University. Saiki returned to the classroom, teaching at Harvard for the spring 1993 term.

During spring break Saiki received another enticing telephone call: a Republican committee in Hawaii called to ask her to run for governor in 1994. "I really felt that with a lifetime that's been gifted with a devoted family, a great husband, good health and a political career which has fulfilled the faith of my supporters, I could do a good job as governor." Saiki lost the race for governor to Benjamin Cayetano, however, in November of 1994.

Sources:

Black, Cobey, "Hilo Girl," campaign literature, Saiki for Governor '94: A Committee, 1994.

"A Fresh Start: Patricia Saiki '94 Governor," campaign literature, Saiki for Governor '94: A Committee, 1994.

"Hawaii Business," *In Focus,* September 1991.

Saiki, Patricia, "The Advantages of Making Loans with the SBA (Small Business Administration)," *Journal of Commercial Lending,* November 1992.

"Women Who Won: Seasoned Politicians with Solid Campaign Financing Make Their Mark," *Ms.,* January 1987.

Richard Sakakida

Counterintelligence agent
Born November 19, 1920, Maui, Hawaii

Richard Sakakida was awarded the Bronze Star for his distinguished, selfless, and crucial service to the American military.

R etired Lieutenant Colonel Richard M. Sakakida of the U.S. Air Force is a career military officer who worked as a counterintelligence agent in the Philippines during World War II. During this time, Sakakida was held as a prisoner by the Japanese, who repeatedly tortured him to find out his position within the U.S. military. He was eventually released by the Japanese but continued to work among them, obtaining useful information and sending it to General Douglas MacArthur's command in Australia.

After the war, Sakakida continued to work for the U.S. military by helping to round up persons suspected of committing war crimes. He later testified as a key witness in war crimes trials. Sakakida was awarded the Bronze Star for his distinguished, selfless, and crucial service to the American military.

Early military training

Sakakida was born November 19, 1920, in Maui, Hawaii. His parents, both of Japanese descent, raised their three children—two sons and one daughter—in Honolulu. His father was a boilermaker and his mother was a homemaker who stayed at home to raise Sakakida and his two siblings.

Sakakida began his military training at Honolulu's McKinley High School, where he achieved the rank of cadet colonel during his senior year. He graduated from McKinley in 1939, two years before the United States entered World War II. Sakakida's instructor at McKinley, Major Jack Gilbert, recruited him into the Corps of Intelligence Police (CIP), the counterintelligence agency of the U.S. Army. In 1941, nine months before the Japanese bombing of Pearl Harbor, Sakakida was sworn in as a sergeant in the CIP.

Protecting U.S. interests

Along with another Japanese American, Arthur Komori, Sakakida was sent to the Philippines on April 7, 1941. The United States had still not officially entered the war, but the government was worried that Japan would use its military power to take over weaker territories in Asia and the Pacific. The United States had a longtime colonial interest in the Philippines and wanted to protect it from the Japanese. Sakakida's mission was to pose as a deserter from the American military and to keep tabs on Japanese nationals living in the Philippines.

Sakakida moved into the Nishikawa Hotel in downtown Manila, where he posed as a representative of the Marsman Trading Company, Sears and Roebuck's outlet in the Philippines. Sakakida blended well into the hubbub of Manila. A key opportunity came on July 25, 1941, when the United States froze Japanese assets, including those in the Philippines, in protest of Japan's military aggression throughout Asia. Sakakida

Richard Sakakida

volunteered to help Japanese nationals adhere to the new financial rules. During interviews with Japanese Filipinos, Sakakida would ask questions that were not actually required, such as those about their military training, if any. He would then pass this information on to his superiors.

On December 8, 1941, the Japanese air force bombed Manila, beginning their invasion of the islands. In the aftermath of the bombing, Japanese nationals were rounded up for detention by American officials. Sakakida, whose mission was secret even to

American officials in Manila, was arrested on suspicion of being a spy for Japan. He spent a few days in prison with his fellow agent Komori before being released. After his release, he began working openly, in uniform, translating Japanese prisoners' responses to questions and signals intercepted from the enemy.

Early in 1942 the Japanese began making significant advances in fighting to control the Philippines. U.S. General Douglas MacArthur ordered the translators who remained on the islands to evacuate, and arrangements were made to send Sakakida and Komori to headquarters in Australia. Sakakida, however, felt he would be better able to help in the Philippines and persuaded his superiors to let another man take his seat on the evacuation plane. On May 6, 1942, U.S. forces in the Philippines surrendered to Japan. Sakakida was arrested and spent six months in jail being interrogated by the Japanese, who doubted his cover story of being an American deserter. They considered him a traitor and tortured him cruelly throughout his imprisonment, burning him with cigarettes and purposely dislocating his shoulders. Sakakida never wavered from his story despite the torture.

Finally, the Japanese gave up on Sakakida, released him from prison, and sent him to work in the office of Colonel Nishiharu, an important official in the Japanese army. His duties would be to assist in the office in any way he could and then to serve as the colonel's houseboy when not at the office, even living at the colonel's residence. His work at Nishiharu's office allowed him access to top-secret information that he used to free Filipino resistance fighters who were imprisoned by the Japanese. The daring prison break he arranged was a remarkable and brave endeavor, and it led to the freedom of nearly five hundred fighters.

Jungle escape

In December of 1944 the United States launched its invasion of the Philippines. Sakakida joined up with a band of Filipinos in the jungle. During a fight with a Japanese unit, Sakakida was wounded and separated from his group. He wandered through the jungle until he came upon an American unit. The Americans were suspicious of Sakakida's story, but the major in charge checked it out and within hours a jeep from the counterintelligence corps was sent for him.

After the war, from 1948 to 1975, Sakakida served the air force in its Office of Special Investigations (AFOSI). At the time of his retirement on April 1, 1975, he was commander of AFOSI in Japan.

In 1994 Sakakida was honored by the government of the Philippines with the Legion of Honor (Degree of Legionnaire) presidential award in recognition of his exceptionally meritorious service to the Filipino-American Freedom Fighters and as a U.S. Army undercover agent.

Sources:

Bray, Ann, "Undercover Nisei," in *Military Intelligence: Its Heroes and Legends,* U.S. Army Intelligence and Security Command, Arlington Hall Station, Virginia.

Sakakida, Richard, written interview with Jim Henry, July 18, 1994.

"WWII Nisei MIS Vet Receives Legion of Honor Award," *Nichi Bei Times,* May 5, 1994.

Lea Salonga

Actress, singer
Born February 1971, Manila, the Philippines

In 1991 Lea Salonga received the Tony Award for best leading actress in a musical—for her performance in Miss Saigon—*in front of a loudly cheering Broadway audience and 12 million television viewers around the world.*

Lea Salonga

I n 1988 17-year-old Lea Salonga was at home in the Philippines attending the Jesuit university, Ateneo de Manila. By then she had amassed 11 years of show business experience in the theater and on TV. Nonetheless, she was planning to become a doctor. But when British theatrical producer Cameron Mackintosh came to Manila to find the female lead for his stage production of the musical *Miss Saigon*, Salonga decided to audition. She won the part and became an international celebrity. Later, in 1992, she provided the singing voice of Princess Jasmine in the Disney hit movie *Aladdin*.

Family guidance and support

Salonga's musical interests had always been encouraged by her parents. Her father, who also loved music, helped to launch Salonga's career. Her mother, Joy, has kept a strict watch on her daughter's professional and social life. Salonga's first stage role was in the Manila production of *The King and I*, after which came *Fiddler on the Roof,* and the title role in *Annie*. When she was 12 years old, she hosted a TV musical variety show for children, *Love, Lea,* for two years.

At the time of the audition for *Miss Saigon*, Salonga's mother wasn't sure Lea should even try out for the part; she was afraid that the casting directors had come to the Philippines to take advantage of young girls. Salonga first had to overcome her mother's objections before she was able to captivate the musical's producers with her pure, sweet, soprano voice at the tryouts. According to those who heard her, Salonga gave a stunning audition and then went on to give remarkable performances.

Salonga's work in the musical was praised by one and all. In 1991 she received the Tony Award (America's highest theater honor) for best leading actress in a musical in front of a loudly cheering Broadway audience and 12 million television viewers watching the award ceremonies around the world. Her role in *Miss Saigon,* however, also raised controversy: when the popular London show headed for Broadway, the Actors' Equity theatrical union demanded that Salonga be replaced because she was Asian and not American. Though it was eventually decided that she would not be replaced, the event almost caused an international incident.

Future plans

Salonga's mother reportedly chaperoned her daughter's dates until she reached the age of 21. Amid such scrutiny, she learned to entertain herself by reading Robin Cook mysteries and watching Charlie Brown and Garfield cartoons. Salonga is interested in working in television and film. She has also released an album of pop songs, titled *Lea Salonga.* Salonga hopes that the story of her success will be inspirational to others.

Sources:

Goodman, Mark, "The New Princess Lea," *People Weekly,* June 17, 1991, p. 55.

Henry, William, "Last Exit to the Land of Hope," *Time,* April 8, 1991, p. 72.

"Lea Salonga: The Fifty Most Beautiful People in the World," *People Weekly,* July 1991, p. 63.

Sheward, David, "Saigon, Rogers, in Tony Tie with Eleven Nominations Each," *Back Stage,* May 10, 1991, p. 1.

"A Whole New World for Lea Salonga," *Science World,* November 19, 1993, p. 16.

Allen Say

Author, illustrator
Born August 28, 1937, Yokohama, Japan

"I consider myself a uniquely American artist and author because I certainly would not have done this kind of work had I stayed in Japan, or had I been born here. It's like [German poet Johann Wolfgang von] Goethe saying that in order to truly know your own language, you must know another. It gives you perspective."

Allen Say is an award-winning author and illustrator of children's books, whose works often explore the experience of being an immigrant in the United States. In 1989 he won the Caldecott Honor Award, the most prestigious award bestowed for the illustration of a children's book, for his illustrations for *The Boy of the Three-Year Nap,* written by Dianne Snyder. The success of the book brought enough recognition for Say to begin illustrating and writing full time. In 1993 Say published *Grandfather's Journey,* which tells the story of his grandfather's life in Japan and America. The book uses Say's vivid paintings to beautifully illustrate the sense of being an outsider in America. In 1994 *Grandfather's Journey* won the Caldecott Medal for most distinguished children's picture book.

Say's books often incorporate moral messages delivered in simple, elegant prose. His paintings, however, are what set his books apart. In an interview with *Booklist,* Say discussed how the two elements of his books come together: "The pictures come first. I do them in sequence. I didn't used to, but this is my way of resolving the story. I start out with a very nebulous idea. I don't really know the nature of the problem at the beginning, but then I start painting, and when the scenes and the characters become real to me, then somehow words ... well, happen. I came late to the English language, and I always have this tremendous fear of writing it. I have no confidence."

A difficult childhood

Say was born in Japan to a Korean father and a Japanese American mother. He began drawing at an early age but was discouraged from artistic pursuits by his father, who wanted his son to devote himself to learning something more practical, like business. Say has many unhappy memories of his childhood, especially those concerning his father. He told *Booklist,* "You notice that I hardly ever talk about my father, whom I really hated all my life. I still do to this day, and that's why he just hovers in the background." His mother was born into a very strict aristocratic family and, according to Say, married his father to get away from the stifling confines of her class and home. She was disowned for doing so.

Say's parents were divorced when he was 12, and he was sent to Tokyo to live with his grandmother, a woman he described in *Booklist* as someone who "turned out to be just a monstrous, horrible woman ... [who] ruined the lives of everyone she came in touch with." Soon after he moved in with her, Say's grandmother told him that if he worked hard at his studies she would get him his own apartment where he would be free to read and draw as much as he wanted. "I thought at first she was kidding," he said,

"but she wasn't." So Say got his own apartment and went off to live on his own in one of the biggest cities in the world at the age of 12.

Say's apprenticeship

Say was smart enough to realize that he couldn't really make it on his own—he knew that he would need some guidance. So one day he showed up at the studio of a famous Japanese cartoonist named Noro Shinpei. The young man thought he was looking for a master in the traditional Japanese sense, but looking back, he now sees that he was "effectively trying to replace my father. Noro Shinpei turns out to be my spiritual father to this day. Each time I send him a book of mine to read, he sends a three-page critique of color, composition, etc. He wrote me about *Tree of Cranes:* 'Not only have you become a master, but poetry has entered your work.' Of course I cried."

Say stayed with Shinpei for four years, learning much from the great cartoonist. At the age of 16, Say was sent to the United States, where he was "deposited at a military academy in Southern California. The idea was that I was going to work my way through school." Say didn't speak a word of English and had to force himself to learn it quickly and mostly on his own. He found a lot of anti-Japanese sentiment at the school, left over from World War II, which had ended only eight years before. He was primarily interested in art, yet the majority of his schoolmates had never heard of the great Spanish painter Pablo Picasso or the Frenchman Henri Matisse. Not only did he feel ostracized for being Japanese, he felt he was with a group who did not share his values.

Allen Say

Cover, *Grandfather's Journey*

As soon as he graduated from the school, Say returned to Japan, saying he hated Southern California. "I thought that Japan was a motherland I was going to return to. I was there for a year; then I eventually came back [to the United States]. I couldn't live in Japan either."

Say's two careers

In Los Angeles Say met a woman he wanted to marry, but they were forced to elope when the woman's father, outraged that she was dating an Asian, threatened Say with a pistol. Then he was drafted and spent two years in the army stationed in Germany. Afterwards, his marriage fell apart and he began looking for a viable way to earn a living. He had all but abandoned painting by this time, having turned his attention to photography, which he'd taken up as a hobby in the army. Soon, he became one of the most successful, highest-paid photographers on the West Coast.

Say continued dabbling in illustration and writing, however, but with no great critical success. In 1968, he illustrated his first children's book, *A Canticle of Waterbirds,* written by Brother Antonius. Four years later he wrote and illustrated his own book, *Dr. Smith's Safari.* In 1979, *The Inn-Keeper's Apprentice,* which he wrote and illustrated, received the American Library Association's Notable Book Award and Best Book for Young Adults citation. The book tells the story of a young Japanese man who apprentices himself to a great comic strip artist. A reviewer, writing in *Horn Book,* said, "The dialogue is lively, the characters are sharply drawn, and the episodes of the loose, realistic narrative are significant events in the maturing of a self-reliant Japanese adolescent."

The Boy of the Three-Year Nap

Throughout the rest of the early 1980s, Say continued to have limited success, but by the middle of the decade he had grown discouraged with publishing and had made up his mind to devote all his energy to photography. Then, in 1987, he was persuaded by his publisher to illustrate one more book. Written by Diane Snyder, *The Boy of the Three-Year Nap* became a hit. In 1988 Say was awarded his first Caldecott Honor for illustration. Say also won the *Boston Globe-Horn Book* award for best picture book of the year. But more importantly, the experience of illustrating this particular book convinced him that, at age 50, he had found what he wanted to do with his life.

In 1989 Say wrote *The Lost Lake;* in 1990, the critically acclaimed *El Chino;* in 1991, *The Tree of Cranes;* and in 1993, *Grandfather's Journey,* which won the 1994 Randolph Caldecott Medal. *School Library Journal* described the book as "flawless in execution" and reported, "Say has chronicled three generations of a family whose hearts are divided between two nations." It went on to explain, "The paintings are astonishingly still ... each translucent watercolor is suffused with light ... offering a glimpse into another world. The effect is bittersweet and reflective." *Publishers Weekly* asserted, "Say transcends the achievements of *A Tree of Cranes* and *A River Dream* with this breathtaking picture book, at once a very personal tribute to his grandfather and a distillation of universally shared emotions."

In describing his place in America as a non-European immigrant, Say told *Booklist,* "I know that I am categorized as an ethnic, as a multicultural artist, but that's not really where I'm coming from. All I'm trying to do is art. I consider myself a uniquely American artist and author because I certainly would not have done this kind of work had I stayed in Japan, or had I been born here. It's like [German poet Johann Wolfgang von] Goethe saying that in order to truly know your own language, you must know another. It gives you perspective."

In his 1988 acceptance speech for the *Boston Globe-Horn Book* award, Say described how he sees his growth as an artist: "I look at my work as a personal tree-ring, a growth record. It is wonderful to be my age and realize that I am growing as an artist."

Sources:

Olendorf, Donna, ed., *Something About the Author,* vol. 69, Detroit: Gale, 1992, pp. 181-83.

Roback, Diane, "Houghton Mifflin Sweeps Newberry, Caldecott Awards," *Publishers Weekly,* February 14, 1994.

Rochman, Hazel, "The *Booklist* Interview: Allen Say," *Booklist,* October 1, 1993, pp. 350-51.

Junior Seau

Football player
Born January 19, 1969, San Diego, California

"There's not another linebacker who does the things he does. But what really sets him apart is he plays with so much enthusiasm and emotion."—Warren Moon

In his three years in the National Football League (NFL), Tiaina "Junior" Seau has become one of the finest, most discussed linebackers in professional football. With the retirement of Mike Singletary of the Chicago Bears and Lawrence Taylor of the New York Giants, Seau is becoming one of the stars of the NFL, the kind of player for which offensive lines make special arrangements. He was a first-round draft pick (fifth overall) in 1990 by the San Diego Chargers after his junior year at the University of Southern California, where he was a consensus All American and the Pac-10 Defensive Player of the Year. He has already played in three pro-bowls in his short career, missing out only in his rookie season.

Growing up in poverty

Seau's parents were native Samoans from the island of Aunuu. They had gone to the United States in the mid-1960s seeking medical attention for Seau's older brother, David, who had been diagnosed with a lung disease at the age of four. The elder Seaus spoke no English and were forced to take menial jobs to support the family and pay for David's medical bills. As a child, Seau and his three brothers slept in the garage, which had been converted into a bedroom. The Seaus instilled a strong moral sense in their children, combining traditional Samoan values with Christianity. Seau told *Sports Illustrated,* "Dad taught us about morals, values, and goals. Having a tight-knit family was important to him. The one question he always asked us was, 'How do we protect the Seau name?'"

Seau began taking an interest in athletics and weightlifting at an early age. Many mornings he would get up before his brothers and lift weights. At the end of the day he would do sit-ups and push-ups by the hundreds. His brothers were athletic as well, but Seau's father recognized in Junior a unique talent and saw the prospect of it taking him somewhere. In recognition of his special talents, the elder Seau did not require that Junior find part-time work as his brothers had to.

Early athletic career

Seau went to school at Oceanside High School, where he played football and basketball. He led the football team to the city's AA championship, was voted the San Diego area's player of the year in both sports after his senior season, and was named defensive MVP of San Diego County and offensive MVP of the Avocado League. Reflecting his versatility as an athlete, *Parade* magazine named him to its All-American team of high school athletes simply as an athlete, with no specification as to sport or position.

Following his graduation, Seau was recruited by the University of Southern California (USC), traditionally a football

Junior Seau

powerhouse. His first two years at USC, however, were marked by setbacks; in his freshman year he was not allowed to play because he scored ten points below the NCAA-mandated score of 700 on his Scholastic Aptitude Test (SAT), a standardized test that most colleges require before admitting a student. This was a major humiliation for Seau; he felt the weight of his family's reputation on his shoulders.

Seau showed great determination, however, in enduring this letdown. In the spring of his freshman year he defeated the entire team in USC's annual Superman Contest, a multi-event test of strength, physical endurance, and speed. But in his sophomore year, Seau injured his right ankle during pre-season practice, and he sat out that season as well. His break came in his junior year, when he was healthy and ready to play and two starters were injured. Seau was put in just weeks before the season began. He had an excellent season and was named a consensus All-American and the Pac-10 Defensive Player of the Year.

Seau decided to leave school after his junior year to be eligible for the professional draft, an increasingly common trend among top-rated college players. He was signed by the San Diego Chargers, for whom he has played ever since.

Accolades in the NFL

Seau has established himself as one of the top defensive players in the league and has become a national celebrity as well. He remains a remarkable all-around athlete; weighing in at 225 pounds, he runs the 40-yard dash in under 4.6 seconds, making him an awesome defensive weapon, able to pursue laterally at or near the speed of many running backs. *The Sporting News* quoted several NFL players about their impressions of Seau and his performance in the league. Kevin Gilbride, the Houston Oilers offensive coordinator, said, "He can hurt you in more ways than any other defensive player in the league. Not only can he be a significant force as a pass rusher, but he has tremendous range against the running game and he's very good on pass coverage."

Warren Moon, the former Oilers quarterback, who was traded to the Minnesota Vikings in 1994, testified, "There's not another linebacker who does the things he does. But what really sets him apart is he plays with so much enthusiasm and emotion. That helps him get to the ball a little faster. It's almost like he's possessed." Chargers coach Bobby Ross says Seau could be used to return punts and kickoffs, and general manager Bobby Beatherd thinks that he could be a tight end or full back. Beatherd went on to say, "And that is not blowing smoke.... He truly is that gifted. That's what makes him different from the classic linebackers from the past. None of them were as athletic as this guy. He has all their tools plus the speed."

Still living simply

Becoming a star professional football player has brought Seau notoriety and a large income, which, unlike many young, wealthy celebrities, he does not spend lavishly. He lives simply, telling *Sports Illustrated,* "Just give me a shack on the beach and couple of tuna fish sandwiches and I'm happy." In 1991 he started the Junior Seau Foundation, the mandate of which is "to promote the protection of children by supporting child-abuse prevention efforts, drug and alcohol awareness, and anti-juvenile delinquency programs." Seau has become a role model in the San Diego community. His success has special meaning for inner-city youths because he was raised in a poverty-stricken, gang-infested neighborhood.

Sources:

Lieber, Jill, "Hard Charger," *Sports Illustrated,* September 6, 1993, p. 64.

San Diego Chargers, "Junior Seau," press release and publicity, San Diego, California, 1994.

Sichan Siv

Investment banker, presidential aide
Born 1948, Phnom Penh, Cambodia

"Success means being able to help others. President Bush said it best, 'The definition of a successful life must include serving others.' To me, volunteerism is an important part of a successful life."

When Sichan Siv first arrived in the United States in 1976 as a Cambodian refugee, he knew no one—not even the Peace Corps officer who had sponsored his trip to America. Thirteen years later, Siv became the highest-ranking Asian American on the White House staff when he was appointed deputy assistant to the president as part of the administration of George Bush, a post he held from 1989 to 1992. He served as deputy assistant secretary of state for South Asian affairs from 1992 to 1993. Siv has been described as "a wily immigrant" who survived the horrors of the brutal Khmer Rouge government in Cambodia, escaped via Thailand to the United States, and managed to work his way from picking apples in Connecticut and driving a taxicab in New York to working with foreign governments and international organizations.

Siv lost his government job when Bush was defeated in the 1992 election. In his new position as a senior vice president at a New York banking company, Siv maintains the same philosophy that has guided him through both his nightmarish wartime experiences and, later, the fulfillment of dreams: "Success means being able to help others. President Bush said it best, 'The definition of a successful life must include serving others.' To me, volunteerism is an important part of a successful life."

The roots of Siv's success

Sichan Siv—*Sichan* means "beautiful moon" in Khmer, the language of Cambodia—was only nine years old when his father, a police chief, died. His mother, a devout Buddhist, was left with limited resources to raise him, his brother, and his two sisters. Siv and his brother did what they could to help by fetching water and firewood for the house while the girls assisted their mother inside the home. From his mother he learned to be calm and to endure throughout difficult times. Siv told *Asian American Biography (AAB)* that he remembers standing by his mother's side as she cooked, listening to her words. She would say, "Remember Sichan. Whatever happens, never give up hope."

When he was 15 Siv was admitted to a highly regarded high school in Phnom Penh. After graduating in 1968, he became a flight attendant for the commercial Cambodian airline, Royal Air Cambodge. The job allowed him to improve his English. Eventually he would learn French and Spanish in addition to English and his native Khmer. In 1970, when air travel declined because of continuing civil war in Cambodia and neighboring Vietnam (the governments of both countries were battling Communist uprisings), Siv decided to go to college in Phnom Penh. After graduation, he studied law briefly but eventually became an English teacher. In 1974 he went to work for CARE, a U.S. relief agency.

By April 1975 Phnom Penh, the capital of Cambodia, was full of people from the countryside trying to escape the war raging outside the city. After years of war, the Communist fighters, called the Khmer Rouge, were threatening to overrun the city and destroy anti-Communist supporters. Siv, then 27, was given the chance to escape through the U.S. Embassy on April 12. But, wanting to leave with "a clear conscience," he drove that day to meet with a government official about delivering more rice and medical supplies to the refugees who needed them. As a result, he missed the last evacuation helicopter by 30 minutes. Five days later, Phnom Penh was overtaken by the Khmer Rouge. One of the Khmer Rouge's goals was to return Cambodia to the simple agricultural society it had been before the colonial rule of the French, and thus the insurgent group viewed the most educated

Sichan Siv

members of Cambodian society as the most politically dangerous. Aware of this outlook, Siv quickly threw away his eyeglasses, convinced, perhaps rightly, that the Khmer Rouge would mark him for death.

Siv and his family were relocated to their father's native village and put to hard labor in the fields. Obtaining forged passes and a bicycle, Siv decided to leave Cambodia. He said good-bye to his family and headed toward Thailand. On his way, he saw daily evidence of the bloodbath that was sweeping his country. For three weeks, Siv slept in bushes and escaped notice, showing false papers to Khmer Rouge soldiers. But only a few miles from the Thai border peasants reported him, and he was arrested and sent to various slave labor camps. Siv was forced to work 18 hours a day digging ditches and fixing roads, returning exhausted to camp at night to a bowl of rotten soup. Through it all he never forgot his mother's words, "Whatever happens, never give up hope," and he continued to seek an opportunity to escape.

One day Siv was assigned to a lumber crew near the border and managed to escape into the jungle. His second night without food or water, he fell into a deep hole after hearing loudspeakers announcing a Buddhist festival. At first Siv feared he was still in Cambodia. It was not until he climbed out of the hole the next morning and discovered fruit cans with Thai labels, saw footprints of sneakers, and observed people wearing colored clothes that he sensed he had made it across the border; sneakers were banned by the Khmer Rouge in Cambodia, as were colored clothes.

But Siv's problems were not completely over. He was arrested by the Thai border police. Only after a friend came to bail him out was he transferred to a refugee camp. Industrious as ever, he proceeded to organize English classes. A U.S. Embassy official contacted by the relief organization CARE eventually found Siv in the camp and made arrangements for his immigration to the United States. Before coming to America, Siv became a Buddhist monk. He remains a Buddhist, though he gave up the priesthood when he moved to the United States. Siv later learned that almost all of his family—his mother, his older brother and sister, and their families—had been brutally murdered by the Khmer Rouge. Friends say that his faith in Buddhism has helped him emerge from his gruesome experiences in Cambodia without unbearable bitterness.

A new life

Siv supported himself in America with various jobs: picking apples, cooking hamburgers at a chain restaurant in Connecticut, and after moving to New York City, driving a cab. Eventually he got a job counseling refugees for a Lutheran organization. In 1979 he wrote passionate letters to several U.S. universities describing his background and goals. Columbia University offered him a full graduate scholarship.

In 1982 Siv became an American citizen and a year later married Martha Pattillo, a native Texan who works for the World Bank. After earning a master's degree in international relations, Siv worked for a bank, the Episcopal Church, the United Nations, and later, the Institute of International Education in New York.

In 1987 Siv volunteered for the Bush campaign, which marked a turning point in his career. He worked hard for the campaign in New York and became friendly with a Bush aide who, impressed by Siv's knowledge and personality, recommended him for the job of presidential aide. Soon after an interview for the position, Siv was offered the $65,000-a-year job with the historic distinction of being the first Asian American to become a ranking presidential aide. "It's a tremendous honor," he said, "not just for me, but for all Cambodians, for all Asian Americans, for all refugees."

The drive to always be better

Siv made every effort to assume leadership positions. He was the president's representative to key public interest groups and spoke regularly on the president's behalf to explain administration policies. He was also the leader of the White House Communications Task Force on national security issues, co-chair of the U. S. delegation to the Geneva conference on refugees, and senior adviser to the U.S. delegation to the Paris conference on Cambodia. Bobby Kilberg, another White House deputy assistant, said about Siv, "You can trust him with your life. He tells you what he really thinks, and often in politics that's not what happens."

Siv's next appointment was as deputy assistant secretary of state for South Asian affairs. Among his duties was addressing U.S. policy toward Afghanistan, Bangladesh, Bhutan, India, the Maldives, Nepal, Pakistan, and Sri Lanka. In the summer of 1993, after the Republican party lost the national election and relinquished control of the White House to Democrat Bill Clinton, Siv joined Commonwealth Associates, a New York-based investment bank and brokerage firm, as a senior vice president heading the firm's Asian and Pacific department.

Siv has received many awards, including the Outstanding Asian American Award from the Asian Pacific American Heritage Council, the Twice the Citizen Award from the Reserve Officers Association of the United States, and the CARE Honor for "Selflessness and Courage in Pursuit of his Lifelong Commitment to Human Freedom, Opportunity, and Dignity." Siv is a lieutenant colonel of the U.S. Air Force Auxiliary Civil Air Patrol, and he also serves on the boards of the United States Committee for Immigration and Refugee Services of America, the Center for Migration Studies, the Smithsonian Institution Arthur M. Sackler Gallery, and the National Council for Christians and Jews.

"My success," Siv told *AAB*, "is based on my belief that I had to adapt and to be adopted (that is, accepted) by my new country. My advice to others is adapt and be adopted." According to Siv, America is a nation "where you have the right to dream and the ability and opportunity to make your dream come true."

Still, Siv's adaptation to his new country did not mean cutting ties to Cambodia. Siv has remained involved with events concerning his birthplace; he recently visited Cambodia during the United Nations-supervised election campaign there.

Through all the difficult moments in his life, Siv has recalled his mother's advice to never give up hope, and he never has. "I am a strong believer that dreams do come true. I have every right to be," he said.

Sources:

Commonwealth Associates, "Sichan Siv," press release, September 27, 1989.

McAllister, Bill, "A Cambodian Emigre's Route from the Killing Fields to the White House," *Washington Post,* March 31, 1989.

Nugent, Tom, "Escape from the Inferno," *People,* March 27, 1989.

Ryan, Michael, "I Survived on Hope," *Parade*, July 8, 1990.

Siv, Sichan, "Help Can Work in Renascent Cambodia," *International Herald Tribune,* April 8, 1994.

Siv, Sichan, telephone interview with Susan Gall, April 16, 1994.

Cathy Song

Poet
Born August 20, 1955, Honolulu, Hawaii

"I tell my students that true freedom and power come from getting ahold of language and your feelings."

Cathy-Lynn Song is a prominent American poet who was awarded the Yale Series of Younger Poets Award in 1982. The award, perhaps the most prestigious for young poets in the country, drew considerable attention to Song, who has published her poems in such magazines and journals as *American Poetry Review, Michigan Quarterly Review, Ploughshares, Poetry,* and *Shenendoah.* In choosing Song's first collection of poems to be published as part of the Yale prize, Richard Hugo wrote that "her poems are flowers: colorful, sensual, and quiet, and they are offered almost shyly as bouquets to those moments in life that seemed minor but in retrospect count the most. She often reminds a loud, indifferent, hard world of what truly matters to the human spirit." Since winning the Yale prize, Song has published two more collections of her work to generally glowing reviews in such important national publications as *USA Today,* the *Washington Post,* and the *Los Angeles Times.*

A prolific writer as a child

Song is the middle of three children born to Andrew and Ella Song. Andrew Song is a second-generation Korean American whose father had emigrated to Hawaii in the 1920s with the first wave of Korean laborers; Ella Song is a Chinese American. "My father was a pilot," Song recalled in an interview with *Asian American Biography (AAB),* "so we did a lot of traveling. Our family travels started my writing. I guess I was about nine when I decided I wanted to be the family chronicler." She wrote constantly, creating magazines and books for herself. She made so many of these books that her father began buying army surplus target paper, so Song's earliest works are backed by a bull's-eye. Much of this writing was in the form of a journal. In an interview with *Honolulu Weekly,* Song remembered that when she was young, "an experience didn't feel complete until I wrote about it."

After an education in public schools, Song went on to two years of college at the University of Hawaii (UH) at Manoa. While there, Song, who described herself as a "hippie type" during this period, met the first professor who encouraged her to work on her writing. The noted poet and biographer John Unterecker "was someone who encouraged me from early on," Song explained. "Generosity—I was lucky to find such generosity. I remember the first poem I wrote for him, he just wrote on the bottom, 'See me.'"

After two years at UH Manoa, Song transferred to Wellesley College in Wellesley, Massachusetts, where she earned a bachelor's degree in English literature in 1977. She then went on to earn a master's degree in creative writing from Boston University in 1981. While at Boston, Song studied with Kathleen Spivack, another professor who would have a strong impact on the young writer. It was Spivack who encouraged Song to send her poems to mainstream presses as well as the Asian American and ethnic presses, where she had been concentrating her early efforts at publication.

Success

One year after she received her master's degree, Song's collection of poetry was selected as the 1982 winner of the Yale Series of Younger Poets Award. The award judges manuscripts submitted by poets under the age of 35 from all over the United States. To win is an incredible honor and assures a young poet national attention as the winning entry is then published by Yale University Press and is traditionally reviewed by the major book reviewers around the country. Song's collection, *Picture Bride,* was published in 1983. The name refers to the practice among mid-century Asian immigrant men of marrying women from their homelands after choosing them from photographs. The book received glowing reviews from the national media. *USA Today* said reading *Picture Bride* was "a sensual experience with pleasures on almost every page.... Song writes intensely specific, exposed poems." The *Washington Post* described Song as "obviously devoted to the most scrupulous craftsmanship (there are no excesses in these poems, no unpolished corners)." The *Los Angeles Times* described the poems in the collection as "both beautiful and timely" and "the fruit of East-to-West transplanting." *Picture Bride* was a finalist for the 1983 National Book Critics Circle Award.

Song's next book, *Frameless Windows, Squares of Light,* was published in 1988 by

Cathy Song

W. W. Norton, a major New York publishing house. This book, too, was widely reviewed and highly praised. *Library Journal* wrote, "At her best [Song] gives us poignant visions of childhood, the family, and moments of perception that become 'a study of small pleasures' to be recalled and savored." The *Minneapolis Star Tribune* said, "Song works to capture the events and characters in the manner of a skilled and sensitive photographer." Song's *School Figures* was published by the University of Pittsburgh Press in 1994.

Subjects and images

Some of the criticism Song has received over the years addresses the perception that she is a "middle-class poet." She told *Honolulu Weekly,* "I think it's very unfair. We all suffer in different ways. I don't have to have grown up on the plantation speaking pidgin and having someone beat ... me to write good poetry."

Song's most current work focuses on women's issues. She discussed this in an interview with *AAB:* "Being a woman and an Asian American has only helped my work as an artist. You have to be on the periphery, on the outside looking in, marginalized in some way, to gain a different perspective, a perspective which only provokes your art because there is no way you can possibly accept the party line."

Song also writes about motherhood—she is the mother of two. "I try to deal with the complexities of the many roles of women," she told *AAB.* "I believe women can take full possession of their lives by finding ways to articulate through art, or other *meaningful* work, their right to define their own existence without being trapped in the male-dominant cultural ideal."

Poet as teacher

Since 1987, Song has been participating in Hawaii's well-known "Poets in the Schools" program. This program enables public school children from kindergarten through high school to work with and learn from working poets. Song finds her work with children especially rewarding. She told *Honolulu Weekly,* "I tell my students that true freedom and power comes from getting ahold of language and your feelings.... Monetarily, you don't get compensated very well [in the program].... But I get so much back. What these students give to me is so life-enhancing."

In 1993 Song won the Hawaii Award for literature, becoming the prestigious award's youngest recipient. That year the Poetry Society of America awarded Song the Shelley Memorial Award. And in 1994 she was invited to travel to South Korea and Hong Kong with the United States Information Agency's Arts America program. Song married Douglas McHarg Davenport while she was studying in Boston. In 1987 the couple moved to Hawaii, where they have lived since.

Song's advice for young poets is not to be afraid to start at the top when trying to publish their work and to take advantage of the help of mentors. She recounted to *AAB:* "As Kathleen Spivack told me, 'Your voice has just as much importance as any other American writer.' Young poets and writers should remember that ethnic background doesn't make your voice any less American. Don't limit yourself—when you feel it's ready, send your work to the best publication you know."

Sources:

Choo, David, "Cathy Song," *Honolulu Weekly,* June 15, 1994, pp. 6-8.

Lee, Li Young, correspondence with Cathy Song, August 1994.

Nye, Naomi Shihab, correspondence with Cathy Song, August 1994.

Roddy, Kevin M., "Sister Stew: Fiction and Poetry by Women," *Library Journal,* July 1992, p. 85.

Song, Cathy, telephone interview with Susan Gall, July 28, 1994.

Somtow Sucharitkul

Author, composer, conductor
Born December 30, 1952, Bangkok, Thailand

"[The work of Somtow Sucharitkul] provokes thought ... more often than many a contemporary 'serious' novel.... It is easy to predict great things for so accomplished and talented a writer as this."—Washington Post Book World

Somtow Sucharitkul is an author —under the name S. P. Somtow— of science fiction and a composer and conductor of modern, forward-looking music who made his international conducting debut at the age of 19 with the Holland Symphony Orchestra. He has since had his compositions performed by major orchestras around the world. Sucharitkul began writing science fiction in 1979, publishing his first novel, *Starship and Haiku,* in 1981. It was well received critically and won two prestigious awards. Sucharitkul has since written several novels and short story collections and continues to compose.

A privileged childhood

Sucharitkul's father, Sompong, was a career diplomat with the Thai government, a post that allowed Sucharitkul access to a good education and an upper-middle-class upbringing. He was educated in Thai private schools and went to college at Cambridge University in England, where he received both his bachelor's and master's degrees from St. Catherine's College, one of the many colleges that make up Cambridge.

By 1974 Sucharitkul had established himself as an important composer, and he was chosen by his country as its representative at two international music fairs: the Asian Composer's Conference-Festival in Kyoto, Japan, and the International Music Council of UNESCO. In 1977 Sucharitkul was named director of the Bangkok Opera Society. He also began working with other orchestras around the world, including the Cambridge Symphony, the Holland Symphony, and the Florida Atlantic University New Music Ensemble. In 1978 he was named artistic director of the Asian Composer's Conference-Festival, held that year in his native Bangkok. That same year, Japanese television made a documentary about the rising young star.

The writer emerges

In 1979 Sucharitkul moved to the United States and began turning his attention to writing. Since he was a child, he had been fascinated with science fiction. His first novel, called *Starship and Haiku,* was published in 1981. The book relates the story of an earth that has been wiped out by nuclear holocaust, leaving only the Japanese alive. The surviving humans struggle with their predicament and battle over what to do. Half the population begins planning to take human civilization to another, as-yet-undiscovered planet, while the remainder advocates suicide as the only rational response. *Starship and Haiku* won the John W. Campbell Award for best new writer and the Locus Award for a best first novel from

Locus magazine and was a selection of the Science Fiction Research Association. The *Washington Post Book World* faulted the budding writer for using too many trendy gimmicks to tell his story, such as telekinetic (able to move things without touching them) whales, but admitted that "the waters [Sucharitkul] probes are deep."

In the early 1980s, Sucharitkul wrote a sequence of related novels collectively entitled *Chronicles of the High Inquest.* This series consists of the novels *Light on the Sound* (1982); *The Throne of Madness* (1983); *Utopia Hunters* (1984); and *The Darkling Wind* (1985) and tells the tale of a race of mutilated humans who try to destroy a race of whale-like beings. The humans operate under the direction of an astral species known as the Inquestors who are steadily demonized throughout the series and eventually die in an apocalypse. Writing about the series, Tom Easton of *Analog* magazine said Sucharitkul "writes of worlds and beings just far enough from our lives to feel strange, yet with echoes of a familiar past. He is a myth-maker." The *Washington Post Book World* was impressed as well, suggesting that Sucharitkul "may yet give us the best [science fiction] novel of all time."

Sucharitkul's next series was called *The Aquiliad,* a richly imagined play based on the classic Greek epic *The Iliad.* In *The Aquiliad,* however, the ancient Romans discover and colonize America and invent the automobile. The series, consisting of *The Aquiliad* (1983); *The Aquiliad #2: Aquilia and the Iron Horse* (1988); and *The Aquiliad #3: Aquilia and the Sphinx* (1988), established Sucharitkul as a master of irony and dark humor. The books are full of characters whose Indian names have been Latinized, as well as characters with names that are references to contemporary science fiction writers. He even presents the mythical figure of Bigfoot as the leader of a group of mutated Jews. The *Washington Post Book World* again praised the writer, saying that although "Sucharitkul does not want you to take this world seriously at all" there is "a perverse elegance" in the writing.

Fantasy and horror

In 1985 Sucharitkul began publishing under the name S. P. Somtow and embarked on a change of focus from science fiction to fantasy and horror. His first series in this new genre are the *Valentine* books: *Vampire Junction* (1984) and *Valentine* (1992). Both novels center on Timothy Valentine, a two-thousand-year-old vampire and rock star. The *Washington Post Book World* wrote that *Vampire Junction* "provokes thought ... more often than many a contemporary 'serious' novel.... It is easy to predict great things for so accomplished and talented a writer as this."

In addition to these novels, Sucharitkul has written dozens of short stories, many of which have been anthologized. In 1982 he was nominated for a Hugo Award, science fiction's highest honor, for his stories "Absent Thee from Felicity Awhile" and "Aquila." He writes book reviews for various magazines and newspapers, including the *Washington Post Book World,* and writes about music for *Tempo* and *Musical Newsletter.* He is also a contributing editor and columnist for *Fantasy Newsletter.* In addition, Sucharitkul writes children's books and has published novelizations of episodes of the short-lived television series *V.* He currently divides his time between his Los Angeles, California, home and his native Bangkok.

Sources:

May, Hal, ed., *Contemporary Authors,* vol. 118, Detroit: Gale, 1986, pp. 456-57.

Anna Sui

Fashion designer
Born c. 1955, Dearborn, Michigan

"For many years I couldn't decide between styling and designing. It's kind of a youthful fantasy that you can do everything, but you have to learn the business you're in."

Anna Sui is one of the up-and-coming young fashion designers in New York today, having made a name for herself in this highly competitive field with her eclectic designs, which often combine the influences of periods as diverse as the English Victorian era and the counterculture of the 1960s. The *New York Times* described some of the inspirations for her work as coming from "a [fashion designer Cristobal] Balenciaga suit in an old magazine, from a Barbie doll's travelling costume, from a photograph of Lady Diana Cooper working in her garden, or from a length of vintage fabric." Her designs are especially popular among trendy young women and celebrities like Madonna, Sandra Bernhardt, Lady Miss Kier of the dance group Deee-Lite, and supermodels Linda Evangelista and Naomi Campbell. She has also managed to keep her clothes priced well below those of her competitors, demonstrating her belief that fashion is for fun. Kalman Ruttenstien, vice president of fashion direction at Macy's, the giant New York retailer, was quoted in the *New York Times* as saying, "She probably offers more fashion for the price than anyone else at [her] price range."

This philosophy has worked well for Sui, and her business has grown quickly and dramatically. Since beginning with a bare-bones operation in 1980, Sui now heads a $1.75 million business, selling her fashions in more than 200 department stores in the United States, Canada, Japan, and Europe, and she has her own retail store in Manhattan's Soho district.

An early dream

Sui's parents immigrated from China. Her father, Paul, is a structural engineer and her mother, Grace, is a homemaker who once studied painting in Paris. Her mother was very stylish, and Sui says she was influenced by her fashion sense from an early age. Even as a very young child, Sui wanted to be a fashion designer. In *Harper's Bazaar,* James Laurie wrote, "During her childhood in Detroit, Sui devoured magazines like *Mademoiselle* and *Seventeen,* even hunted down copies of *Women's Wear Daily.* She fantasized about the glamorous fashion world they presented, clipping articles and stylish advertisements—most of which she still has today, meticulously maintained and organized in manila folders she calls the Genius Files."

Sui was an eccentric dresser even as a child. She told *Harper's Bazaar,* "I was the one in the big frilly lavender party dress in class pictures." She began making her own clothes in junior high, beginning in those days what would become a Sui trademark: outfits with matching shoes, hats, and handbags. She was voted the best-dressed student in her ninth-grade class.

Parsons School of Design

After graduating from high school Sui chose to go to New York to study at the Parsons School of Design. She'd heard about the school when reading an article about a couple of young designers who had gone there and then gone on to brilliant careers. Her parents were dismayed by her decision; her mother especially wanted Sui to become a doctor or a nurse, but the Suis eventually gave in and their daughter moved to New York City.

While in school, Sui befriended Steven Meisel, now one of the world's top fashion photographers. Her first job was with a sportswear company as a junior designer. She also worked as a stylist for Meisel's increasingly prestigious fashion shoots for magazines such as the Italian *Lei.* (A stylist is the person who selects clothes, accessories, and even hair and makeup styles for a fashion shoot, thus helping to determine the overall look of the photos.) This was a fun, experimental time for the young fashion designer and her photographer friend. When they weren't working together on a shoot, they would often play with ideas and looks, using as models friends and even people off the street whom they would lure into Meisel's studio for a "makeover."

Sui learned a lot during this period, and she met several prominent models, including Evangelista and Campbell, both of whom

Anna Sui

would later play important roles in helping Sui publicize her designs. Sui told the *New York Times* about her days as Meisel's stylist, remarking, "For many years I couldn't decide between styling and designing. It's kind of a youthful fantasy that you can do everything, but you have to learn the business you're in."

The beginnings of success

The business Sui ultimately decided she wanted to pursue was fashion design. She continued working for various designers throughout the 1970s and into the 1980s. In her free time she created her own designs. In 1980 she showed six original Lycra garments (lycra is a stretchy material used frequently in exercise clothes) and received an order from Macy's, which used one of the designs in an advertisement in the *New York Times*. This early success encouraged Sui, and that year she started her own business, which she ran out of her apartment. "There were boxes piled up to the ceiling, and we were shipping clothes out of here," she told *Vogue* in 1992.

Sui's business grew steadily throughout the 1980s, and she was able to sell through more and more retailers. In 1991 she reached a landmark in the fashion business when she had her first solo runway show. The show created a stir: the *New York Times* reviewer commented, "There was a fashion collision Wednesday evening. It looked as if [the rock band] Sly and the Family Stone crashed into [French designer] Coco Chanel and then got rear-ended by [French designer] Christian Lacroix. The show, the first by Anna Sui, was a riot."

The success of the show was a major turning point for the young designer. She was finally able to move her business out of her apartment and rent office space in New York's garment district. She continued showing her designs to rave reviews and Macy's gave Sui her own boutique in its flagship Herald Square store in 1992. In February of 1993 Sui was awarded the coveted Perry Ellis Award for new fashion talent.

Sui continues to be very successful and also manages to keep her prices down. She told *Women's Wear Daily,* "Raising the prices would take away the humor of my clothes—if they were more expensive they would be too precious. It's not my outlook; Lacroix and Chanel can do that better." She also designs her clothes with the intention of letting the personality of the wearer come through. Sui says, "I don't want to make [my customers] my walking [advertisement] sandwich boards.... So many of today's dresses make you look like your mother. My dresses are not overconstructed; they're easy enough for anyone to wear."

Sources:

Doppelt, Gabe, "Vogue's View," *Vogue,* February 1992, pp. 90, 92.

Hochswender, Woody, "Anna Sui's Slam-Bang Look: A Wistful Glance at the 60s," *New York Times,* April 12, 1991.

James, Laurie, "Sui Success," *Harper's Bazaar,* September 1992, p. 274.

Schiro, Anne Marie, "Nostalgia with a Look That's Now," *New York Times,* December 1, 1991, p. 68.

Ronald Takaki

Academician, historian, writer
Born April 12, 1939, Honolulu, Hawaii

"I wanted Americans of each group to learn about themselves and each other. In the sharing of their various stories, Americans from different shores create a community of a larger memory."

R onald Takaki is a pioneer in the field of ethnic studies. Through his teaching, research, and writing, Takaki has encouraged young Americans to learn about cultural diversity and to be tolerant of ethnic differences. At the University of California at Los Angeles (UCLA), Takaki taught the school's first African American history course. During his five years at UCLA, he helped found its centers for African American, Asian American, Chicano, and Native American studies. In 1972, Takaki moved to the University of California at Berkeley, where he served as chairperson of the ethnic studies department and where he helped found the first Ph.D. program in ethnic studies in the United States. In addition to his academic work, Takaki has published several critically acclaimed books and has appeared on such television shows as NBC's *Today Show,* ABC's *Good Morning America,* CNN's *International Hour,* PBS's *MacNeil/Lehrer NewsHour,* and many others.

Island son

Born on April 12, 1939, Takaki grew up in a working class, multiethnic neighborhood in Honolulu, Hawaii. His mother was second-generation Japanese American and his father was first generation. "I can remember when I was young going to friends' houses and hearing the parents speaking in Portuguese, Japanese, Chinese, etc. As kids, we thought that was normal. But at school, we were not taught why we were so diverse," recalled Takaki in an interview with *Asian American Biography (AAB).*

When he was five years old, Takaki failed the entrance exam of the local English standard school, part of a school system he would need to enter if he wanted to attend college. "I was one of the kids who flunked because my English was so bad. I spoke mostly Pidgin English." (Pidgin English is a simplified form of English used for communication among people who speak different languages.) In the fifth grade, Takaki's parents transferred him to a private school so he "could be on the college track." In spite of his parents' encouragement, Takaki remembered, "as a teenager, I wasn't much of an academic. I have to confess this. I was more interested in surfing. My parents owned a hot-plate lunch restaurant on Waikiki Beach and I would help out, cutting onions and peeling shrimp. Then when I was done, I would just surf. I used to be a pretty good surfer."

During his senior year in high school, a teacher recommended that Takaki go to a small liberal arts college on the mainland. The first person in his family to go to college, Takaki was one of only two Asian Americans in a student body of about one thousand at the College of Wooster in Ohio. At Wooster, Takaki studied history and eventually decided to attend graduate school at the University of California at Berkeley instead of becoming an Episcopal priest as he had planned.

Takaki attended Berkeley during the civil rights movement of the 1960s. Many students there, including Takaki, organized peaceful protests against racism and campaigned for free speech. The movement inspired him to write his first book, *A Pro-Slavery Crusade.* Published in 1970, the book was a study of how Southerners defended the existence of slavery.

A professor's life

In the fall of 1967, Takaki joined the faculty of the University of California at Los Angeles, where he taught the school's first African American history course. "At first I was met with skepticism," he told *AAB.*

Ronald Takaki

"There were four hundred students enrolled and when the black and white students first saw me, their first reaction was, 'Gee, he doesn't look black.' I had to prove that I had something to teach." He became very active in organizing the Black Students Union, acting as the group's faculty adviser. He was also involved with Chicano and Asian American students. After two years of teaching African American history, Takaki developed another groundbreaking course, "The History of Racial Inequality," a study of inequality across various minority groups. Takaki returned in 1972 to his alma mater, the University of California at Berkeley, after accepting an invitation to join the ethnic studies department there. Today,

Berkeley is recognized as the center of America's ethnic studies.

Author, author

Though Berkeley is still his home, Takaki has been invited to lecture at universities throughout the United States, including Cornell University in upstate New York. In addition to receiving much praise as a teacher, Takaki is also a noted writer. "Writing is a chance to redefine America, what America means to different people, to make sure that African Americans, Asian Americans, Chicanos, and Native Americans all get included in the definition of America," he stated. "It's not enough to be only teachers."

"My books are all related to my teaching and to my politics," Takaki explained. "My scholarship was initially influenced by my involvement in the 1964 free speech movement and my horror at the murder of the three civil rights workers in Mississippi and the bombing of [black] churches in Alabama [during the civil rights movement]. So I wrote *A Pro-Slavery Crusade* and *Violence in the Black Imagination* [a study of nineteenth-century African American novelists, published in 1971]." In 1979 Takaki published *Iron Cages: Race and Culture in Nineteenth Century America,* an analysis of African Americans, Asian Americans, Chicanos, and Native Americans.

While writing *Iron Cages,* Takaki returned to his native Hawaii. "I had three young kids at the time and I wanted to teach them Pidgin English and how to surf." When Takaki described his writing projects to one of his favorite uncles, the uncle replied, "Why you no go write a book about us, huh? Why you just write books about mainland folks? Your history is here on Hawaii's plantations." Takaki saw that his uncle was right.

Published in 1983, *Pau Hana: Plantation Life and Labor in Hawaii* was a different kind of history book from those Takaki had written previously. "Before *Pau Hana,* I had used a very academic style, very philosophical language," he revealed. "But now I was writing a book for my uncle and people like him in Hawaii, and so I decided to use a narrative storytelling style with the voices of the people telling their own stories. By letting people tell their own stories, they thereby reclaimed their own history.

"*Pau Hana* taught me a new way to challenge traditional scholarship. It showed me how to contribute to the community. After it, I was finally ready to write *Strangers from a Different Shore,* a study of Asian Americans in the islands and on the mainland. Again, it was a book filled with the stories of people with minds, wills, and voices." *Strangers from a Different Shore: A History of Asian Americans* received numerous awards, including a 1989 Pulitzer Prize nomination for nonfiction, the Gold Medal for nonfiction from the Commonwealth Club of California, and a Notable Book of 1989 citation from the *New York Times Book Review.* Takaki's latest book, *A Different Mirror: A History of Multicultural America,* covers the years from the founding of the Jamestown settlement in Virginia in 1607 to the end of the Cold War (a period in American history marked by extreme political tension between the United States and the Soviet Union) in the 1990s.

A scholar abroad

During the past decade, Takaki has traveled extensively to share his views and expertise with many universities and organizations. "I enjoy the lecturing and traveling, for it means learning from other cultures," Takaki said. "And I also enjoy sharing what I know about U.S. society and culture. Ethnic conflict, after all, is a global issue." In past years, Takaki has lectured in Japan and the former Soviet Union. His plans include a U.S. State Department-sponsored trip to South Africa during which he will lecture on multiculturalism in the United States.

With his many international visits, it is not surprising that the focus of Takaki's next book reaches beyond U.S. borders; the new work will be a study of multiculturalism in relation to World War II. "I believe histori-cal scholarship has overlooked the multicul-tural dimension of World War II—it was the first time that many ethnic groups went to war for the U.S.," Takaki pointed out. "They included Navajos from the reservations, Chicanos from the barrios, African Ameri-cans from the ghettos, and even Japanese Americans from the internment camps."

Sources:

Takaki, Ronald, telephone interview with Terry Hong, June 10, 1994.

George Takei

Actor
Born April 20, 1940, Los Angeles, California

"Whatever time period we live in, man needs an affirmative sense of his future. Right now, people have a feeling that their efforts are futile and that the human race is foredoomed. Star Trek did ... help reaffirm the intrinsic strengths in man—our capability to wrestle with society's problems. If we don't have that confidence in our inventive genius and adventuresome spirit to overcome our troubles, then we won't be able to come up with the solutions."

George Hosato Takei is a television, theater, and film actor who is best known for his portrayal of the helmsman Sulu in the *Star Trek* television series of the late 1960s and the Star Trek feature films that followed. He is also politically active in the Democratic party in California, where he ran for office on two occasions. Not lim-iting himself to these endeavors, though, Takei is also the author of a science fiction novel, *Mirror Friend, Mirror Foe.*

Disrupted childhood

Takei was born on April 20, 1940, in Los Angeles, California, to second-generation Japanese Americans. When he was one year old the United States entered into war with Japan. It was not long before the U.S. gov-ernment—in obvious violation of the consti-tution—sent Japanese American citizens who lived on the West Coast to internment camps in various parts of the country, far from their homes, because the government feared they might aid the Japanese in the event of an invasion. Takei and his family were sent to a camp in Arkansas. He said in an interview for *Starlog* magazine in June 1981 that he has few memories of his fam-ily's imprisonment, and that the ones that he has are mostly pleasant. "You have to remember though," he said, "that I was just a very little boy. For my parents it was a ter-rible time."

Takei's mother believed the camps vio-lated her country's promises of justice and liberty for all citizens, so she joined with many other imprisoned Japanese Americans and renounced her American citizenship. Takei explained, "It was a symbolic gesture, but for my mother, being a citizen of a country that was doing this to her family was intolerable." In retaliation for his mother's outspokenness, the family was transferred to an even harsher prison camp in California, where they lived for the remainder of the war.

After the war ended and the Takeis were allowed to return to a normal life, Takei proved to be an excellent student with an outgoing personality. He attended Mount Vernon Junior High and Los Angeles High School. He was active in extracurricular activities—including the drama club—and was elected student body president at both schools. After graduation he enrolled in the University of California at Berkeley. He intended to study architecture to please his parents, who had convinced him that acting was not a substantial enough career.

His first roles

While at Berkeley, Takei got his start in acting by dubbing English words over the soundtracks of Japanese science fiction films. After his second year of college, Takei transferred to the University of California at Los Angeles (UCLA) and switched his major to acting. Shortly thereafter he was contacted by an agent he had met while dubbing the Japanese films. The agent landed him a television role in a *Playhouse 90* episode called "Made in Japan." Takei later was signed by another agent who had seen him perform in a college production. He was soon being cast in small parts in television shows like *Hawaiian Eye* and *77 Sunset Strip.*

In addition to his studies at UCLA and his television work, Takei was studying acting at the Desilu Workshop, a school for television and film studies. At UCLA Takei starred in classmate Francis Ford Coppola's student film *Christopher.* Coppola would later become a prominent film director.

After graduating from UCLA in 1960, Takei lived briefly in New York, where he starred in a small production of the play *Fly Blackbird.* He then spent a summer in Europe, studying Shakespearean drama at the Shakespeare Institute at Village of Stratford-upon-Avon in England. After completing this program, he returned to the United States and UCLA, where he enrolled in the master's program in theater arts. It was then that his agent called him to say that producer Gene Rodenberry wanted to interview him for a role in a new series called *Star Trek.*

Star Trek

Takei met with Rodenberry about playing the part of the astrophysicist Sulu. Recalling the meeting for *Starlog*, Takei said, "My feeling was that [it] wasn't successful because of the way it was carried on. Gene didn't ask me a thing about my experience. We just discussed current events and the movies we had recently seen. I figured Gene was being polite, but that he wasn't interested in me." As it turned out, Rodenberry was indeed interested, and Takei was offered the part. Early in *Star Trek's* first season, however, his role was changed from that of an astrophysicist to a helmsman. This was done partly to get Takei's character into the thick of the action on the bridge with the other main characters.

In 1968, after only two seasons, NBC announced that it was canceling the show. But *Star Trek's* devoted fans sent so many letters of protest that the network reversed its decision. Still, the show was aired at a very unpopular time, Friday nights at ten o'clock, when few of its fans would be home to watch it. *Star Trek* was cancelled in 1969 after its third season.

Star Trek had a tremendous cult following, however, that would not accept the show's demise. Conventions of "Trekkies," as devoted fans came to be known, were held around the country for years after the show was cancelled—and continue to be held today. Actors from the show, including Takei, often appear at the conventions.

Takei clearly found meaning in his role as Sulu. He remarked, "Whatever time period we live in, man needs an affirmative sense of his future. Right now, people have a feeling that their efforts are futile and that the human race is foredoomed. *Star Trek* did ... help reaffirm the intrinsic strengths in man—our capability to wrestle with society's problems. If we don't have that confidence in our inventive genius and adventuresome spirit to overcome our troubles, then we won't be able to come up with the solutions. "

Politics

After the cancellation of *Star Trek,* Takei became involved in civic and community affairs in a more visible way. He began hosting a local talk show on the Los Angeles public broadcasting station called *Expressions: East/West.* He also became active in local Democratic politics and served as a delegate to the 1972 Democratic National Convention in Miami Beach, Florida. In 1973 Takei ran for a Los Angeles city council seat. In an interview with *Starlog*, he said: "My campaign for public office held a *lot* of surprises. I had always known that there were a lot of people who would stoop to any level to win an election, but I really saw them in action for the first time.... Someone in the opposition even

George Takei

accused my father of having been a communist—which of course he was not—so therefore *I* must be a communist as well." Takei lost the bitterly fought election by three percentage points.

For the remainder of the 1970s Takei worked in a variety of television shows including *Kung Fu, Ironside, The Six Million Dollar Man, Chico and the Man,* the *Hallmark Hall of Fame* series, and *The Blacksheep Squadron.* He also continued his interest in public service; during this period Takei organized and served as the founding chair of the Friends of Far Eastern Arts at the Los Angeles County Museum of Art, as national cultural affairs chair of the Japanese American Citizens League, and on the Academy of Television Arts and Sciences' Blue Ribbon Committee for the Emmy Awards. Additionally, he served as vice president of the board and chair of the personnel committee of the Southern California Rapid Transit District.

In the late 1970s, Takei also worked on his book, *Mirror Friend, Mirror Foe*, with science fiction writer Robert Asprin. Published by Playboy Press in 1980, it sold remarkably well. That same year, Takei ran for a seat in the California assembly, though he abandoned his campaign before the election after his opponents claimed he had an unfair advantage because of his famous role as Sulu.

The *Star Trek* films

With a huge body of dedicated—some might call them obsessed—fans, it was only a matter of time before another *Star Trek* project was put together. In 1979 Paramount released *Star Trek—The Motion Picture,* in which Takei revived his role as Sulu. Reviews were unfavorable. But despite poor critical notices, the film did well at the box office, and Paramount released a series of sequels: *Star Trek II: The Wrath of Khan* in 1982; *Star Trek III: The Search for Spock* in 1984; *Star Trek IV: The Voyage Home* in 1986; *Star Trek V: The Final Frontier* in 1989; *Star Trek VI: The Undiscovered Country* in 1991; and *Star Trek: Generations* in 1994.

Other work

Aside from his work on the *Star Trek* films, Takei has acted in several foreign film productions and in the theater in New York City. In 1991 he starred in *The Wash,* a play written by **Philip Kan Gotanda,** a prominent Asian American playwright. He also won high critical praise for his role as a Japanese admiral in the Australian film *Blood Oath,* a movie about an Australian captain's attempt to bring Japanese officers to justice for atrocities committed against prisoners of war in World War II. In an article published in *Drama-Logue,* Takei discussed *Blood Oath* and another recent foreign role and the difficulty of finding nonstereotypical roles as an Asian in America: "I have to go abroad to get producers to cast me in challenging, dimensional roles. *Return to the River Kwai* is British, and *Blood Oath* is Australian. There's an interesting message there."

Sources:

Burns, James H., "George Takei: Part I," *Starlog,* June 1981, pp. 37–39, 62.

Burns, James H., "George Takei: Part II," *Starlog,* August 1981, pp. 44–47.

Scaffadi, Richard, "This Star Is Still Trekkin'," *Drama-Logue,* January 24-30, 1991, p. 30.

Amy Tan

Writer
Born 1952, Oakland, California

"[Amy Tan has] a wonderful eye for what is telling, a fine ear for dialogue, a deep empathy for her subject matter, and a guilelessly straightforward way of writing."—New York Times Book Review

Amy Tan is one of the most successful fiction writers to emerge in the literary field in the last several years. In 1989 Putnam published *The Joy Luck Club,* a novel that had originally been a collection of short stories detailing the lives of several Chinese American women and their American-born daughters. The book was a tremendous commercial and critical success, catapulting Tan to the top of the American literary scene in a manner that seldom benefits unknown, first-time writers. *The Joy Luck Club* was a mainstay on the *New York Times* bestseller list from April through November 1989, a finalist for the National Book Award and the National Book Critics Circle Award, and won the Bay Area Book Reviewers Award. It has been translated into 17 languages, including Chinese.

In 1991 Tan published her second novel, an event eagerly anticipated by her readers. Entitled *The Kitchen God's Wife,* it, too, became a bestseller and earned excellent reviews. This is especially noteworthy because second novels are often exposed to much more intense scrutiny than first novels by critics who seem at times eager to prove early success a fluke.

Family tragedy

Amy Tan's parents, John and Daisy Tan, were Chinese Americans who met and married in the United States. John, an electrical engineer, had worked for the United States Information Service during World War II, before immigrating to the United States. Tan's family moved around the San Francisco Bay Area for much of her early childhood, finally settling in Santa Clara, California. They remained there until a bizarre tragedy struck the family in 1968: within a period of eight months, both Tan's father and older brother died of brain tumors.

The family was devastated by these deaths, and Tan's mother took her and her younger brother to Switzerland to escape the horror of the events. Tan finished high school in Switzerland, becoming somewhat wild and rebellious. She began spending time with some suspicious characters. Tan's mother believed these people were involved in drug dealing and even hired a private detective, who confirmed her suspicions and discovered that Tan's boyfriend had escaped from a mental hospital. Tan's mother then went to the police and instigated a major drug arrest involving Tan's boyfriend. The seriousness of the situation straightened Tan out.

In 1969 the family left Europe and returned to the Bay Area. Tan enrolled in Linfield College, a small Baptist school in Oregon. Her mother had chosen both the school and her daughter's course of study: she would be a premed major. Tan spent only a year at Linfield; in 1970 she moved with her boyfriend and future husband, Lou DeMattei, to San Jose, California. There she enrolled in San Jose City College and changed her major to something that interested her instead of her mother: English and linguistics. She earned a bachelor's degree in 1972 and then went on to earn a master's in 1974. Tan intended to earn a doctorate at the University of California at Santa Cruz, but she dropped out in 1976 to take a job with the Alameda County Association for Retarded Citizens as a language development consultant.

The writer emerges

Tan's first writing experience was as a business writer, producing pamphlets, reports, and speeches for such corporate giants as IBM, Apple, and AT&T. She became very successful in this field and earned a substantial income from it. As she became more successful, however, she also became increasingly consumed by her work, eventually realizing that she was turning into a workaholic. As a way to distract herself from her work, she joined a local fiction writers workshop that was run by a professor at the University of California at Irvine. The very first story she wrote for the workshop was published by *FM* magazine and later reprinted by *Seventeen.* Buoyed by her success, Tan continued writing, and in 1986 she signed with the literary agent Sandra Djikstra.

In 1987 Tan took a trip to China with her mother to visit relatives she had never met before. She took the trip in an effort to connect with her Chinese heritage, something she had not been exposed to in her family, which wanted to become Americanized. When she returned to the United States she found that her agent had sold a collection of her short stories to the publisher G. P.

Putnam for a $50,000 advance, a very high sum for an unknown writer. Tan finished a series of stories to complete the collection and then wove them together in such a way that they became more of a novel than a collection of unrelated stories.

The Joy Luck Club

Published in 1989, *The Joy Luck Club* was an immediate success. The book, in a series of related vignettes, focuses on the story of Jing-mei Woo and the journey she takes to China to meet her mother's daughters from a previous marriage. The *New York Times Book Review* described the young writer as having a "wonderful eye for what is telling, a fine ear for dialogue, a deep empathy for her subject matter, and a guilelessly straightforward way of writing." He went on to say that the stories that make up the novel "sing with a rare fidelity and beauty." Other critics echoed these sentiments, and Tan became a national celebrity.

But Tan had difficulty with her second novel. She feared her reputation had made her a target for literary critics eager to discredit her status as a serious writer. After much agonizing and a few false starts, she finally decided on telling a story much like that of her mother's. Tan's mother had come of age during World War II, a particularly chaotic and violent time in Chinese history. The mainland was under attack from the Japanese, who occupied large parts of the country and were massacring hundreds of thousands of innocent Chinese. Yet her mother had rarely spoken about her experiences during those years. Tan pushed her for information and was given the material for her next book. In 1991 she

Amy Tan

The *Wall Street Journal* wrote, "Where *The Joy Luck Club* was a group portrait, *The Kitchen God's Wife* above all tells the story of [one person] ... the most richly imagined character Ms. Tan has yet created. The story—which describes a brutal first marriage set against turbulent times—is closely based on her mother's life in China before, during and after World War II, and the wartime scenes, especially, have the force of a compelling oral history. But this is fundamentally a novel: its power lies in the author's impressive ability to create a world."

Other projects

In 1992 Tan published a children's book called *The Moon Lady*. The book received warm praise but was not as successful as her adult writing. The *New York Times* called it "a story with deep, satisfying meanings, a tale of a lost child who for a prolonged and terrifying moment risks losing even her sense of self."

In 1993 the film version of *The Joy Luck Club* was released. Tan wrote the screenplay in collaboration with Ronald Bass, a veteran film writer. The movie was true to the spirit of the novel—an accomplishment in itself—and marked a sort of milestone in becoming the first major Hollywood production starring a nearly 100 percent Asian American cast. It was also directed by an acclaimed Asian American director, **Wayne Wang**.

Fame

In an interview with the *New York Times,* Tan described her feelings about her fame and what it has done to her life. She said that

published *The Kitchen God's Wife* to generally good reviews.

The *New York Times Book Review* said, "Amy Tan's second novel is a harrowing, compelling and at times bitterly humorous tale in which an entire world unfolds in a Tolstoyan tide of event and detail. No doubt it was daunting to attempt a second book in the wake of the enormous success of [her first], but none of Ms. Tan's fans will be disappointed. *The Kitchen God's Wife* is a more ambitious effort, and, in the end, more gratifying."

she has created a second personality she puts on when playing the role of celebrity, a role she frankly does not much like. She claims her private personality is "sillier ... and a lot bitchier" than her public personality and admits she is most comfortable "walking around back home with my husband, or when I'm having a private conversation with him and he's sort of drifting off trying to read the paper and I say, 'Well, this is good; I'm as boring as I ever was.'"

Sources:

Dew, Robb Forman, "Pangs of an Abandoned Child," *New York Times Book Review,* June 16, 1991, p. 9.

Just, Julie, "A Mother's Lifetime of Secrets Revealed," *Wall Street Journal,* June 17, 1991, p. A8.

Rothstein, Mervyn, "A New Novel by Amy Tan, Who's Still Trying to Adapt to Success," *New York Times,* June 11, 1991, p. C13.

Schechter, Ellen, "Girl Overboard," *New York Times Book Review,* November 8, 1992, p. 31.

Schell, Orville, *New York Times Book Review,* March 9, 1989.

Chang-Lin Tien

Educator
Born July 24, 1935, Wuhan, China

"All obstacles or challenges are opportunities."

Chang-Lin Tien is the chancellor of the University of California at Berkeley. The first Asian American to head a major U.S. university, Tien arrived on campus in July 1990 during troubled times. Tien's appointment was hailed—and criticized—as a response to the growing diversity of the university's student population. He pledged to transform Berkeley from a huge, faceless institution into a warm, personal educational community that cares deeply about its students. "Excellence Through Diversity" became his theme.

Tien's years at Berkeley have been marked by controversy stemming from his style of leadership and disagreement about what he has accomplished. To give him inner strength in the face of these difficulties, Tien relies on Buddhism (the religion or approach to life derived from the teachings of Siddhartha, or the Buddha, who lived from around 563 B.C. to 483 B.C. Buddhism is practiced by over 300 million people, mainly in Southeast Asia and Japan.) Tien maintains an unwavering optimistic belief that "all obstacles or challenges are opportunities."

Frequent moves during youth

An appreciation for diversity is something Tien understands well. Born July 24, 1935, in Wuhan, China, Tien was the son of a wealthy government banking official. During World War II his family fled to Shanghai to escape the invading Japanese. After the war, the family fled again, to the island of Taiwan, following the Communist revolution in 1949. (Taiwan became the home of Nationalist, or non-Communist, China.) Tien's life changed drastically after each move. In Shanghai, he recalls having chauffeur-driven cars, maids, butlers, and servants; in Taiwan, he and his parents lived in cramped conditions. Though his father reestablished himself in the government and

Tien's sweetheart (later his wife), Liu Di-Hwa, was the daughter of a top army general, Tien's family fell into poverty when his father died in 1952.

Living as a refugee in Taiwan, Tien learned the value of education. He did well in his studies and graduated from National Taiwan University in 1955 with a degree in mechanical engineering. Though only 5-foot-6, he achieved some success shortly after graduation playing basketball for a military academy. Later, he decided to pursue a career in education. He borrowed $4,000 from relatives and traveled to the United States to attend the University of Louisville, Kentucky, and then Princeton University in New Jersey, where he ultimately earned his Ph.D. in mechanical engineering.

Tien became a teacher at Berkeley in 1959, working in what would become his field of specialization, thermal radiation. As a teacher and researcher, he earned many awards, grants, and honorary positions. Over the years, he held several administrative posts, serving as chair of the university's thermal systems division and later of the department of mechanical engineering.

In 1983, Tien became vice chancellor of research at Berkeley, only to resign in 1985 because he wanted to return to research and teaching. But in 1988, when the University of California at Irvine offered him the position of vice chancellor, he decided to accept it. He stayed for two years, until he was offered the position of chancellor at Berkeley. He returned to Berkeley with his wife and four children, all of whom have graduated from the University of California.

Chang-Lin Tien

New land, new problems

Tien's firm commitment to diversity can be traced to his experiences as a newly arrived immigrant. When he came to the United States in the late 1950s, the country was considered the land of hope and prosperity. He quickly learned that it was also a land of racial discrimination. On a bus to Louisville, he noticed washroom signs at bus stop stations marked "Colored" and "White." Barely able to speak English, he was confused; he was not sure which washroom he should use. He was told to use the

"White" washroom, but he later learned that institutionalized American prejudice did not stop there. A college professor insisted on calling him "Chinaman." When Tien learned that this was not a flattering term, he asked the professor to call him by his name, Chang-Lin Tien. "The professor came right back and said, 'How can I remember all those strange names, Ching, Chong, Tong, Cong,'" recalled Tien in an interview with *Asia Inc.* in 1993. "I got so mad, I said, 'If you can't call me by my name, don't call me.'" The professor did not call him by any name for the next nine months.

These memories linger. Tien wants no student to suffer the indignities he did, and his policies at Berkeley reflect his efforts to be sensitive to all races and cultures. At times, this sensitivity has drawn criticism from some conservative Californians.

Not the type to shut himself inside an office, Tien frequently strolls around campus, greeting students and socializing in crowds. "When I first became chancellor and started walking around, nobody said anything to me," Tien said in an interview with *World Monitor* magazine. "They'd never seen a chancellor."

The budget battle

Tien has been criticized for avoiding tough questions and talking about—rather than solving—problems. But he has succeeded in some of his efforts at improving Berkeley's financial condition. Shortly after his appointment as chancellor, the Tang Foundation in San Francisco awarded Berkeley a $1 million grant, which has since been increased to more than $4 million. Tien also travels frequently to Asia to promote organizations of Berkeley graduates and build relationships with Asian governments and corporations. These efforts have resulted in numerous additional grants to the university.

Sources:

Curtis, Diane, "New Chancellor Takes Command at UC," *San Francisco Chronicle,* July 2, 1990.

DeVoss, David, "Berkeley's Asian Connection," *Asia Inc.,* September 1993.

"Facing 4th Year of Cuts, Berkeley Chancellor Leads Budget Revolt," *New York Times,* May 12, 1993.

Gordon, Larry, "Chang-Lin Tien: Maintaining Berkeley's Excellence at a Time of Stiff Budget Cutbacks," *Los Angeles Times,* September 13, 1992.

Hallanan, Blake, "Excellence in Ethnic Diversity," *Time,* April 1, 1991.

Schoch, Russell, "A Conversation with Chang-Lin Tien," *California Monthly,* September 1990.

Shao, Mario, "He's Seen our Future, And ..." *World Monitor,* July 1992.

Wood, Daniel B., "Preaching Excellence in Diversity," *Christian Science Monitor,* October 24, 1990.

Tamlyn Tomita

Actress
Born 1966, Okinawa, Japan

"We need to counter the myth of the model minority.... [As] a group we have to emphasize we're Asian Americans, but we have to emphasize more that we're Americans first."

Tamlyn Tomita is one of the best-known Asian American actresses working in Hollywood today. Her first big break came in 1986 when she was cast to play Ralph Macchio's girlfriend in

The Karate Kid, Part II. Then, in 1990, she played Dennis Quaid's wife in *Come See the Paradise,* a film about the internment of Japanese Americans during World War II. Most recently, she played the adult Waverly in the movie based on **Amy Tan**'s hugely successful novel *The Joy Luck Club.*

Tomita has earned high praise for her acting and her dynamic on-screen presence. Alan Parker, director of *Come See the Paradise,* said of the actress, "You can look at her one moment and you see an all-American girl from the San Fernando Valley. Then if you blink, you see a very sophisticated Japanese woman. Off set, she's just fun. Yet she has a sort of patrician dignity onscreen."

Born in Japan

Tomita was born in Okinawa, Japan, to a second-generation Japanese American father and a Japanese Filipino mother. Her parents brought her to the United States when she was just three months old. In an interview with *Asian American Biography (AAB),* Tomita said she grew up an "all-American girl" in the San Fernando Valley, a largely upper-middle-class suburban area of Los Angeles, California. Tomita was a good student and went to the University of California at Los Angeles (UCLA), where she studied history. "A lot of research is needed in such a discipline," she told *AAB,* "research that I've been able to apply to much of my acting. The acting has brought to life that research, what I've seen and read about historical events."

Initially, Tomita did not intend to become an actress. The idea was suggested to her by Helen Funai, a woman Tomita met while attending a Japanese American film festival in Los Angeles when she was a student at

UCLA. Funai suggested that Tomita audition for a role in the upcoming *Karate Kid, Part II.* Tomita went to the open audition and won the part, playing the beauty who captivates Macchio's heart. She told *AAB* that this was her "favorite role ... because it was first, it was brand new."

Acting as a career

After the success of her first role, Tomita began seriously pursuing acting as a career. She began taking acting lessons and working in television, including a regular role on the soap opera *Santa Barbara.* She made guest appearances on such prime-time television shows as *Quantum Leap, The Trials of Rosie O'Neill, Raven,* and *Tour of Duty,* while continuing to work in films. She had a starring role in *Vietnam, Texas,* the story of Vietnamese refugees living as fishermen along the Texan shore of the Gulf of Mexico, and was in *Hawaiian Dream,* the first Japanese-produced film shot entirely in the United States.

In 1990 Tomita starred in her second major Hollywood film. The movie was *Come See the Paradise,* and its theme marked a turning point in film and in American popular culture. It was the first major film to address a subject many in America would just as soon pretend never happened: the imprisonment of 120,000 Japanese Americans on the West Coast during World War II. This "internment" of American citizens was intended as a security measure. It was reasoned that in the event of a Japanese invasion of the West Coast, Japanese Americans may have been tempted to assist the Japanese, though prominent studies had indicated that Japanese Americans were among the most loyal citizens of the United States. This national outrage is downplayed in history books and largely ignored in discussions of World War II.

Come See the Paradise, while notable for telling the story, was nonetheless criticized by many in the Asian American community for its casting of a white person (Dennis Quaid) in a starring role in what is an Asian American story. Despite this criticism, Tomita defends the film. "Not everyone is going to be pleased," she told *AAB*. "People have to take it with a grain of salt. They have to understand that the studio thought they needed a star with recognition to pull in audiences.... It's not the perfect film, but it does say something and it's out there for posterity's sake. The film is a beginning point to legitimizing the arguments that will make sure that something like this will never happen again." She went on to say that despite the fact that the film stars a white person, "it tells a story that needs to be told." Many Americans, she said, still know nothing of this dark chapter in American history.

Personally, the making of *Come See the Paradise* was an emotional journey for Tomita. "My father and father's family were interned at Manzanar, California [one of the many internment camps], during the war years, so it's always been a part of my legacy," she told *American Film* magazine in 1991. "I recall when I was a little girl in elementary school reading about World War II and seeing a very small paragraph saying, 'On the West Coast, in Hawaii, and in portions of Canada, 110,000 Japanese Americans were evacuated under Executive Order 9066.' And there were no details furthering the story. So I went home and asked my father, 'Did this really happen? Were you guys interned?' And he goes, 'Yes.' And it shocked ... me."

The Joy Luck Club

Two years later Tomita was cast in one of the most eagerly awaited films of its time: the screen adaptation of Amy Tan's bestseller *The Joy Luck Club*. Tan's novel had been a great success, catapulting Asian Americans and Asian American issues to the forefront of American popular culture. The film version of the novel, produced by Oliver Stone and Janet Yang and directed by the notable Asian American film director **Wayne Wang**, would be the first mainstream Hollywood film with a virtually all-Asian cast. Tomita was cast to play the adult character Waverly, a former child chess star who aspires to be the best she can be at everything, letting nothing stand in her way. The film received generally glowing reviews—*People* called it "painfully moving"—though it disappointed some at the box office.

Tomita also enjoys working in theater. Most recently she appeared in the January 1994 world premiere of highly regarded playwright **Philip Kan Gotanda**'s *Day Standing on Its Head* at the Manhattan Theater Club in New York City. Tomita played Nina, a role she described for *AAB* as "both physically and emotionally demanding because it was not bordered by the paradigm of a normal person's world: the character existed in someone's head." The play received horrible reviews, though the writer, not the actors, was singled out for criticism.

Other theater credits of Tomita's include the premiere of *Nagasaki Dust* at the Philadelphia Theater Company, *Don Juan: A*

Meditation in Los Angeles, and the title role in *Winter Crane* at the Fountain Theater, for which Tomita received a *Drama-logue* Award. While most of her roles have been serious, Tomita is fascinated by comedy. "With a dramatic character," she told *AAB,* "there's a set process. You go through the ups and downs, you build, peak, and experience a sense of retribution. Comedy is much more of a challenge and I'm scared to death of that. You have to go out of yourself. It's timing and listening to the audience. There's an internal dialogue going on between yourself and the character you play, the other characters, and the audience. You have to always be aware of all that."

So few good roles

One of Tomita's great concerns as an actress is the absence of good roles for people of color. "We need to push for more Asian Americans to be seen in roles. Just because people see one Asian face, that face isn't the face for all Asians. It's the face of one individual," she told *AAB.* "We need to break the notion that we are all children of long-suffering parents who gave up everything for us. We need to break the notion of the heroic Asian. We need to counter the myth of the model minority.... [As] a group we have to emphasize we're Asian Americans, but we have to emphasize more that we're Americans first."

Sources:

Seidenberg, Robert, "*Come See the Paradise*: Tamlyn Tomita Relives Her Family's History," *American Film,* vol. 16, January 1991, pp. 48-49.

Tomita, Tamlyn, telephone interview with Terry Hong, January 3, 1994.

Tritia Toyota

Television journalist
Born Pacific Northwest

Tritia Toyota's work reflects her commitment to the large, ethnically diverse Asian American community in Southern California.

Tritia Toyota is one of the best-known television news anchors and reporters in Southern California. (An anchor is the person who reads the news.) She anchors both the 6:00 P.M. and 11:00 P.M. news at KCBS in Los Angeles and serves as the station's principal reporter for major political events. She has covered important stories around the globe, from Bosnia-Herzegovina to Seoul, South Korea. Toyota scored a major victory in 1995 when she became the first newsperson to conduct a television interview with Judge **Lance Ito,** who was then presiding over the sensational O.J. Simpson double murder trial.

Toyota's work reflects her commitment to the large, ethnically diverse Asian American community in Southern California. She frequently speaks at community and professional events and has earned a reputation as a dignified, professional representative of Asian American interests and concerns. In 1981 Toyota helped found the Asian American Journalists Association (AAJA).

American with Asian roots

A fourth-generation Japanese American, Tritia Toyota was born and raised in the

Tritia Toyota

Pacific Northwest. She attended public schools and earned a bachelor's degree in communications and home economics from Oregon State University. After graduation, Toyota continued her education at the University of California at Los Angeles, where she received a master's degree in electronic journalism.

Toyota's first job in broadcasting was with KNX-CBS radio in Los Angeles, a local news station. She started as a copy person, maintaining the texts read on the air, and eventually worked her way up to on-air reporter. She also worked as a writer and producer.

In 1972 Toyota joined KNBC television in Los Angeles, where she worked as a general assignment reporter. In 1975 she was promoted to weekend anchor, and in 1977 she was named anchor of the daily 5:00 P.M. news broadcast. The next year she took on the additional duty of anchoring the 11:00 P.M. broadcast. Toyota combined her anchoring responsibilities with continued work as a reporter. As KNBC's head reporter for the coverage of elections, special events, and investigative series, she reported and produced *Asian American*, a one-hour documentary focusing on the Asian Pacific American community in Southern California. This groundbreaking television broadcast was the first serious journalistic examination of the huge Asian American community in Los Angeles. Toyota moved to KCBS-TV in 1985.

Asian American Journalists Association

In 1981 Toyota and Bill Sing, a reporter with the *Los Angeles Times,* founded the Asian American Journalists Association. Under Toyota's guidance and leadership, the AAJA has grown from the original Los Angeles chapter to an organization with more than 15 chapters across the country. Toyota served the organization loyally for more than ten years in a variety of positions. She stepped down as president of the board of directors in 1991, but she maintains influence through unofficial contacts and advisory positions. She also continues to speak on behalf of the organization and remains deeply committed to its ideals.

Respected celebrity and mentor

A well-known member of Southern California's Asian American community, Toyota speaks at colleges whenever she can and makes herself as available as possible to young journalists looking for advice or inspiration. Many Asian American journalists point to their contact with Toyota as an important influence on their careers.

Toyota has received several Emmy awards for her work as a journalist and has earned many other honors, including the Golden Mike for best news broadcasts, the Outstanding Young Woman of America citation, the Los Angeles Human Relations Commission Achievement Award, the Greater Los Angeles YWCA Communicator of the Year Award, the Los Angeles City Asian American Association Person of the Year Award, the Asian American Journalists Association Lifetime Achievement Award, and the U.S. Asia Institute Achievement Award.

Toyota currently is studying for a doctorate in cultural anthropology.

Sources:

Asian American Journalists Association, "Tritia Toyota."
Toyota, Tritia, telephone interview with Helen Zia, August 22, 1994.

Eugene Trinh

Physicist, astronaut
Born September 14, 1950, Saigon, South Vietnam

"The best thing [an astronaut] can do going around the earth is to look down at the ocean and the earth."

E ugene Huu-Chau Trinh is a physicist and astronaut who served as a payload (the cargo and equipment for the particular mission) specialist aboard NASA's first long-duration space shuttle flight in June 1992. As a member of the first microgravity (a virtual absence of gravity) laboratory mission, Trinh spent 14 days aboard the shuttle and circled the earth 350 times. As a payload specialist, he was responsible for conducting more than 30 experiments in the sciences of fluid dynamics and space manufacturing. In addition to his work for NASA, Trinh is a highly regarded physicist in the field of fluid dynamics. He holds three patents and has been widely published in scientific journals.

Born in Vietnam

Although Trinh was born in Vietnam, his father, a civil engineer with the United Nations, sent his family to live in Paris when Trinh was only two years old. Vietnam at the time was involved in an increasingly violent anticolonial war against the French, and the elder Trinh wanted to spare his family the violence.

Trinh was educated in Paris in the French public school system and then went to the

Eugene Trinh

homeland. Having grown up in Paris, he had "been pretty much won over by the Western perspective of things."

Trinh graduated from Columbia in 1972 with a bachelor of science degree in mechanical engineering and applied physics. He went on to Yale University in New Haven, Connecticut, for graduate work. In 1974 he earned a master of science degree in applied physics. A master of philosophy followed in 1975, and he received a Ph.D., also in applied physics, in 1977. After completion of his doctoral dissertation, Trinh remained at Yale, where he worked as a postdoctoral fellow for one year. He then moved to the Jet Propulsion Laboratory (JPL) at the California Institute of Technology, where he worked in laboratory-based experimental research in fluid mechanics. Fluid mechanics is the study of the motion of fluids ("fluids" can refer to either liquids or gases) and the laws of physics that govern it. This field of science is key in describing the effects the motion of the atmosphere or the ocean has on the earth. On a smaller scale, fluid mechanics, or dynamics, can describe the motion of aerosols and other small particles of liquids and gases.

United States in 1968 to attend Columbia University in New York City, to which he had won a full academic scholarship. Columbia University at that time was the site of some of the country's most virulent anti-Vietnam War protests. In an interview with *Asian American Biography (AAB)*, Trinh recalled the protests as tame compared to the student strikes of Paris in 1968, a violent series of clashes between students and government officials that rocked French society that year. He also said that he was very sympathetic to the American students who did not want to fight in Vietnam, his

In this area of scientific inquiry, weightlessness is often required to perform experiments on the behavior of gases and liquids in a containerless state. To this end, Trinh established experiments to be conducted aboard NASA KC-135 airplanes. These specially designed and outfitted airplanes would fly in what are referred to as "low-G" curves, in which weightlessness is achieved for short periods of time in the cargo bay as the airplane essentially free-falls from tremendous heights. Of course, experiments of this type are extremely limited in time.

The ideal conditions for experiments in weightlessness occur naturally in outer space. One of the rationales behind the development of the space shuttle program was that it would greatly benefit just the type of science Trinh was interested in by making space flight cheap and routine. With the introduction of the space shuttle program, NASA began doing scientific research beyond the reach of the earth's gravity.

Applying to the Space Program

Trinh first applied to work aboard the space shuttle in 1983 as one of a group of physicists headed by **Taylor Wang** that was preparing the Drop Dynamics Module experiment for Spacelab 3. Wang was selected as the payload specialist for the 1985 flight, and Trinh was his backup. The next NASA mission in which Trinh was involved was the United States Microgravity Laboratory 1 (USML-1), scheduled to be launched in June 1992. He applied to be a part of the crew and was accepted as a payload specialist.

Trinh told *AAB* that the experiments he performed in space concerned fluid dynamics generally and the surface tension of liquids in low gravity specifically. Surface tension is created by the forces that dictate the shape of a liquid in low gravity. These experiments allow scientists to probe surface tension and to test its strength in a liquid that is dominated by surface tension's force—a condition that does not occur on earth, where the force of gravity far exceeds that of surface tension.

The experiments also allowed Trinh to observe the dynamics of oscillating (moving back and forth between two points) liquid globes or bubbles. The science of surface tension is used in the production of surfactants (surface-active substances), which, in turn, allow for the production of such diverse products as mayonnaise, pharmaceuticals, cosmetics, detergents, and a wide array of industrial products. Another practical application of Trinh's work is in environmental science. The type of information he uncovers is useful in understanding the motion of the ocean and the way it transfers gases to the atmosphere—and the way they are transferred back to the ocean—which sheds light on the nature of climates.

Trinh greatly enjoyed his time in space, though the workload was very hard. Payload specialists conduct experiments in 12-hour shifts, during which time they are almost constantly busy. Despite this, Trinh did take a lot of time to look out the window, which he said was "the best thing one can do ... going around the earth, being able to look down at the ocean and the earth." The most surprising thing about his flight, he added, was how well he got along with his fellow astronauts, considering that they didn't know each other very well and were confined to such a small area for an extended period of time. "It's surprising how humans can interact so easily," he said, "so there's hope for most of the interaction we have on this planet as it gets more crowded."

Trinh believes strongly that one should keep oneself open to opportunities. He told *AAB* that he never imagined that someday he would be able to fly in outer space as an American astronaut. The fact that he did is proof that there really are no limits to what one can achieve, unless those limits are self-imposed. He also emphasized the importance of work and education. Although he believes that schooling is vital, he contends it's possible to have a good time along the way.

Trinh remains associated with NASA, and there are opportunities ahead for him to fly aboard another mission. But he is careful to balance his desires in this area with his family commitments. Trinh and his wife, Yvette, have a daughter, Claire, who celebrated her first birthday while Trinh was in space.

Sources:

NASA, "Eugene Trinh," biographical materials and press releases, 1993.

Trinh, Eugene Huu-Chau, telephone interview with Jim Henry, June 1, 1994.

Yoshiko Uchida

Author
Born November 24, 1921, Alameda, California
Died June 21, 1992, Berkeley, California

"I have ... tried to evoke the strength and courage of the first-generation Japanese whose survival over countless hardships is truly a triumph of the human spirit. I hope today's young people can learn from [their] sense of purpose, affirmation, and hope in life, and will cherish the traditions of values and of the past."

Yoshiko Uchida was one of the most prominent and successful writers of children's literature reflecting the Asian American experience. Between 1948

and 1991, she wrote 29 books, all but two of them for children. Among her more prominent works are *The Best Bad Thing, The Bracelet, New Friends for Susan,* and *Journey to Topaz: A Story of the Japanese-American Evacuation.* Her two books aimed at an older audience were her 1991 memoir written for young adults, *The Invisible Thread,* and *Desert Exile: The Uprooting of a Japanese American Family,* first published in 1982.

Daughter of a poet

Although Uchida was born in Alameda, California, she spent much of her childhood in the nearby city of Berkeley. Her mother was a poet and instilled a love of all literature and Japanese traditions in Uchida and her older sister, Keiko. Her father was a very popular businessman who regularly brought home friends and visitors, enlivening the house with diverse characters, many of whom provided the basis for characters in Uchida's books.

Uchida began writing as a child, completing her first book when she was ten years old. She also began what would be a lifelong practice of keeping a diary. Focusing so much of her attention on the written word taught Uchida the power of writing; she reported in her memoir *The Invisible Thread* that after writing in her diary about the death of a family dog, she realized "that writing was a means not only of holding on to magic, but of finding comfort and solace from pain as well. It was a means of creating a better ending than was sometimes possible in real life."

Executive Order 9066

Uchida went to high school at the predominantly white, affluent University High School in Oakland, California, and it was there that she experienced her first real taste of prejudice. She was a native-born American, like virtually every other student at the high school, but was seen as an outsider because of her name and her Asian features. She was an excellent student, however, and she graduated from high school in 1938 at the age of 16. She then went on to college at the University of California at Berkeley, where she chose to study English.

In December of 1941, during her senior year at Berkeley, Japan bombed the American naval base at Pearl Harbor, Hawaii. This event spurred a hysterical response in the American media and government, and the result of this "yellow scare" was the issuance by President Franklin D. Roosevelt of Executive Order 9066, which authorized the imprisonment of Americans of Japanese descent on the West Coast for the duration of World War II. The reasoning the government provided for this unconstitutional and inhumane act was that in the event of a Japanese invasion of the West Coast, Japanese Americans might aid the Japanese. No such action was taken against Americans of German or Italian descent, though the United States was at war with both Germany and Italy. The Uchida family, along with 120,000 other Japanese Americans, was rounded up and sent to internment camps.

Life in the camps

The Uchidas were first sent to Tanforan race track in San Mateo, California, which had been converted into what was called an

Yoshiko Uchida

"assembly center." The family lived in Stall Number 40, and it was to this address that Berkeley sent Uchida her diploma, rolled in a cardboard tube. At Tanforan, the prisoners organized hospitals, churches, and schools. Uchida was appointed a teacher and was given a class of second graders. For this work she was paid $16 a week.

After five months the family was moved to Topaz, a dilapidated stretch of barracks in Utah's Sevier Desert. The Uchidas lived in an 18-by-20-foot room outfitted with four cots. Life was extremely difficult and unpleasant in this barren land, where prisoners were subjected to isolation, unreliable water and heat sources, and endless dust storms. Of this time Uchida wrote in *The Invisible Thread,* "The Japanese endured with dignity and grace and it is that spirit which has made me especially proud of my heritage."

Release from the camps

In May of 1943 Uchida was awarded government clearance to leave Topaz. She had taught throughout her imprisonment and, with the help of the Quaker-backed National Japanese Student Relocation Council, was awarded a full graduate fellowship to study at Smith College. In 1944 she received a master's degree in education and took her first teaching position, at the Frankford Friends School, a Quaker school near Philadelphia at which she taught elementary school classes.

In 1952 Uchida received a Ford Foundation Fellowship, which she used to live in Japan for a year. There she was introduced to her Japanese roots and was afforded the opportunity to explore the culture, art, and spiritualism of Japan. When she returned to the United States she settled in Berkeley, where she had lived as a child. She brought with her a deep desire to share with third-generation Japanese Americans the same sense of pride and self-esteem she felt about their shared cultural history.

Uchida as a writer

As a child, Uchida had noticed that there were no books about Asian American children. As an adult, she made it her life's work to rectify this situation. She published her first book in 1949 while she was teaching at Frankford Friends School. Called *The Dancing Kettle and Other Folk Tales,* it received warm reviews and was reissued in 1986. In 1951 she published *New Friends for Susan,* and in 1955 *The Magic Listening Cap,* which won Uchida her first literary prize when it was awarded a Children's Spring Book Festival honor award. In between these children's works, Uchida also published a critical study of a Japanese folk artist, *We Do Not Walk Alone: The Thoughts of Kanjiro Kawai.*

Uchida's mother died in 1966, which inspired the author to write a book telling the story of her mother's generation and all it had endured as immigrants in the United States. Titled *Journey to Topaz: A Story of the Japanese-American Evacuation,* the book won a medal for the best juvenile book by a California author from the Commonwealth Club of California when it was published in 1971.

Uchida continued writing prolifically for the remainder of her career. Her work has been widely anthologized and her writings have been translated into German, Dutch, Afrikaans, and Japanese. In 1976 she was cited by the Japanese American Citizen's League for outstanding contributions to the cultural development of society. She was awarded the Best Book of 1985 Award from the Bay Area Book Reviewers for her very popular *The Happiest Ending.* Two years later, she published *Picture Bride,* her first adult novel.

Her legacy

Uchida's life work has helped many young people of both Asian and European descent understand and cope with ethnic differences in America's highly diversified society. Her books embody the Japanese American spirit as she experienced it during her lifetime, a period marked by racism and conflict. She was especially proud of how the Japanese spirit had endured unbroken through the nightmare of World War II. In an epilogue to *The Invisible Thread,* she wrote, "I have ... tried to evoke the strength and courage of the first-generation Japanese whose survival over countless hardships is truly a triumph of the human spirit. I hope today's young people can learn from [their] sense of purpose, affirmation, and hope in life, and will cherish the traditions of values and of the past."

Yoshiko Uchida died in June 1992 in her Berkeley, California home.

Sources:

"Author, Yoshiko Uchida, 70, Related Japanese-American Life," *Chicago Tribune,* June 28, 1992, p. 6.

The Regents of the University of California, "Nisei Author and Philanthropist, Yoshiko Uchida, Evokes the Traditions of the Past to Promote Cross-Cultural Understanding," *Cal Futures,* vol. 1, no. 4, pp. 2-4.

Uchida, Yoshiko, *The Invisible Thread, A Memoir,* New York: Julian Messner, 1991.

Huynh Cong Ut

Photojournalist
Born March 29, 1951, Long An Province,
    South Vietnam

Ut's now-legendary photograph of a nine-year-old Vietnamese girl running down a dirt road after she and her family home had been hit by napalm ... was widely reproduced around the world, won nearly every major photojournalism award including the Pulitzer Prize, and helped the antiwar movement win wide support with the American public.

H uynh Cong "Nick" Ut is an award-winning photojournalist best known for his work with the Associated Press (AP) during the Vietnam War. During that time he distinguished himself as a reliable combat photographer who was unafraid of work in hostile areas. He was wounded twice while covering the joint American and South Vietnamese invasion of Cambodia: once in the stomach and once in the upper chest. Another time, he said, "a rocket parted my hair. I was very, very lucky." Such risks are par for the course for a combat photographer.

The highlight of Ut's career came in 1972 when he took a now-legendary photograph of a nine-year-old Vietnamese girl running down a dirt road near Trang Bang, Vietnam, after she and her family home had been hit by napalm—the chemical defoliant developed in the United States to destroy the thick jungle foliage the North Vietnamese used so effectively for cover. The photo, so clearly documenting the horror that the war was indiscriminately inflicting on the impoverished civilian population of Vietnam, was widely reproduced around the world, won nearly every major photojournalism award including the Pulitzer Prize, and helped the antiwar movement win wide support with the American public. For many, Ut's photo became the symbol of the Vietnam War.

A country divided by war

Ut was born on March 29, 1951, to a family of rice farmers in rural Long An Province, southwest of Saigon in the Mekong River Delta. Vietnam had been divided after World War II. North Vietnam was occupied by the Chinese until guerrilla leader Ho Chi Minh, who followed the teachings of Chinese Communist leader Mao Zedong, took over. South Vietnam was occupied by the British and the French. The European colonial powers initiated many attempts to unify the country, but these ultimately deteriorated into wars fought by the French, the pro-Western puppet governments of the South, and, beginning with the French withdrawal in 1954, the United States. As a young man, Ut moved to Saigon, the capital of South Vietnam, where he lived with his brother.

One of Ut's nine brothers (he also had six sisters), Huynh Thanh My, was a photographer for the Associated Press who was killed in 1965 covering combat in the Mekong Delta. Ut was only 14 at the time, but he persuaded some of his brother's friends at the AP bureau in Saigon to give him a job working in the darkroom. He was a good worker and showed interest in all aspects of photography. He was especially interested in following in his brother's

Huynh Cong Ut

footsteps as a combat photographer. His boss, Horst Faas, the AP photo editor in Saigon, was reluctant to let the young man do such dangerous work. "Horst was afraid I'd get killed, too," Ut recalled years later. By 1966, though, Faas relented and assigned Ut as a combat photographer.

While covering the Vietnam War, Ut, who by this time was going by the name "Nick" Ut, traveled all over Indochina to Laos, Cambodia, Thailand, and both North and South Vietnam. The war had spread to all these countries, though the American public was largely unaware of this. On several occasions Ut worked alongside veteran AP war correspondent Peter Arnett, whose texts his photos often accompanied.

The photo

The photograph that made Ut's reputation came in June of 1972. The South Vietnamese air force was dropping napalm near the village of Trang Bang, and some villagers' homes were inadvertently hit, as was often the case in such bombings. After the raid, Ut photographed a nine-year-old girl named Kim Phuc running down Route 1, her naked body seared and nearly smoldering from the napalm dropped on her home. The photograph was reproduced all over the world and stood as a symbol of the random brutality of the war. After taking the picture, Ut rushed the girl to the hospital. The Saigon bureau of the Associated Press opened a bank account to help pay for her medical expenses.

Ut's photograph earned him an international reputation and several prestigious awards. Among them were the Pulitzer Prize for photography, the World Press Photo Award, and the George Polk Memorial Award. Recognition also came from the Overseas Press Club, the National Press Club, and Sigma Delta Chi.

Ut continued to cover the war for the Associated Press until the fall of Saigon to ,the forces of the North in 1975. During those tense days, the photographer was airlifted out of Vietnam and ended up living for a time in a refugee camp set up at the Camp Pendleton Marine Corps base in Southern California. He lived there for a month before being reassigned by the Associated Press to their Tokyo bureau as a general assignment photographer. In 1977 he was transferred to Los Angeles, again as a general assignment photographer, where he worked with distinction on a variety of stories. In 1993 Ut was sent to Hanoi, Vietnam, to open the AP's new bureau there, marking the country's opening to the West after years of isolation.

While in Vietnam, Ut met with the family of Kim Phuc, the young girl whose photograph had made his reputation. They still lived in Trang Bang, although the girl whose photo had gripped the world had left the country. She had gone to study in Cuba and had later married and defected to Canada. Ut stayed at this temporary assignment in Hanoi for several months and told *Asian American Biography (AAB)* in an interview that he found the people very friendly and was thrilled to be back in his home country. He added that when his children are old enough (Ut married in Tokyo and has two teenage children), he intends to return to work in the Hanoi bureau permanently.

Ut told *AAB* that he feels very gratified to have worked in a field in which he was able to show the world the horror of the Vietnam War, which he described as "probably one of the largest and most unforgotten wars of this century." Although American involvement in the war came primarily in the late 1960s and early 1970s, with a loss of life of near 60,000, the Vietnamese people had been fighting colonial domination since the end of World War II, with a loss of life numbering in the millions and with most of the country left in virtual ruin. His advice for aspiring photojournalists is to study the art of photojournalism and, specifically, the work of those photojournalists they admire.

Sources:

Associated Press, "Bio of Nick Ut," press release, Los Angeles, California, 1994.

Ut, Huynh Cong, telephone interview with Jim Henry, June 30, 1994.

Urvashi Vaid

Attorney, community activist
Born October 8, 1958, New Delhi, India

"The movement I work in might be called a gay and lesbian movement, but its mission is the liberation of all people."

Urvashi Vaid is a community organizer and grass-roots activist who has been involved in the gay/lesbian and feminist movements since the early 1980s. Her most prominent position was as executive director of the National Gay and Lesbian Task Force (NGLTF), one of the nation's oldest and most influential gay rights organizations. She served as executive director for three years and worked as that organization's director of public information for an additional three years.

Vaid has not limited her community service to gay/lesbian rights, however. She is a former staff attorney with the American Civil Liberties Union (ACLU), where she worked on behalf of prisoners in the ACLU's National Prison Project. She described what she sees as the nature of her work for *Vanity Fair,* explaining, "The movement I work in might be called a gay and lesbian movement, but its mission is the liberation of all people. To me, my mission is about ending sexism, about ending racism, and about ending homophobia."

A very young activist

Vaid was born in India in 1958, but when she was eight her family moved to the United States because her father, a novelist, was offered a teaching position at the State University of New York at Potsdam. Vaid was an intellectually curious child and at a very young age became involved in the antiwar movement then sweeping through America's campuses in protest of U.S. involvement in the war in Vietnam. At the age of 11 she participated in an antiwar march, and at 12 she gave a speech praising George McGovern, the 1972 Democratic nominee for president who was beaten by Richard Nixon in a landslide.

In general, though, Vaid was an outsider as a child. She told *Vanity Fair,* "I was a very awkward young girl. I spoke with an Indian accent. I had these very thick glasses. I had long hair, very thick, straight hair, Indian hair, down to my waist. I was such an intellectual. I read voraciously, and by the time I was 12 I was going through my parents' library.... I lived a lot in my head." Vaid graduated from high school in only three years and attended upstate New York's Vassar College on an academic scholarship.

The climate at Vassar at this time was politically charged, as was Vaid herself, and she was heavily influenced by it. She was especially attracted to the feminist movement, though she was concerned about oppression in all its forms. "I've gotten criticized throughout my political life for having a multi-issue agenda," she told the *Boston*

Phoenix. "All I can say is that that agenda derives from the oppression I experience. As a woman who is a lesbian, who's out [open about her sexual orientation], and who's a woman of color—it's not possible for me to divorce the prejudice I experience one from the other."

Political organizing

Vaid began political organizing in college, working to form a variety of groups to address the discrimination she felt. In 1979 she graduated with a bachelor's degree in English and political science, then spent three months as a volunteer intern with the Women's Prison Project. After graduation, she worked as a legal secretary and administrative assistant for a small criminal and business law firm in Boston while also serving on the steering committee of the Allston-Brighton Greenlight Safehouse Network, an anti-violence neighborhood project that she had cofounded. In 1980 she enrolled in law school at Northeastern University in Boston. Two years later, she cofounded the Boston Lesbian/Gay Political Alliance, a nonpartisan political organization that interviews and endorses candidates for political office and supports and speaks out for Boston's gay community.

She graduated from law school in 1983 and went to work as a staff attorney with the ACLU's National Prisons Project in Washington, D.C. In this position Vaid conducted class action civil rights lawsuits to improve conditions in the nation's prison system. In 1984 she initiated the National Prisons Project's work with prisoners who had contracted the HIV virus, which is generally believed to cause AIDS.

Urvashi Vaid

National Gay and Lesbian Task Force

Vaid became involved with the NGLTF in 1985 when she served on its board of directors. In 1986 she became the group's director of public information and brought with her a degree of professionalism and media savvy it had not known before. She increased coverage of NGLTF's activities and agenda and established the organization as a principal source of information on issues concerning gay and lesbian rights. She told the *Boston Phoenix,* "We concentrated on making sure that gay issues were going to be really, really in the media's face, and hatched a lot of plots to do that."

In 1989 Vaid became executive director of NGLTF's Policy Institute in Washington, D.C. There, she tripled the group's operating budget and increased staff while beginning major fund-raising and public outreach programs. As always, Vaid was working to increase visibility, believing that the more gays and lesbians are seen by the media as ordinary citizens participating in society just like anyone else, the fewer barriers there will be to acceptance. She also cofounded the NGLTF's Creating Change conference, which remains the only national gay and lesbian political conference, making news during the 1988 and 1992 presidential campaigns.

After NGLTF

Vaid is acknowledged to have had a major impact on NGLTF's efforts to increase the visibility of gays and lesbians on the national scene. She is seen in the gay community as a fiery orator, someone who strongly supports the kind of direct action politics advocated by groups like ACT-UP and Queer Nation, who use radical public confrontations and heavily symbolic acts of civil disobedience to draw media attention to their cause. In 1990, for instance, she disrupted President Bush's first policy speech on AIDS by holding up a sign that read, "Talk Is Cheap, AIDS Funding Is Not" and was removed from the audience by police. In 1991 she was arrested in front of the White House along with 16 others protesting the Supreme Court's *Webster* decision granting states the right to enact laws limiting access to abortion in certain proscribed

ways. These are just two examples of the hundreds of local and national protests she has organized over the years.

In 1992, however, Vaid resigned her position and moved to Provincetown, Massachusetts, to work on a book about the history of the gay civil rights movement. It is tentatively titled *Margin to Center: The Mainstreaming of Gay and Lesbian Liberation* and is scheduled to be published in the fall of 1995. She has also written extensively in the gay and mainstream press and has been published in magazines like the *Nation,* the *New Republic,* and the *Advocate.*

The closet

Like nearly all lesbians and gays, Vaid has felt the terror of coming out of the closet (admitting her sexuality to her family, friends, and society at large). When she told her family, her father was not surprised, but her mother was devastated. Vaid told *Vanity Fair,* "I think I would have been a lesbian whether I grew up in India or America. Eventually I would have found it. This is how I feel about my sexuality. It's very very deep in me, and it was formed at an early age, and once I could name it and accept it, it became fixed."

On a broader level, the closeting of homosexuals by social mores is something Vaid sees as having a crippling effect on political organizing. "Why is it so hard for us to build?," she asked in *Vanity Fair.* "Because of the closet. Because so many of our people are hidden from us. Many women leaders still feel the need to be closeted to protect their access or their status. They feel if they come out of the closet as lesbians in the women's movement they will somehow lose their leadership." It is a dilemma Vaid has been fighting for nearly two decades.

Sources:

Galst, Liz, "Homo Beat: On Guard," *Boston Phoenix,* January 9, 1993, p. 16.

Khan, Surina A., "Still Out Front," *Metroline,* June 10, 1993, pp. 22-24.

Torregrosa, Luisita Lopez, "The Gay Nineties," *Vanity Fair,* May 1993, pp. 124-29.

Vaid, Urvashi, resume, provided by Vaid, August 1994.

Vaid, Urvashi, telephone interview with Jim Henry, August 8, 1994.

John D. Waihee

Attorney, governor of Hawaii
Born May 19, 1946, Honokaa, Hawaii

Waihee has grand dreams for Hawaii. He says he would like Hawaii to be a state filled with thousands of trees, where lands once used to raise sugar cane are restored to native forest.

J ohn David Waihee was Hawaii's fourth elected governor and the first of Hawaiian ancestry. Described by political insiders as an idealist and an activist, Waihee transformed an early interest in politics into a long-standing career. He took office in 1986 after edging out a favored Democrat in the state's primary. Waihee promised a new generation of leadership that would offer tax breaks, innovative solutions to traffic problems, a strong economy, and a top-quality education system.

Waihee left office after the 1994 election. (State laws do not allow a two-term governor to run for re-election.) While some of his promises appear to have been kept, many of his decisions caused controversy.

Mainland education

Waihee was born on May 19, 1946, in Honokaa, on the island of Hawaii. His father worked as a telephone company line worker. His mother, born Mary Parker Purdy, was a descendant of a Massachusetts sailor who eventually became an adviser to Hawaii's King Kamehameha I. Waihee earned his bachelor's degree in history and business from Andrews University in Michigan and then returned to Hawaii. There he became a member of the first graduating class of the William S. Richardson School of Law. His classmates included a number of future prominent state lawmakers. He practiced law at a Hawaiian firm for four years before starting his own law practice in 1979.

Hawaii's voters tend to vote Democratic, and most politicians who want to serve in state offices maintain close ties with those already in power. Waihee, however, decided to make a name for himself through other means. In 1972, at age 26, he joined a renegade political force, Coalition 72, which attempted to challenge the Democratic party leadership at the party's state convention. The challenge failed and landed Waihee firmly outside the political establishment. Six years later, at the state's 1978 Constitutional Convention, he proved he had learned a lesson; he worked to unite the old-time political establishment with young activists and emerged from the convention as a clear leader. During that time, he began to identify

John D. Waihee

Waihee built a grass-roots political following throughout many of the state's smaller islands and wound up winning the race. Four years later, he entered the governor's race. Once again he faced a political favorite and, despite being outspent, won the election, though the margin of victory was narrow.

In his eight years as governor, Waihee was instrumental in promoting a tax-reduction program that resulted in the return of $700 million to taxpayers. He has also worked to reform education so that schools are managed at the local level. Additionally, a $200 million program championed by Waihee resulted in increased levels of affordable housing. And while Waihee was in office, Hawaii grew rapidly and boasted one of the lowest unemployment rates in the nation. The governor strongly supported a rapid-transit system planned for Honolulu and the development of alternative energy.

However, Waihee has experienced his share of controversy. He was severely criticized for his choice of a nominee for the state supreme court. Later, the press and public were critical when Waihee's office ordered a $10,784 desk at a time when the state was approaching a massive budget crisis. Waihee defended himself by saying that it was his openness that caused the problems; before he took office, many now-public records were confidential.

The future

Waihee has grand dreams for Hawaii. He says he would like Hawaii to be a state filled with thousands of trees, where lands once used to raise sugar cane are restored to native forest. He dreams of state environmental plans that preserve watersheds and

with a political movement known as Palaka Power, which argued that the power of government rests with local activists. Even as governor, Waihee continued to oppose any proposals that might challenge the strength of local governments.

Triumph as the underdog

Waihee was elected to the state House of Representatives in 1980. Two years later, he joined the race for lieutenant governor, challenging a front-runner, then-state senator Dennis O'Connor. Though an underdog, of beaches that are free for all people to use, without having to maneuver through crowded hotels to get to his state's spectacular coastal areas. He is also committed to the promotion of superior education for Hawaiian students and to Pacific Rim trade in which engineers from Hawaii can help to develop China and other growing Asian economies. Ultimately, though, Waihee's long-range plan for the state can be summed up thus: "I hope the Hawaiian people are happy in Hawaii," he said in a recent interview with *Honolulu* magazine. "I really do."

Sources:

Honolulu Advertiser, November 15, 1990; January 13, 1993; January 19, 1994.
Honolulu magazine, January 20, 1993.

An Wang

Inventor, entrepreneur, philanthropist
Born February 7, 1920, Shanghai, China
Died March 24, 1990

"Those of us working on computers in the late 1940s ... did not have a sense that we were making history."

From an initial investment of $600, An Wang, inventor of the magnetic core memory (a component of early computers), built one of the most rapidly growing, successful businesses in American history. Founded in 1951 in Lowell, Massachusetts, Wang Laboratories became one of the giants in the computer business. In 1984 Wang was estimated by *Forbes* magazine to be the fifth-richest person in America.

Wang gave generously from this wealth. He donated millions to fix the roof of the Boston Performing Arts Center. He supplied $15 million to construct a factory in Boston's Chinatown that provided jobs for impoverished city residents. He also supported education, giving millions to Harvard University and Wellesley College, and spending $6 million to create the Wang Institute of Graduate Studies in Tyngsboro, Massachusetts, for software engineers and China scholars.

For his achievements Wang was awarded the Medal of Liberty on July 3, 1986, during ceremonies for the relighting of the Statue of Liberty on its centennial. Wang was honored along with 11 other Americans who had been born abroad but who had made great contributions to American society.

Traditional Chinese childhood

An Wang was born on February 7, 1920, in Shanghai, China, to Yin Lu and Zen Wan (Chien) Wang. His father taught English at a private elementary school in Kun San, about 30 miles from Shanghai. He also practiced traditional Chinese medicine, using herbs and other organic substances to treat common illnesses. Because of his father's education and status, the Wang family lived a relatively middle-class existence. Until the time he was 21, Wang lived in either Shanghai or Kun San, where his father's ancestors had lived for six hundred years. In keeping with Chinese tradition, the Wang family maintained a book of recorded family history that claimed to be accurate for 23 generations, back to the time of the explorer

Marco Polo's journeys from Europe to China. Writing about these books in his 1986 autobiography, *Lessons,* Wang said, "[They] gave our families a sense of continuity and permanence that I don't see in the more mobile West."

Wang's father was very strict and believed in the value of education. The young Wang became a good student, excelling in math and science. He graduated from high school at age 16. In 1936 he began studying electrical engineering and communications at Chiao Tung University in Shanghai.

The age of confusion

While Wang studied, China was going through a period of struggle that is sometimes referred to as the Age of Confusion. There was civil war between feudal warlords (military leaders who came from powerful families that ruled areas of China, sometimes for centuries) and the Nationalist forces of Chiang Kai-shek, and between the Nationalists and the Communists under Mao Zedong. (Mao would emerge victorious in 1949.) Even worse was the brutal invasion of the militarily superior Japanese army. During the various battles in this wartorn era, Wang lost both his parents and one sister. He remained safe at the university, however, which was inside a French-held district of Shanghai.

After his graduation in 1940, Wang spent a year as a teaching assistant in electrical engineering. Thinking the Japanese would soon control all of Shanghai, he volunteered along with eight of his classmates to secretly find a way into the interior of China, then under Japanese control. In spite of continuous Japanese bombing of the area, he

An Wang

worked at the Central Radio Works in Kweillin from 1941 until 1945, designing and building transmitters and radios for Nationalist troops.

Immigrant to inventor

After the war Wang applied and was accepted to a program set up by the Nationalist government to send highly trained engineers to the United States to learn about management and technology. He was to serve a two-year apprenticeship with an American corporation, then return to help rebuild war-ravaged China. In June 1945 he arrived in Newport News, Virginia. Six years later he would found Wang Laboratories.

Once in the United States, it occurred to Wang that he might learn a lot more and be of more service to his country if he continued his studies at an American university. He chose Harvard and was accepted. Although after one year the Chinese government stopped funding the program that was supporting his education, Wang remained at Harvard, where he earned a master's degree in 1946 and a doctorate in applied physics in 1947.

From 1948 until 1951 Wang worked as a research fellow in the Harvard Computation Laboratory under Howard Aiken, one of the pioneers of modern computer science. In 1944 the Computation Lab had designed the first binary (a system of numbers having two numbers as its base, specifically the digits one and zero) computer in the United States, a noisy machine 51 feet long and eight feet high that used thousands of mechanical relays. Aiken and his employees had been trying for some time to discover how the machine could record and access large amounts of information without mechanical motion. In only three weeks Wang found the solution. His invention, the magnetic memory core, revolutionized computing and served as the standard method for memory retrieval and storage until the invention of the microchip in the 1960s. (A microchip is an integrated circuit that features a tiny complex of electronic components and their connections, produced in or on a small slice of material.) Wang took his groundbreaking work in stride. "Those of us working on computers in the late 1940s ... did not have a sense that we were making history," he commented.

The beginning of Wang Labs

On July 10, 1949, Wang married Lorraine Chiu. They settled in Boston, Massachusetts, to begin their family, which eventually included two sons, Frederick and Courtney, and a daughter, Juliette. In 1951 Wang left the Harvard Lab to begin Wang Laboratories. His first office was a 200-square-foot unfurnished loft in Boston. One of his first jobs was to build the new scoreboard at New York's Shea Stadium. He then began marketing desktop calculators. In the 1970s Wang developed a typewriter with electronic memory that was priced below the standard IBM model of the time. He then introduced what has become a standard in home and office computing: the television-like monitor. Wang Labs became known in the media as "the word processing company."

Wang Laboratories continued its incredible growth, developing such systems as the Office Information System (OIS), which integrated word and data processing. But competition in the computer business was growing stronger, and by 1985 a depression in the computer market forced Wang Labs to lay off 1,600 workers. In August of 1989 the company announced losses of $374.7 million. A series of drastic restructuring moves were initiated, however, which has led to the partial comeback of Wang Labs today.

Wang died of cancer of the esophagus on March 24, 1990.

Sources:

"An Wang," obituary, *New York Times,* March 25, 1990.

"Forum, On the Medal of Liberty," *Omni,* July 1986.

Wang, An, with Eugene Linden, *Lessons: An Autobiography,* Reading, Massachusetts: Addison Wesley, 1986.

Taylor Wang

Physicist, astronaut
Born June 16, 1940, Shanghai, China

"When we started out, the spacecraft was pretty cramped for all seven of us. But once you get into space, you find you don't have to live on the floor; you can live off the ceiling, or you can live off the wall, so the spacecraft becomes very spacious. I picked the ceiling for my home base."

Taylor G. Wang is one of the growing number of scientist/astronauts who work with NASA and perform experiments in outer space aboard the space shuttle. He is also the Centennial Professor of Applied Physics and director of the Center for Microgravity Research and Applications at Vanderbilt University in Nashville, Tennessee. In 1985, Wang flew aboard the space shuttle *Challenger* as a payload specialist, performing containerless experiments in fluid dynamics.

Born in pre-revolution China

Wang was born in China in the midst of World War II, during the Japanese occupation of his country. After the Japanese were defeated in the war and forced to retreat from its empire, a civil war broke out in China between the Nationalist forces of Chiang Kai-shek and the Communist insurgency led by Mao Zedong. It was a long, brutal war that ended with Mao's victory. Many Chinese then fled the mainland and established a "second China" on the island of Taiwan. The Wangs were one such family.

Wang's father was a wealthy businessman, and it was expected that one day Wang would grow up to take over the family business. By the time he was 12, however, he had decided he wanted to be a physicist. In an interview with *Asian American Biography (AAB)*, Wang recalled how his early natural curiosity played itself out. "I was a destroyer, always curious about how things worked. I used to take things apart, but was never quite able to put them back together properly. Consequently, a lot of things in my house started falling apart prematurely. An act of sabotage on my part."

As a child, Wang had two role models. The first was his mother, whom he described as a "very intelligent woman [who has] the wisdom of focusing on the big pictures and just causes, establishing in me, early on, the proper responsibilities and duties of an individual." His other model was the great Chinese general Yua Fay, who "believed that each individual has responsibilities from a higher calling. For China, he defied his emperor, and for his emperor, he gave up his own life. I admire his spirit and selflessness."

A wake-up call

As a student, Wang was always at or near the top of his class, but he took his abilities for granted and didn't really apply himself. After high school, students in Taiwan are required to take a college entrance exam. Wang just assumed he would pass and didn't bother preparing himself properly. "Confidently, I took the exam, and bombed miserably. It made me realize that I had to settle down and work hard to achieve my goals. It made me look at my life a little more seriously," he told *AAB*.

Barred from entering college in Taiwan, Wang went to the United States to study at the University of California at Los Angeles (UCLA), where he did all his academic work. He earned his Ph.D. in 1971. In 1972, Wang accepted a position at the Jet Propulsion Laboratory (JPL) at the California Institute of Technology in Pasadena, where he worked in applied physics. In 1974, NASA accepted a proposal he had made for an experiment to be conducted in space. By 1980, Wang's team had finished designing the mechanical hardware required to conduct the proposed experiments.

For years, NASA had been accepting proposals from scientists for experiments to be conducted in space. They were eagerly anticipating the beginning of the space shuttle program, which would allow routine flights in space. The extremely technical nature of these experiments, however, presented NASA officials with a dilemma. Wang explained in an article published in *Engineering and Science:* "NASA ... asked the question: 'Is it better to train a career astronaut as a scientist, or to train a career scientist as an astronaut?' NASA headquarters finally opted for the latter, since this mission would be primarily science oriented." NASA announced an open selection for astronauts and Wang was chosen.

Experiments in space

Wang was trained in all aspects of space flight before being fully accepted as a payload specialist. He had to learn everything about the shuttle, including how to fly it home in the event of an emergency. Wang described his experience for *Engineering and Science,* relating, "It was a very good

Taylor Wang

launch.... It took about two hours for the spacecraft to get into stable orbit. When you first get into orbit and experience zero gravity, something very interesting happens. For the first time in your life your body says, 'I don't need my legs.' And so the brain says, 'Since I have no need for the legs, let's shrink them.' And your legs actually shrink about an inch in diameter very quickly."

When it came time for Wang to begin work on his experiment, there was trouble. "I started to turn on the experiment," he wrote in *Engineering and Science,* "and it didn't work." Wang spent the next two days trying to fix the machinery needed to conduct the experiment. He was finally successful. "Although there wasn't a high degree of probability of fixing it, with good support from my team on the ground we were able to discover the problem and find a way around it."

Wang also described his impressions of space flight for *Engineering and Science:* "For one thing, there's no up and no down. So you can live on any of the six surfaces. When we started out, the spacecraft was pretty cramped for all seven of us. But once you get into space, you find you don't have to live on the floor; you can live off the ceiling, or you can live off the wall, so the spacecraft becomes very spacious. I picked the ceiling for my home base." He went on to describe sleeping in space. "When you sleep, you don't lie on something, you just float. So when you're tired you just close your eyes and you can go to sleep wherever you want to. It's very comfortable. The only trouble is that sometimes you float too far and drift into your friends."

Wang married his high school sweetheart, Beverly, in 1965, and the couple has two children. Wang told *AAB* he believes that to succeed in life it is necessary to "do your best, but never accept failure as a conclusion." He added, "Life is very short. We should not waste it on frivolousness."

Sources:

Wang, Taylor G., "A Scientist in Space," *Engineering and Science,* January 1986, pp. 17-23.

Wang, Taylor G., interview with Jim Henry, April 7, 1994.

Vera Wang

Fashion designer
Born 1949, New York City

Vera Wang has created wedding gowns for members of the Kennedy clan and pop singer Mariah Carey (with a 27-foot train). She has designed dresses that actresses Sharon Stone, Marisa Tomei, Penelope Ann Miller, and Holly Hunter have worn at the Academy Awards ceremonies, and created costumes for Olympic figure skater Nancy Kerrigan.

Vera Wang went into bridal design in 1989 after searching for a wedding dress for her own wedding. She found the market overloaded with loud and garish designs, and very sparse in taste and creativity. Since Wang had a longtime interest in fashion, her frustrated search for a dress gave her an idea: to start a business designing creative, nontraditional bridal gowns.

Wang opened the Vera Wang Bridal House on New York City's Madison Avenue in 1990. She also started a separate couture (custom-made clothing design) business called Vera Wang Made to Order, which custom designs both bridal and evening wear. By the mid-1990s, Wang had a thriving business selling her designs through her own shop and through the upscale, New York City-based Barneys department store. In 1994 she added a line of evening clothes, which is sold through high-end retailers such as Saks Fifth Avenue, I. Magnin, and Neiman Marcus.

A privileged childhood

Wang's father, Cheng Ching Wang, is chair of the U.S. Summit Company, a pharmaceuticals distribution and trading concern, and her mother, a former United Nations translator, is the daughter of one of the last feudal warlords—the landed royalty—in China. As a child, Wang studied ballet at New York's School of American Ballet and later became a nationally competitive figure skater. She was educated at private schools and went to Sarah Lawrence College in New York, spending her junior year at the Sorbonne in Paris, the world's oldest college. She earned a bachelor's degree in art history and later did graduate work at Columbia University in New York.

Wang's first job after college was at *Vogue,* where, at age 23, she was made an editor, one of the youngest in the magazine's history. That she chose to pursue a career instead of starting a family was a sore point with Wang's mother. The designer told the *New York Times Magazine:* "When I was made a *Vogue* editor my mother was very sad. 'Why work so hard?' she wanted to know, 'Why don't you want to make a family?'" At that point, Wang had different goals. "I was the Beatles generation, the 1960s, S.D.S [Students for a Democratic Society, a politically active student group of the 1960s].... I was driven in my career, afraid of what marriage and children might really mean to me." Her job at *Vogue* was as a sittings editor, which meant she was responsible for choosing the photographs that, in fashion publishing, essentially *are* the magazine. Wang worked at *Vogue* for 16 years and then moved into fashion design, something she had always wanted to do.

Vera Wang

Moving into design

Her first job in design was with Ralph Lauren, where she was creative director, involved in ten of the designer's lines. Discussing her introduction to the design world in *Asian Week,* Wang said, "Lauren was my mentor." She stayed with Lauren for two years, leaving in 1990 to form her own company.

Wang opened her business, as she told *Asian Week,* because "I was trying to find a wedding gown in 1989 when I was planning my wedding. I couldn't find anything that I really liked, and that inspired me to open my bridal shop in September 1990." The new business was financed by her father, who remains her major investor. And although Wang's businesses have yet to show a profit, she expects 1995 to be her turnaround year. Indeed, she does a brisk and high-profile business. She has created wedding gowns for members of the Kennedy clan and pop singer Mariah Carey (with a 27-foot train). She is also well respected among celebrities for her couture designs. She has designed dresses that actresses Sharon Stone, Marisa Tomei, Penelope Ann Miller, and Holly Hunter have worn at the Academy Awards ceremonies. Also, in 1992 and 1994, Wang designed figure skater Nancy Kerrigan's Olympic costumes.

Bridalwear success

One often-stated reason for Wang's success in the bridal market is the tendency among those in fashion to stay away from this highly formalized, tradition-bound specialty. It is usually considered an area with little room for creativity. But Wang, defying conventional wisdom, followed her instincts on this matter. She commented in the *New York Times Magazine:* "If I were to listen to many other voices I would have done a safe product. Would anyone believe that a sheer illusion low-cut-back slinky dress would ever have sold in the bridal market? Ten out of ten people would say you are out of your mind. I said there've got to be girls like me who are not 23 and want to look sophisticated and sexy."

According to *Asian Week,* "Wang has established a style for women with under-stated, modern tastes ... who are body conscious without being obvious. Wang's bridal collections for the spring and summer represent a tour de force of draping, detailing, silhouette and sophistication. It is the most comprehensive collection of wedding dresses to be found anywhere. Her dresses have the tradition of white as well as touches of color, but are known for their sexy cuts, exquisite gown trimmings and bows, illusion sleeves and bareback simplicity with style."

A new line

In the late spring and early summer of 1994, Wang introduced her much-anticipated line of ready-to-wear evening clothes to generally positive reviews in the fashion press. Her clientele is still composed largely of the well-to-do, with basic black dresses priced from $900 to $3,000. Putting together her line of ready-to-wear was stressful for Wang. There were countless details to look after, and they seemed to multiply as the time to show her designs neared. She told the *New York Times Magazine,* "I see myself as a madwoman scrambling to keep 100 marbles on the table before they fall off." In spite of this pressure, however, Wang counts herself lucky to have gotten to where she is in the incredibly competitive, cutthroat world of fashion design.

Wang has been honored with a number of awards for her achievements. In 1993 she was the Chinese American Planning Council's Honoree of the Year. In 1994 the Girl Scout Council of Greater New York honored her with a Women of Distinction award. That same year, Wang was elected to membership in the elite Council of Fashion Designers of America.

Sources:

Ku, Beulah, "Designs of Elegance and Style from Vera Wang," *Asian Week,* January 21, 1994, pp. 12-13.

Witchel, Alex, "From Aisle to Runway: Vera Wang," *New York Times Magazine,* June 19, 1994, pp. 22-25.

Wayne Wang

Filmmaker
Born 1949, Hong Kong

"I don't think most of America knows that Chinese Americans are just as American as they are."

When Wayne Wang's father named his son after one of his favorite Hollywood stars, actor John Wayne, he could not have known that one day his son would become perhaps the most powerful Asian American director in Hollywood. Wang, the director of the blockbuster hit *The Joy Luck Club,* has developed a career filled with both critical and financial hits. Many of them reflect his experiences with racism and with the problems immigrants face in the United States.

From Hong Kong to the United States

Wayne Wang was born in 1949 in Hong Kong, six days after his family arrived in the city after fleeing the Communist Revolution in their homeland of China. Wang's father was an engineer and businessman who spoke fluent English. "My father named me after seeing John Wayne in *Red River,*" Wang told the *New York Times.* "What appealed to him, I think, was the freedom and righteousness, the whole American mentality. My father loved to play football. He loved anything American."

In Hong Kong, Wang was educated at Roman Catholic schools by Jesuits (members of the Roman Catholic Society of Jesus, which is dedicated to missionary and educational work), learning English as a child. At age 18, he left for the United States to escape political unrest in Hong Kong. He enrolled at Foothill College near Palo Alto, California, to study painting. Wang recalled his first college experience to Tony Chiu of the *New York Times*: "It was a very lily-white, suburban, country-club type of junior college. I developed a lot of insecurity about being Chinese here. There was no direct prejudice—people didn't call me 'Chink' or look down at me. But indirectly, I felt that out of fear, out of not knowing the Chinese, out of media stereotypes, a lot of them were locking me in as this or that."

After two years at Foothill, Wang enrolled at the California College of Arts and Crafts in Oakland. There he earned a master's of fine arts in film and television. "My parents wanted me to go into medicine or become an engineer. My parents said, 'Oh, no!' when I went into art. I lived mostly on scholarships. When I got into film, my dad was actually glad because he loved movies so much; and he said at least I wasn't going to be a painter starving in the streets," recalled Wang in an interview with Bernard Weinraub of the *New York Times.*

With his new degree, Wang returned to his native Hong Kong. He quickly found work as a director on small films and television series. When he felt he needed a greater challenge, he returned to the United States, settling in San Francisco's Chinatown. His first film, *Chan Is Missing*, was about his experiences with the immigrant community there. Completed in 1982, it was Wang's first feature and his first success. Made for just $22,000, the film quickly earned some 50 times its initial investment.

Establishing a film career

In 1984 Wang completed the acclaimed film *Dim Sum* with a budget 20 times that of *Chan*. It centered on the relationship between a Chinese-born mother and her American-born daughter. Gentle and sentimental, the film used both the Cantonese and English languages to illustrate the cultural differences experienced by mother and daughter.

Three years later, Wang directed his first film with a non-Asian cast. *Slamdance*, a mystery thriller starring Tom Hulce and Mary Elizabeth Mastrantonio, was well received at the prestigious Cannes Film Festival, but it was not a commercial success. The film quickly disappeared and was released on video without making it to the big screen.

Wang returned to the world of Chinese America with his 1989 film *Eat a Bowl of Tea*, based on the novel of the same name by Louis Chu about a newlywed couple in 1949. Later Wang was inspired to create *Life Is Cheap ... but Toilet Paper Is Expensive*, in which he explored for the first time the cultural clash that occurs when the two worlds of an Asian American collide.

Making history

Wang was the only director considered by *The Joy Luck Club* author **Amy Tan** when she decided to bring her blockbuster novel to the screen. Wang and producer Oliver Stone worked together to make the movie the most commercially successful Asian American film produced thus far. In spite of rave reviews from critics, this 1993 film about four Chinese-born mothers and their American-born daughters has remained controversial in the Asian American community; it has been attacked for criticizing Asian American men, and both the novel and the film have been accused of distorting Chinese traditions and myth.

Regardless of the controversy, with its mainstream praise and big-dollar studio backing, *The Joy Luck Club* paved the way for future Asian American-focused films. Wang told the *Washington Post* in 1993 that he hoped his movies about Asian America will reach "the heart of America," adding, "I don't think most of America knows that Chinese Americans are just as American as they are."

Sources:

Chiu, Tony, "Wayne Wang—He Made the Year's Unlikeliest Hit," *New York Times*, May 30, 1982, pp. 17, 35.

Hsiao, Andy, "The Man on a 'Joy Luck' Ride," *Washington Post*, September 27, 1993, pp. B1, B3.

Kasindorf, Martin, "Wayne Wang's Subtle Film Punch," *New York Newsday*, August 3, 1989, pp. 3, 13.

Mandell, Jonathan, "Culture Clash," *New York Newsday*, August 20, 1990, pp. 8-9, 16.

Weinraub, Bernard, "'I Didn't Want to Do Another Chinese Movie,'" *New York Times*, September 5, 1993, Sec. 2, pp. 7, 15.

Michiko Nishiura Weglyn

Costume designer, writer, activist
Born November 29, 1926, Stockton, California

"As I look back, I ... credit both the Vietnam war ... and the civil rights movement ... for the transition that took place within me.... I was enraged by democracy's flagrant disregard for elemental human rights, especially as they related to ethnicity and skin color, and by America's shocking disregard for a reverence for life which we had been taught to hold sacred."

Michiko Nishiura Weglyn was a very successful costume designer during the 1950s and 1960s. She was the first nationally prominent Japanese American to work in the field, contributing designs to such popular television variety shows as *The Jackie Gleason Show, The Patti Page Show, The Tony Bennett Show,* and *The Dinah Shore Show.* She eventually went on to establish her own design studio.

Then, in the late 1960s, Weglyn wrote a groundbreaking book that changed the way Americans view their history. During the 1960s, many assumptions about the U.S. government were being questioned; the Vietnam war was increasingly viewed as immoral and ill-conceived, the civil rights movement was revealing that large segments of the population were considerably less free than others, and early feminists were questioning the structure of a male-dominated society. One day, the U.S. attorney general, Ramsey Clark, in an appearance on national television, said that there never had been and never would be concentration camps in the United States. (The term concentration camp was generally associated with the death and forced-labor camps set up by the Nazis during World War II.)

Weglyn heard this statement and was enraged, having been imprisoned for two years in a concentration camp established and maintained by the U.S. government in the desert in Arizona. In an interview in the magazine *Rafu Shimpo,* Weglyn recalled her feelings after hearing this "outright lie," remarking, "I decided they were not going to get away with that. That was the catalyst for my book." The resulting volume, *Years of Infamy: The Untold Story of America's Concentration Camps,* exposed to the general public what academics and politicians had known and politely declined to mention for decades—that some 120,000 Americans of Japanese descent spent the better part of World War II imprisoned in concentration camps known as "internment" camps. Writer and activist Frank Chin called *Years of Infamy* "the only Asian American book to change Asian American history."

Early life on the farm

Born Michiko Nishiura, Weglyn was one of two daughters of Tomojiro and Misao Nishiura. The family lived in a run-down house on a 500-acre farm in Brentwood, a small town about 50 miles east of San Francisco, California. As a child, Weglyn worked on the farm for a few hours before going to school each morning. In grade school, she found friends among the Filipino and Mexican children. Her parents had instilled in her a shyness when it came to mixing with white people. She told *Asian American Biography,* "The terror of having to enter grammar school without the ability to speak English had me in tears that unforgettable first day. From that humiliating day forward, I yearned to overcome my handicap and speak like others."

Weglyn had just turned 15 when the Japanese bombed the U.S. naval base at Pearl Harbor, Hawaii, in 1941, which officially marked America's entry into World War II. She felt very anxious about going to school after that day. Her teacher was understanding of what she and other Japanese Americans must have felt, however, and cautioned her students not to blame Japanese Americans for what the Japanese Air Force had done. On February 19, 1942, President Franklin D. Roosevelt signed Executive Order 9066, which called for the evacuation of all persons of Japanese descent on the West Coast to what were termed "relocation centers," but what were essentially prisons, or concentration camps. Families were given six to ten days to dispose of their property and businesses.

Weglyn recalled the horror of those days in an interview with Harriet Shapiro: "People wanted to buy our bicycles and automobiles for next to nothing, and the chickens for a quarter apiece. At that price my Mom decided it would be better to eat as many chickens as we could before we left. To this day, when my sister and I talk about that period, the hurried killing and eating of our pet chickens was one of the most traumatic aspects of the evacuation. Our father and mother were losing everything they had worked for, but my sister and I had little realization of that. For us it was parting with our animals: our cats, dogs, chickens, our possum, and our parrot. Most were left abandoned. I guess that's what war is like. But these are the things that are not written up in the history books."

Life in an American concentration camp

Weglyn and her family were sent to Gila, Arizona, to a camp in the desert that was plagued by unremitting heat, dust storms, overcrowded housing, and communal bathrooms providing virtually no privacy. Despite these conditions, the young Weglyn thrived, feeling for the first time in her life that she was among her own people. She emerged as a leader among her peers. She became president of the Girl Scout troop that she organized. She held a day-long Girls League Convention, which brought some 500 high school girls from various Arizona cities to the camp, where they participated in a talent show, were given a tour of the camp, ate together in the mess hall, and discussed timely issues. Weglyn felt this was an important event, in which the girls were shown that there was nothing subversive about the Japanese American population, that they were, in fact, very much like any other group of Americans of immigrant descent—of which, after all, most Americans are.

In 1944, after two years in the prison camp, Weglyn was given the opportunity to take an entrance examination for Mount Holyoke College in Massachusetts. Just before her exam, she stopped at a nearby drug store for a soda; she was asked to leave by the storekeeper, who would not serve her because she looked Japanese. Weglyn was accepted to Mount Holyoke and attended the prestigious private school on a full

Michiko Nishiura Weglyn

scholarship. She studied design and won a campuswide contest with costumes, sets, and scenery she had created for a college production. Then, in her second year, Weglyn was forced to leave school and enter a sanitarium for tuberculosis, which she had contracted at Gila.

In 1947, Weglyn returned to school, this time attending Barnard College in New York City. But she was again forced to leave for health reasons. In 1948, she began studying at New York's Fashion Academy. Two years later, she married Walter Matthys Weglyn, a perfume chemist who came to

the United States in 1947 after having survived the Holocaust (the Nazi's systematic attempt to destroy European Jewry during World War II).

Beginning in the 1950s, Weglyn began working in the entertainment industry as a costume designer. She achieved great success in the field, working with some of the most popular entertainers of the time. Her longest stint was as the costume designer for *The Perry Como Show,* a position she held from 1956 through 1965. From 1964 until 1967, Weglyn was head of costume manufacturing and design for Michi Associates Limited, a company she had founded.

An outpouring of activism

Weglyn retired from design in the late 1960s, a time of almost unprecedented political participation and activism in American history. People were speaking out on a wide range of issues; long-held and previously unquestioned beliefs about the nature of American democracy were publicly challenged and held up to critical analysis. Weglyn was deeply affected by these events. She recalled their impact in a commencement address she gave in 1993 at California State Polytechnic University in Pomona, which was reprinted in *Rafu Shimpo:* "As I look back, I would first have to credit both the Vietnam war—when the use of technological savagery on the lives, habitats, and ecosystem of a small Asian nation was shocking the entire civilized world—and the civil rights movement ... for the transition that took place within me. From an apolitical innocent I became a traumatized citizen. I was enraged by democracy's flagrant disregard for elemental human rights, especially as they related to ethnicity and skin color, and by America's shocking disregard for a reverence for life which we had been taught to hold sacred."

Weglyn decided to research a book on the experience of Japanese Americans who had been interned in concentration camps after hearing then-attorney general Clark deny on television that America had ever sponsored such camps. She spent eight years working on what would become *Years of Infamy: The Untold Story of America's Concentration Camps*. The book was published in 1976 to wide acclaim. Carefully researched, it documented institutional racism and blatant disregard for democracy at the highest levels of government. One of the book's revelations was that instead of the official reason behind the imprisonment—that in the event of a Japanese invasion of the West Coast, the loyalty of Japanese Americans could not be guaranteed—the camps were actually intended as hostage colonies and the Japanese Americans who lived there were to be used, if necessary, as hostages of the American government. The government, according to Weglyn's book, thought it could use these hostages as a bargaining tool to persuade the Japanese government to treat American prisoners of war humanely—and even as possible incentive for the return of American prisoners.

Years of Infamy helped inspire a new social activism among Japanese Americans in the areas of civil and human rights. This, in turn, eventually led to the redress movement of the 1980s and early 1990s, in which Japanese Americans lobbied for, and eventually won, a financial settlement and formal apology from the U. S. government.

Weglyn has been a consultant to countless projects, including the Japanese American Museum in Los Angeles, the Japanese American Library in San Francisco, Loni Ding's award-winning film *Color of Honor*, and the Congressional Study on the Commission of Wartime Relocation and Internment of Civilians.

Sources:

Nakayama, Takeshi, "Nisei Author Honored by Cal Poly Pomona," *Rafu Shimpo*, June 14, 1993.

Perkins, Robert, "U.S. 'Infamy' Recalled," *Springfield Union*, March 11, 1977.

Seko, Sachi, "Digging for Roots," *Pacific Citizen*, February 27, 1976, p. 4.

Weglyn, Michi Nishiura, biographical information, July 1994.

Anna May Wong

Actress
Born 1907, Los Angeles, California
Died 1961

As a young child, Anna May Wong began skipping Chinese school in the evenings to watch such movies as The Perils of Pauline *(1914) at the local theater. By the time she was 11, Wong decided she was going to be a movie actress. Against all odds, she got her first part at age 12 when an agent hired three hundred Chinese girls as extras in the 1919 film* The Red Lantern.

A nna May Wong became America's first Asian American movie star before films could even talk. In fact, with more than 80 film credits to her name, Wong is the all-time leading Asian American presence on film. She maintained her popularity for more than a quarter of a century and remained one of the highest-salaried stars of her time. She built a career around being the mysterious evil villainess, repeatedly playing stereotypical Oriental roles. She was the exotic slave girl, the powerful dragon lady, the mysterious woman of the Orient with deadly charms.

However, despite her success, Wong was torn between her two cultures. Twice, at the height of her fame, she moved to Europe to protest the limited, stereotypical roles she and other Asians were offered in Hollywood. Yet during a later trip to China to learn more about her native culture, Wong was heavily criticized for her degrading portrayals of Chinese women and was told that many of her films were banned in China.

Hollywood beckons

Born on Flower Street in Los Angeles, California, in 1907, Anna May Wong was named Wong Liu Tsong, which in Cantonese means "frosted yellow willow." Wong was third-generation Chinese American; her father was born in Sacramento and his father had immigrated to California during the Gold Rush.

Growing up, Wong and her six brothers and sisters lived in an apartment over the family's run-down laundry. Her first memories were of constant steam and the strong odor of hot-ironed linen. As a young child, Wong became fascinated with the brand-new world of movies. She began skipping Chinese school in the evenings to watch such movies as *The Perils of Pauline* (1914) at the local theater. By the time she was 11, Wong decided she was going to be a movie actress. Against all odds, she got her first part at age 12 when an agent hired three hundred Chinese girls as extras in the 1919 film *The Red Lantern.* Hardly visible in the film, she went on to get a few more minor roles.

For two years, Wong worked after school as an extra without telling her parents, who, she knew, would not approve. At age 14, her father found her a job as a secretary, but Wong was fired as unqualified one week later. When she returned home, fearing her father's anger, she found a letter from a director's office offering her a role in the film *Bits of Life* (1921). It would bring Wong her first screen credit. Although Wong's father strongly objected to his daughter's chosen career, he eventually gave in on the condition that an adult escort, often he himself, would chaperone the young Wong on the film sets at all times. When she was not in front of the cameras, her father locked her into her room on the set.

At age 17, Wong had one of the few romantic lead roles she would ever play in *Toll of the Sea* (1923), the first Technicolor feature ever made. As a young village girl who marries an American sailor, Wong captured the media's attention for the first time. Reporters began to appear at the laundry in the hopes of catching Wong for an interview or a photo.

International fame came in 1924 with *The Thief of Bagdad,* in which Wong played an exotic Mongol slave girl opposite star Douglas Fairbanks, Sr. Wong's role embarrassed her family. Although Wong would continue to support her family for many years, she remained close only to her brother, Richard.

Anna May Wong

The movie star's life

The success of *Bagdad* led to countless new offers. She appeared as an Eskimo in *The Alaskan* and a Native American girl in *Peter Pan.* In addition to film roles, Wong also worked as a model. She made a few more films but soon became disillusioned with the roles and with Hollywood's practice of casting non-Asians in the few leading Asian roles. Wong finally fled to Europe where, in London, she costarred with Charles Laughton in *Piccadilly.* After the

film, director Basil Dean produced a Chinese play, *A Circle of Chalk,* specifically for Wong. She successfully played opposite the rising new talent, Laurence Olivier, in London's New Theater.

Wong remained in Europe for three years, where she was hailed for her film and stage appearances. In Germany and France, she made foreign versions of her British films, including Germany's first sound picture. She spoke both German and French so fluently that critics could hardly believe they were hearing her voice instead of a native actress. During her career, Wong taught herself to speak English, Chinese, French, German, and Italian.

In 1931 a leading role on Broadway lured Wong back to the United States. The play, *On the Spot,* ran for 30 weeks, until Wong was called back to Los Angeles when her mother died in an automobile accident.

Wong's next screen role, *Daughter of the Dragon,* cast her in yet another stereotypical role as the daughter of the infamous Dr. Fu Manchu. Wong then appeared in the thriller *Shanghai Express,* starring Marlene Dietrich. Wong's portrayal of the bad-girl-turned-good inspired better reviews than Dietrich received. Years later, Dietrich would complain that Wong had upstaged her.

Wong then made one independent Sherlock Holmes picture and returned to England, where she felt her true audiences were. Like many minority artists at the time, Wong felt Europe was a less racist place to work. There she enjoyed the company of royalty and the wealthy. Wong remained in England for almost three years, appearing in more films and traveling in a variety show.

An early retirement

After failing to win the lead role in *The Good Earth*, which was given to a non-Asian German actress, a furious and frustrated Wong traveled to China, the home of her ancestors. In spite of those who criticized her for playing degrading Asian roles, Wong remained in China for ten months, studied Mandarin Chinese, purchased costumes for films and plays, and wrote articles on her travels. Unfortunately, she learned that she was too westernized for the Chinese stage, and would never be considered American enough for Hollywood's racist views.

After returning to the United States, Wong starred in one sympathetic role before World War II. In *Daughter of Shanghai,* she played a detective. She then appeared in two war epics, *Bombs over Burma* and *The Lady from Chungking.* The war brought another difficult situation for Wong. As more war movies were being cast, she was not hired as an actress, but as a coach to teach Caucasian actors how to be more believable as Asians.

In 1942, finally fed up with the Hollywood system, Wong retired from films at the age of 35. "I had to go into retirement for the sake of my soul. I suddenly found no more pleasure in acting. My screen work became a weary and meaningless chore—and Hollywood life a bore!" Wong told *New York Enquirer* in 1957. Throughout the war, she contributed to the war efforts by working for the United China Relief Fund and touring with the USO. During the 1940s and 1950s, Wong took occasional small parts on television, even starring in her own series, *Mme. Liu Tsong,* in which she played the owner of an international chain of art galleries who was also a sleuth.

Seventeen years after retirement, Wong attempted a film comeback. She returned as Lana Turner's mysterious housekeeper in the 1950 film, *Portrait in Black.* In 1961, while she was preparing for the role of the mother in *Flower Drum Song,* Wong died of a heart attack in her sleep.

Sources:

"Anna May Wong: Combination of East and West," *New York Herald Tribune,* November 9, 1930.

Davis, Mac, "Fled from Fame for 5 Years," *New York Enquirer,* February 18, 1957.

Mok, Michel, "Anna May Wong, with Chinese Courtesy, Makes Newspaper Photographer Blush," *New York Post,* April 26, 1939.

Sakamoto, Edward, "Anna May Wong and the Dragon-Lady Syndrome," *Los Angeles Times* (Calendar section), July 12, 1987, pp. 40-41.

B. D. Wong

Actor
Born October 24, 1962, San Francisco, California

"The representation of Asian Americans in the media means being able to bring a little kid to the theater and having him or her see that Asian people have full human characteristics that are special and derive from a specific kind of culture. It's about affirmation as people, not stereotypes."

B. D. Wong was in his twenties when he won theater's highest prize—a Tony Award for his portrayal of a transvestite Peking Opera star in **David Henry Hwang**'s much-heralded Broadway play *M. Butterfly.* Since then, he has appeared in several movies, including *Father *of the Bride* and *Jurassic Park* and, in 1994, landed a starring role in the short-lived ABC series *All American Girl*. Featuring stand-up comedian **Margaret Cho,** the sitcom was the first network television show to feature an all-Asian American cast.

In addition to his acting, Wong has emerged as a critical voice in the debate over the way Asians are portrayed in the mainstream media. He was one of the loudest critics of the producers of the musical *Miss Saigon* when they decided to use a white actor made up to look Asian in a starring role. The controversy was very divisive in the acting community, and Wong was criticized by some who suggested his interest was in getting the part for himself. For standing up to this decision, Wong and David Henry Hwang each were given a Special Award for Advocacy from the Association of Asian/Pacific American Artists that cited the two "for courageously and unselfishly bringing the issue of discriminatory casting raised by the *Miss Saigon* controversy to national attention through their own visibility and success in the established entertainment community."

Growing up in San Francisco

Wong is the second of Roberta and Bill Wong's three sons. Second-generation Chinese Americans, his parents lived in San Francisco's North Beach area bordering Chinatown when Wong was born. A few years later the family moved to the city's Sunset district, which is now a popular area for Chinese American families, but back then the family was isolated. "We were the second Chinese family on the block," Roberta Wong, a retired telephone company

supervisor, told the *San Francisco Examiner.* Wong and his brothers had a difficult time maintaining a connection to their Chinese heritage in this environment, so they made a point of going to a Chinatown youth group every Saturday and a Chinese American camp every summer. But Wong still had difficulty fitting in. He wasn't particularly good at sports, and the other children teased him because of it.

As a child, Wong loved art and drawing. He considered becoming an architect, but the math and science involved deterred him. He was also interested in acting. As a student at Lincoln High School, Wong performed in a number of school productions, each succeeding role feeding his passion for the stage. His parents supported him in his efforts to make it as an actor as he found roles in community productions, but they were anxious about his ability to really make it as a professional actor. "Being Chinese, we were a little apprehensive because we knew there were very few roles for Asians," Bill Wong, a retired postal worker, told the *San Francisco Examiner.* "Even in our jobs, there were very few opportunities for promotion."

Wong, however, felt that he was capable of playing any role, in part because he didn't think of himself as Asian American. He felt that he was American just like anybody else. When he auditioned for the role of a sailor in *Anything Goes* in a community theater production and was instead offered the part of a "coolie" (a term once used to describe an unskilled and poorly paid worker, usually from Asia), he refused the part. "I was so ashamed of that role," he told *Asian American Biography (AAB)* in an interview. "Probably not unlike a lot of young Asians, I wished that I was white."

Broadway

After graduating high school in 1980, Wong attended San Francisco State University for a year but ended up spending all his time in the drama department and receiving "incompletes" in his classes. What he really wanted was to move to New York and try to make it in the theater, so he saved his money and in 1981 he made the cross-country move, becoming one of thousands of aspiring young actors in New York. He took odd jobs while performing in summer stock and in dinner theater. Then, in 1985, a role in the chorus with the national touring company of the popular musical *La Cage aux Folles* brought him to Los Angeles. He decided to stay on the West Coast and study with a prominent acting teacher. In Los Angeles he got his big career break when he was asked to audition for a new play by David Henry Hwang called *M. Butterfly.*

Wong won the part of Song Lingling, a man who fooled a male French diplomat into believing that he was a woman during their long relationship. The play, remarkably, was based on a true story. Wong received excellent reviews for his mesmerizing portrayal and was awarded a Tony Award for his performance. With his newfound fame in the theater, Wong began landing small roles in Hollywood films. His first jobs were bit parts in the 1989 film *Family Business,* with Sean Connery and Dustin Hoffman, and the 1990 film *The Freshman,* with Marlon Brando and Matthew Broderick.

His first major part in Hollywood was as a drug-ring leader in the 1991 movie *Mystery Date.* The role could have been stereotypical, but Wong played it so well that he came off as a fully formed character. Wong did

B. D. Wong

make a stand against bigotry on the set, however, when a white extra showed up in "yellow face" makeup for a scene. "I had to be the party pooper," Wong told *Premiere* magazine. "Everyone thought it was funny, like Halloween, but they don't have the sensibility of what decades of yellow face in the movies mean. A part of you dies when you watch a Caucasian actor bastardize your existence for the sake of comedy."

Wong's next big role was as Martin Short's assistant in the 1991 Steve Martin film *Father of the Bride.* Short, who was encouraged to improvise in the role, had high praise for his young costar's ability to stay with him. "He was always right there," he told *Premiere.* "Nothing could throw him, because he was very much into the details of creating his character." More recent roles include the nerdy geneticist in *Jurassic Park* (1993) and a gay artist in the HBO cable film *And the Band Played On.*

Wong made inroads into television as comedian Margaret Cho's brother in the show *All American Girl,* which premiered in the fall of 1994. The show received lots of pre-air attention because it was the first network series to feature an all-Asian cast; the Asian American community was hopeful the situation comedy would help Asian Americans further assimilate into the culture. Although the show received disappointing reviews and was cancelled after its first season, Wong's performance was singled out as a bright spot. *Entertainment Weekly* wrote, "The one cast member who ... triumphs over the banal scripts ... is the theater-trained Wong, who exhibits an unearthly poise and authority in his little throwaway role as the brother."

Taking a stand

Wong took a very principled stand when the musical *Miss Saigon* opened on Broadway featuring a white actor in yellow face playing the role of a Eurasian. No Asians had auditioned for the part, and Asian American activists were outraged. In spite of possible repercussions for his own career, Wong spoke up against the casting of the play. Drama critics across the country—from the *New York Times* to *Variety*—attacked him, saying he simply wanted the part. "There was a lot of B. D. bashing," he told *AAB,* "but I got a great deal of respect for my stand. No matter what people said about me, they had to acknowledge that we were raising some real issues about racial stereotypes and images and how casting decisions are made."

After the controversy had blown over, Wong told *Premiere* that he couldn't wait for the day he could dress up in a coolie hat and talk with a funny accent. "I can't wait for the time when I can make fun of my culture and my heritage, but that can't be done until there is a ground-level awareness that we are all equal. Only then can we have a good time fooling around."

Wong is very modest about his achievements. "I'm just an actor, not a Nobel Prize winner," he told *AAB.* But he is committed to seeing roles for Asian Americans evolve. "The representation of Asian Americans in the media means being able to bring a little kid to the theater and having him or her see that Asian people have full human characteristics that are special and derive from a specific kind of culture. It's about affirmation as people, not stereotypes."

Sources:

Chin, Steven, "The World of B. D. Wong," *San Francisco Examiner,* September 5, 1993.

Lin, Sam Chu, "B. D. Wong. Flashing Dino-Sized Talent," *Asian Week,* June 18, 1993.

Raymond, Gerard, "B. D. Wong," *Premiere,* December 1991, p. 54.

Wong, B. D., telephone interview with Helen Zia, July 1994.

Flossie Wong-Staal

Medical researcher
Born 1947, China

Flossie Wong-Staal worked in the field of retroviruses with the prominent researcher Robert Gallo at the National Cancer Institute in Bethesda, Maryland. She is credited as the codiscoverer of HIV, the virus that causes AIDS.

F lossie Wong-Staal is one of the world's foremost authorities in the field of virology, the study of viruses, and is one of America's pioneering researchers of AIDS (Acquired Immune Deficiency Syndrome). Along with her colleagues at the National Cancer Institute, Wong-Staal was the first researcher to clone, or make a copy of, the human immunodeficiency virus (HIV)—the virus that is believed to cause AIDS—which allowed them to decipher its structure. Since moving to the University of California at San Diego in 1990, Wong-Staal has continued her AIDS research, working specifically in gene therapy, one of the most technologically sophisticated areas in medical research. In 1990 she was listed by the Institute for Scientific Information as the top woman scientist of the past decade and the fourth-ranking scientist under age 45.

Growing up in Hong Kong

Wong-Staal was born Yee Ching Wong in mainland China in 1947. Her father was in business and her mother was a homemaker. In 1952 the family fled the Communist mainland and settled in the British colony of Hong Kong, where Yee Ching was enrolled in a Catholic school and her name was changed. The nuns thought that she should have an English name, and her father, who spoke no English, picked Flossie from a newspaper account of Typhoon Flossie, which had hit Hong Kong the week before. "I used to be embarrassed by [it]. Now I'm trying to change the image of the name," Wong-Staal told *Discover* magazine.

Wong-Staal was an excellent student and did especially well in science and math. About her early years, she told *Asian American Biography,* "I did not really have a role model in my family when I was growing up. All the women in the family were full-time housewives. Most of the men were in business, and rarely pursued higher (post-college) education." Her family was very supportive of her, however, and "surprisingly, my being female was not an issue with them."

As she excelled in school, Wong-Staal was encouraged to study science further. At first, she was not that interested in it, but the deeper she got into the field, the more fascinating it became to her. After graduating from an all-girls high school in Hong Kong in 1965, Wong-Staal immigrated to the United States to study at the University of California at Los Angeles (UCLA), where she chose to focus on molecular biology. She earned her bachelor's degree and then went on to graduate work as a research assistant in bacteriology. She attended the University of California at San Diego for postgraduate work in the same field. It was during this period that she married, adding Staal to her name. (She has since divorced.) In the early 1970s, having completed her

Flossie Wong-Staal

Cancer Institute's lab, at which Wong-Staal and Gallo were then working, took up the search, and in 1983 they discovered HIV simultaneously with a French researcher. Wong-Staal was instrumental in this very important work; she was specifically responsible for the first cloning of HIV in 1985 and its first genetic mapping (a representation of genes on a chromosome). This work, and her subsequent research, broke the ground for the development of HIV tests that are used to screen donated blood and test people for the virus.

In 1990 Wong-Staal left the National Cancer Institute to become the Florence Riford Chair in AIDS Research at the University of California at San Diego (UCSD). In that position, Wong-Staal is focusing on discovering a vaccine for the AIDS virus and on therapies to treat those already suffering from the disease.

Her vision for a cure

Wong-Staal and her staff at UCSD, in collaboration with five other research institutions across the United States, are currently working on a scheme to stop HIV from reproducing itself in infected people. Perhaps the most promising area of her current research is in gene therapy. Wong-Staal is also working with several biotechnology companies to develop drugs that might short-circuit the virus's reproductive cycle.

schooling, Wong-Staal took a position with the National Cancer Institute in Bethesda, Maryland, where she worked in the field of retroviruses with the prominent researcher Robert Gallo, credited as the codiscoverer of HIV.

AIDS research

By the time the AIDS epidemic was first recognized in the early 1980s, medical researchers were already working feverishly to isolate the cause of the many illnesses that make up the syndrome. The National

Despite obstacles in her pursuit of a vaccine to immunize healthy people against the baffling virus, Wong-Staal has made progress; recently she began working with a synthetic reproduction of HIV that could cause human cells to reject the actual HIV. She told *Discover,* "Our goal is to make a virus as similar to the real one as possible, but to make sure there's no risk of introducing its dangerous genes into an uninfected population." This is just one of the many areas being researched around the world in an all-out effort to stop the spread of this global epidemic and reduce the suffering of those already afflicted.

Sources:

Baskin, Yvonne, "Intimate Enemies," *Discover,* December 1991, pp. 16-17.

Clark, Cheryl, "Researcher Stays Hot on the Trail of Deadly Virus," *San Diego Union-Tribune,* November 11, 1992, p. C1.

Garrett, Laurie, "On the Front Line," *Sunday Newsday,* November 17, 1991, pp. 4-5.

Johnson, Greg, "Sharpening the Attack on AIDS Virus," *Los Angeles Times,* November 11, 1992.

Wong-Staal, Flossie, interview with Helen Zia, June 14, 1994.

Chien-Shiung Wu

Physicist
Born May 31, 1912, Liuhe, China

In a series of careful experiments, Wu confirmed one of physicist Enrico Fermi's theories. Many people considered this important work worthy of a Nobel Prize.

Chien-Shiung Wu is an award-winning physicist who worked with Nobel Prize-winning scientists on some of the most complicated problems in the field of physics. She overcame both racism and sexism in her path to becoming one of the most influential female physicists in history. Wu is the first living scientist with an asteroid named after her (an asteroid is one of thousands of small planets between Mars and Jupiter), and she has lectured and taught at universities around the world, including China and Taiwan.

Throughout her career, Wu has outspokenly criticized traditional scientists for their old-fashioned attitudes toward women in science. She encourages girls to break the barriers they may encounter and study science even if their teachers don't support them.

Always a top student

Wu was born in Liuhe, a small town near Shanghai, China. Her father, Wu Zhongyi, had participated in the revolution of 1911 that toppled the Manchu dynasty. He was the founder and principal of a private girls school—one of very few in China, where educating girls has never been considered important. Wu attended this school until the age of nine, when she was sent to the Soochow Girls School. This school's curriculum was Western (oriented toward North America and Europe) and professors from major American universities often lectured there. Wu received an excellent education at Soochow and in 1930 graduated at the top of her class.

Wu went on to college at Nanjing University, where she studied physics and, again, became a top student. After graduating in 1934, she spent one year teaching in a university and another year doing research in the field of x-ray crystallography (the study of crystals) at the National Academy of Sciences in Shanghai. There she met a woman scientist who encouraged her to continue her studies in the United States because China did not have a physics program at the post-doctoral level. With the encouragement of her family and the help of a rich uncle, Wu sailed for America in 1936.

Higher education

Her original intention was to study at the University of Michigan, but once Wu arrived in America she stayed in San Francisco for a number of reasons. The University of California at Berkeley was an exciting place to be in the 1930s for a student of physics. Wu had also learned that at the University of Michigan, women were not allowed to use the student union building. Wu thought this policy was disgraceful. She also decided to stay in San Francisco to be with a man she had met on arriving in the United States, Luke Yuan, who would later become her husband.

Wu began her studies at Berkeley in the area of nuclear physics, working with the renowned particle physicist Ernest Livermore. She was an assistant to Emilio Segre, a future Noble Prize winner. After her first year Wu was recommended by the physics department for a fellowship. She was denied the fellowship, Wu believes, because of racist attitudes toward the Chinese. She experienced another blow that year when Japan invaded China. Because of this, she was completely cut off from her family whom, even after the war, she would never see again.

For her thesis work, Wu studied the electromagnetic energy given off when a particle passing through matter slows its pace. She did another study on what occurs when uranium nuclei split. She received her Ph.D.

Chien-Shiung Wu

in 1940, staying on at Berkeley for two years as a research assistant. During this time she became well known in the scientific community as a reliable expert on fission, the splitting apart of atoms. Berkeley nonetheless refused to hire her in a more formal capacity; the only conceivable reasons were racism and sexism.

In 1942 Wu married Yuan and the couple moved to the East Coast. Yuan found a job working at the RCA Laboratories in Princeton, New Jersey, and Wu took a position teaching at Smith College in Northampton, Massachusetts. Smith did not have a research department, however, and research was Wu's primary interest. She soon left Smith for a position at Princeton. That Princeton hired a female instructor was unheard of at that time, as the university had always frowned on females teaching its male students, particularly in the sciences.

In 1944 Wu was recruited by the Division of War Research at Columbia University. She worked at a secret facility in New York on the development of sensitive radiation detectors for the atomic bomb project. After the war, she stayed at the university.

Also after World War II, Wu finally heard from her family. All had survived the war, and she and her husband considered returning to China. But because of a civil war between the Nationalist Chinese and the Communist forces of Mao Zedong, who would be victorious in 1949, they decided to stay in America.

Monumental work

In the late 1940s and early 1950s Wu studied theories about atoms developed by the famous physicist Enrico Fermi. In a series of careful experiments, Wu confirmed one of Fermi's theories. This work was considered extremely important and many people considered it worthy of a Nobel Prize. But because it wasn't an original discovery or invention, the work did not qualify for the award. As quoted in *Nobel Prize Women in Science,* a former graduate student of Wu's said of this work, "She had straightened up a big mess in physics quite elegantly, but it wasn't quite a discovery."

In 1956 Wu began work with **Tsung Dao Lee** of Columbia University and Chen Ning Yang of the Institute for Advanced Study at Princeton. Lee and Yang were concerned with the validity of a concept of nuclear physics known as the principle of parity. This principle states that, on a nuclear level, an object and its mirror image will behave the same way. In 1952 a new particle called a K-meson was discovered. Strangely, it did not seem to behave in the manner described by the principle of parity, a principle that had been universally accepted for 30 years.

When Lee and Yang announced that the principle of parity was flawed, they asked Wu to perform experimentation to disprove the theory. Wu worked independently of Lee and Yang at the National Bureau of Standards, but her experiments were based on their observations. Her laboratory was underfunded and much of the equipment was below standard. Nevertheless, in January 1957, Wu's team had enough proof to say that K-mesons did indeed violate parity. The announcement took the scientific world by storm. Physicists from around the world were stunned by the result. Similar work was begun by physicists throughout the country, who began finding other particles that violated this once sacred law of nature. Wu, Yang, and Lee became national celebrities, their findings reported on the front page of the *New York Times* and in *Time* and *Newsweek.* Later that year, Yang and Lee won the Nobel prize for physics. Again, Wu was not included for her work because the idea behind her experimental research was not original to her.

More research

Wu continued her research in other areas of physics. In 1963 she experimentally confirmed a difficult hypothesis involving beta decay put forth by Richard Feynman and Murray Gell-Mann, two world-renowned American theoretical physicists. (Beta decay research addressed the problem that arises because of the differences in the way that alpha particles and beta particles are emitted from the nucleus of an atom. All alpha particles leaving a particular nucleus have the same energy. But in beta decay, beta particles may have a range of energies.) Feynman and Gell-Mann's theory had been widely tested for years by scientists around the world, but none had been able to confirm or disprove it. In confirming this theory, Wu contributed to the unified theory of fundamental forces.

Wu was given an endowed professorship by Columbia University in 1972. She has through the years received many honors for her groundbreaking work. She was the first woman to receive the Comstock Award from the National Academy of Sciences, the first woman to receive the Research Corporation Award, the first woman to serve as president of the American Physical Society, and only the seventh woman selected for the National Academy of Science. Wu has received honorary degrees from more than a dozen universities, including Harvard, Yale, and Princeton, where she was the first woman ever to receive an honorary doctorate of science degree. Wu retired in 1981 and has since traveled extensively.

Sources:

McGrayne, Sharon Bertsch, *Nobel Prize Women in Science: Their Lives, Struggles, and Momentous Discoveries,* New York: Carol Publishing Group, 1993.

Travers, Bridget, editor, *World of Scientific Discovery,* Detroit: Gale, 1994.

Kristi Yamaguchi

Figure skater
Born July 12, 1971, Hayward, California

"My grandfather didn't talk much about World War II, but he let me know how proud he was to see me make it as an Asian American representing the United States."

K risti Yamaguchi is an international champion figure skater who won the gold medal in the 1992 Olympics in Albertville, France, upsetting the favorite, Japan's Midori Ito. Prior to her Olympic victory, Yamaguchi had been a significant presence in international competition since 1989, when she placed sixth in her first trip to the World Championships, held that year in Paris. The following year she placed second in the National Championships and fourth in the World Championships. Then, in 1991, she won the World Championships in Munich, Germany, earning eight 5.9s (out of a possible 6.0) for technical merit, and seven 5.9s for artistic impression. After winning the gold medal at the Albertville Olympics, Yamaguchi turned professional, beginning a career in exhibition skating, acting, and celebrity endorsements.

Inspired at an early age

Yamaguchi was born in Hayward, California, and raised in nearby Fremont (both in the San Francisco Bay area). Her father, Jim, is a dentist, and her mother, Carole, is a medical secretary. Yamaguchi's parents and grandparents were interned in prison camps established by the U.S. government during World War II along with 120,000 other Americans of Japanese descent on the West Coast, in what has since been acknowledged as an unconstitutional violation of their civil liberties. (The U.S. government justified this action by maintaining that in the event of a Japanese invasion of the West Coast, the loyalties of Japanese Americans could not be guaranteed.) Experiences of internment were rarely discussed in the Yamaguchi home, however. Her parents instead encouraged Yamaguchi and her two siblings to appreciate American values and to work hard. "My grandfather didn't talk much about World War II, but he let me know how proud he was to see me make it as an Asian American representing the United States," Yamaguchi told the *Chicago Tribune* in 1991. "My parents let us know how fortunate we are now. Otherwise, they really don't look back on it too much."

Yamaguchi began taking figure skating lessons at age five, one year after watching skater Dorothy Hamill win the gold medal at the 1976 Winter Olympics. Yamaguchi showed promise early and entered her first competition at eight. By the time she was nine years old, she was getting up daily at 4:00 A.M. to practice at the local skating rink before school. She began training with a professional coach, Christy Kjarsgaard-Ness, who worked with her on her singles routines, and, beginning in 1983, with Jim Hulick, who coached her and partner Rudi Galindo in pairs skating. In 1985 Yamaguchi and Galindo placed fifth in the National Junior Championships; the next year they won the championship. Also in 1986, Yamaguchi began to emerge as a strong singles skater, becoming the Central Pacific

Kristi Yamaguchi

junior champion and placing fourth in the National Junior medal event. In 1988—Yamaguchi's best year as a junior—she won gold medals at the World Junior Championships in both the singles and pairs competitions. That year the Women's Sport Foundation named her Up-and-Coming Artistic Athlete of the Year.

Overcoming obstacles

Yamaguchi's next several years of competition brought her much success. She won the gold medal in pairs at the National

Championships in Baltimore, Maryland, where she also placed second in the singles division. The gold was her first senior title, and winning the silver made her the first woman to win two medals at the nationals in 35 years.

Yamaguchi's performance in the singles dazzled the audience and the judges, and she would have likely won that competition as well were it not for her lackluster performance in the compulsories, Yamaguchi's weakest event. The compulsories, or school figures, were tedious, specific exercises all skaters were required to perform in competition, having to trace precise figures in the ice with the blades of their skates. These figures were then examined on the ice by the judges; skaters were awarded points based on the exactness of the figures. This event continued to plague Yamaguchi until it was removed from competition in July 1990.

In 1989 Yamaguchi placed sixth in the singles competition and fifth in the pairs competition at the World Championships in Paris. In the spring of that year, as Yamaguchi was completing high school, her singles coach married and moved to Canada. Yamaguchi followed her, which put a strain on her relationship with her pairs partner. Then, in December of 1989, Galindo and Yamaguchi's pairs coach, Jim Hulick, died of colon cancer. This was followed by the death of Yamaguchi's maternal grandfather. Yamaguchi and Galindo had trouble finding a pairs coach to replace Hulick. In 1990 they placed a disappointing fifth at the World Championships. These factors led Yamaguchi to withdraw from pairs competition in May 1990, devoting herself completely to singles.

Climb to the top

In July of 1990, to the relief of competitors and fans alike, the compulsories were eliminated from all major figure skating competitions. No one was more pleased with this development than Yamaguchi. At the 1990 National Championships she finished second and at the World Championships she came in fourth. Yamaguchi was becoming a consistent, highly ranked presence on the international figure skating scene. In 1991 she placed second at the National Championships and then went on to Munich, the site of that year's World Championships. At this competition Yamaguchi really stood out; she skated a nearly perfect short program and gave what is generally considered the best free-skate performance of her career, which earned her first place.

The next year Yamaguchi won the National Championships and in February of 1992 she competed at the Winter Olympics as the reigning national and world champion. She was not the favorite to win, however, and many have attributed her eventual victory to the absence of such pressure. Many of the other top skaters fell during competition, leaving the field open for Yamaguchi to win. After finishing the competition, Yamaguchi left the ice knowing she was likely to win, but she felt a sense of loss. She told *Sports Illustrated,* "I knew I'd done well, and I was happy for that, but I remember thinking, 'Is this it? This is the Olympics. You've always dreamed of it, always, your whole life.' I didn't want it to be over yet."

One month after the Olympics, Yamaguchi defended her title as world champion, becoming the first American skater to successfully hold the title for two consecutive years since Peggy Flemming did it in 1967 and 1968.

Life after the Olympics

In September of 1992, Yamaguchi decided to turn professional, a decision that ended her career in amateur competitions like the Olympics and World Championships. As a professional skater, she performs throughout the country with various ice shows. She has lent her name and image to commercial products in lucrative endorsement deals (though some feel that the skater's endorsement potential has been limited as a result of her Asian American heritage) and even took on a small, walk-on part in the Disney movie *D2: The Mighty Ducks.*

Yamaguchi discussed the changes fame has brought to her life in *Sports Illustrated,* remarking, "I'm just an athlete. I don't think I've changed. It's still funny to have other people fussing over your hair, pretending you're a model for a day. I still feel I'm the same old kid, and someone who still wants to be one."

Sources:

Hersh, Phil, *Chicago Tribune,* February 15, 1991, section IV, p. 1.

Janofsky, Michael, *New York Times,* February 20, 1992.

Miller, Cyndee, "Special K Loves Kristi, but Will Asian Heritage Hinder Other Endorsements?," *Marketing News,* March 30, 1992, pp. 1-2.

Swift, E. M., "A Golden Snub?," *Sports Illustrated,* March 23, 1992, p. 7.

Swift, E. M., "All That Glitters," *Sports Illustrated,* December 14, 1992, pp. 70-79.

Bruce Yamashita

Attorney, activist
Born February 22, 1956, Honolulu, Hawaii

Yamashita's case was highlighted in a story on 60 Minutes *that revealed prevailing racism throughout the very structure of the marine corps.*

Bruce Yamashita is an attorney who drew considerable media attention when he sued the U.S. Marine Corps for discrimination after he was denied graduation from Officer Candidate School. During the grueling nine-week training program, Yamashita endured a litany of abuse from his superiors, ranging from being referred to as "Kawasaki Yamashita" rather than "Candidate Yamashita," to having a garbage can tossed at his head. The abuse was persistent, seemingly well-planned, and brutal. By the end of the training, nearly half of the original students had dropped out; of the remainder, there were five minority candidates, of which four—including Yamashita—were "disenrolled" for "lack of proper leadership qualities."

Yamashita's lawsuit, filed in conjunction with the Japanese Americans Citizens League (JACL) attracted national attention as it exposed a pattern of discrimination throughout the marine corps. Major media outlets ran stories on the case, and the television show *60 Minutes* aired an interview with the commandant of the marine corps who said on national television that the reason there were so few minority officers in the marines was very simple: he said they couldn't shoot or swim as well as whites and that if you gave them a compass at night, they got lost.

With this blatant admission of racism at its highest levels, the corps was forced to settle the suit with Yamashita, who was given the rank of captain in the reserves. He is still awaiting the outcome of a motion to award him back pay and to establish guidelines to ensure that such discrimination will not be allowed to occur again.

A happy childhood

Yamashita's father was the son of a Japanese immigrant who had gone to Hawaii in the 1920s to work on the sugar plantations as an indentured servant (a contractual arrangement in which, in return for travel expenses and minimum upkeep, an immigrant agrees to a term of virtual slavery). The family saved its money and was able to send Yamashita's father to college at Purdue University in Indiana, where he received a degree in engineering. He worked for 37 years as a bridge engineer for the state of Hawaii. Yamashita's mother had a graduate degree from the University of Iowa and was a professor at the University of Hawaii. In an interview with *Asian American Biography (AAB)*, Yamashita said his early childhood took place in "a multi-ethnic, multicultural community—it was just a real happy life."

Yamashita was educated in the public school system. He participated in many activities outside of school including the Boy Scouts and Little League baseball. At Honolulu's University High School, he was a varsity athlete in football, basketball, and baseball and was named to the Honolulu All-Star team in football. He also served as student body president of his class. After graduating from high school in 1974, Yamashita enrolled in the University of Hawaii where he studied political science.

Politics and international affairs

While in school Yamashita became interested in politics. During his junior year, the state of Hawaii was scheduled to hold a constitutional convention at which delegates would consider changes to the state charter. This was a major, statewide event that drew some of the biggest names in Hawaiian politics. Yamashita and some friends decided to run as delegates to the convention. Two of them, including Yamashita, were elected. At 22, they were the youngest delegates present. "It was quite an experience, because you were there with the past and future leaders of Hawaii," Yamashita told *AAB*. "One of our colleagues went on to become governor—the governor until 1994, **John Waihee**."

Yamashita graduated in 1979 with a bachelor's degree in political science. After graduation, he decided to move to Tokyo, where he had spent a semester studying during his sophomore year. He moved there "to learn more about my roots, internationalism, and what it is to be an American." He lived in Japan for the next four years. While there he worked for an import-export company for a while and then started what became a fairly successful newspaper for foreign readers. The paper, *Yokomeshi Shinbun,* was written in a simple form of Japanese that made it easy for the foreign population to read while still providing thoughtful news stories. By the time Yamashita left, the paper had a circulation of 10,000.

Bruce Yamashita

Yamashita returned to the United States in 1984 and enrolled in the Georgetown University School of Law, where he studied in a joint program of law and international affairs. While in school, Yamashita met some members of the military who were there studying international affairs. They suggested that he consider a career in the judge advocate general program, the legal and judicial system of the military. Yamashita, who was not sure what area of government or private practice he wanted to pursue, was intrigued by the idea, and after graduating in 1988 with a law degree and a master's degree in international affairs, he applied for admittance to the Marine Officer Candidate School in Quantico, Virginia.

Institutional racism

Yamashita was warned before going off to Quantico that the school was "blood and guts" and that the most important quality the instructors sought was teamwork. The first day he was there, a sergeant began speaking to him in Japanese, drawing attention to his ethnicity in a demeaning way. Later that day, at the mess hall, Yamashita was standing in line for food in a large crowd and a sergeant came up to him from behind and said, "Candidate, do you speak English?" Yamashita politely told him that he did and the sergeant said, "Well, we don't want your kind around here. Go back to your own country." Yamashita recalled for *AAB,* "I remember there was kind of a hush in the mess hall. It was humiliating. It was hurtful."

The abuse continued in the isolated compound in the mountains of Virginia. One sergeant started calling him by the names of Japanese products; where everyone else would be referred to as "Candidate," Yamashita was referred to as "Kawasaki" or "Yamaha," the names of Japanese motorcycles. He was also called Kamikaze Man, a reference to the suicide bombers of the World War II-era Japanese air force. One day, while the candidates were in a platoon formation, a sergeant singled Yamashita out for attention by asking him, out of the blue, if during World War II Russia had been at war with Japan. Yamashita said that he thought they were—the correct answer—and the sergeant said, "No way, because during World War II we kicked your Japanese ass." As the abuse escalated it occurred to Yamashita that it was becoming a contest among the sergeants to see who could abuse him in the most vile way.

At the end of the course, after enduring this unending abuse, Yamashita was disenrolled for "unsatisfactory leadership." Out of five minority candidates in Yamashita's platoon, four were dismissed. Yamashita believes the commanders felt they had to pass at least one of the minority candidates to avoid the appearance of discrimination. Yamashita's initial reaction was shock.

The decision was so obviously unfair, and yet he could see no way at that time to correct it. He had passed up job offers to enroll in the school. He had given himself totally to this regimen in the hopes of becoming an officer in the judge advocate general program. He had endured an extremely demanding course in which he averaged about four hours of sleep a night, was not adequately fed, and turned the other cheek while being relentlessly harassed. And then he had been disenrolled. Meanwhile, a white candidate who had spent five of the nine weeks in sick bay with a bad knee passed the course.

Taking on the marines

Yamashita returned to Honolulu and decided that he had to do something, at least so that others in the future would find some recourse. He wrote a letter to the commandant of the marine corps. Four months later, he received the corps' reply, stating that nothing had happened and that he was making it all up. As an afterword, they said that the sergeant who had spoken to him in broken Japanese was trying to make him feel at home, and the sergeant who had called him by the names of Japanese products had a long history of dyslexia (a reading disorder) and was simply mispronouncing his name. This response nearly defeated Yamashita, but he decided to take one final action: he wrote letters to about ten civil rights organizations asking if they would be interested in taking up his case. The Japanese American Citizens League (JACL) said they would.

Yamashita and the JACL filed a complaint with the Naval Discharge Review Board and the Board for the Correction of Naval Records in 1989. The case had to be tried in the military court system, which is traditionally not friendly toward disputes with the military. Yamashita's legal team knew they had only a slim chance of effecting any change, and then only if they could get the attention of the national media. Yamashita, meanwhile, had gone into private law practice, deciding he could not devote himself to a firm knowing that, for the next several years as the case made its way through the courts, he would need to keep a fairly flexible schedule.

The marines' first official response was that they would reopen the investigation into his original complaint. This took a full year, after which they acknowledged his complaints, apologized, and offered to allow Yamashita to reenroll at the school. The Yamashita team wrote back that this was unacceptable, that the marine corps had broken the law, and that the burden was on the corps to make it up to Yamashita. The marine corps refused to go beyond their initial offer.

Yamashita was finally granted his hearing with the Naval Discharge Review Board in 1992. At the hearing, Yamashita's team presented statistics showing a consistent pattern of discrimination at every level of the marine corps. The story was immediately picked up by the national media, just as the team was hoping it would be. The marine corps then offered to commission Yamashita as a second lieutenant, the rank he would have held had he not been kicked out of the school. Yamashita again was not satisfied. Feeling that he had been wronged, he asked to be commissioned at the rank he would have achieved had he been in the corps for the intervening years. The marine corps refused.

In November of 1993 Yamashita's case was highlighted in a story on *60 Minutes.* The story revealed prevailing racism throughout the very structure of the marine corps. The commandant of the corps admitted as much in plain, simple language, saying that there were so few minorities in the corps because, in so many words, they were inferior. This caused a national uproar, both in the marines and in the media. A month later, Yamashita got a call from the assistant secretary of defense. The marines offered to make him a captain. Yamashita said, "The bottom line is that the marine corps did it, but they did it kicking and screaming."

Sources:

Yamashita, Bruce, telephone interview with Jim Henry, August 1, 1994.

Jeff Yang

Writer, publisher
Born March 14, 1968, Brooklyn, New York

"There is almost a certain amount of rebellion in embracing English if it's the language that was not spoken predominantly by your parents. You work hard to erase any trace of accent from your voice and embrace literature, instead of the technical arts that parents basically claim as the grounds for a stable life and future."

Jeff Yang is the publisher and editor-in-chief of *A. Magazine: Inside Asian America,* the nation's premiere publication for English-speaking Asian

Pacific Americans. He founded the magazine with three friends in 1989, shortly after graduating from Harvard University. Since that time, the magazine has grown from a small regional publication into an international bimonthly with a circulation of over 100,000 in North America and the countries of the Pacific Rim.

Yang is also a feature writer and cultural critic for the respected New York alternative weekly the *Village Voice.* He was that paper's first Asian American columnist and its youngest feature contributor. He writes regularly for other publications of national importance including the *San Francisco Examiner* and *Mademoiselle,* and is a consultant and senior editor for a new magazine called *Flux.*

Generations of doctors

Yang was born in the Park Slope neighborhood of Brooklyn, New York, where his family was living while his father served his residency at a local hospital. As a recent immigrant Yang's father was required to serve as a resident even though he was a full doctor in his native Taiwan. Yang's mother was a social worker. The family moved to Staten Island, New York, when Yang was six. Yang described this move in an interview with *Asian American Biography (AAB)* as "wrenching." Staten Island at that time was a predominantly white suburb, and his was essentially the only Chinese family in the area. He said that as a child, he had no real idea that beyond his family there was any kind of an Asian community, any larger sense of culture to which he could one day belong. He also felt prejudice in this community, though it was not the sort of prejudice

that led to violence. He described it instead as leading to "isolation and exclusion. Having people ask you whether you can speak English, or ask you why you're eating that kind of food for lunch."

Yang was educated at St. Ann's High School in Brooklyn Heights, an alternative-education private high school that emphasized the arts while also giving its students a free hand to study math and science as their abilities allowed. Yang's father, who was descended from a long line of doctors, had, Yang said, "essentially decided that I would follow in those footsteps." Yang went along with this until his second year of college at Harvard University, to which he had won an academic scholarship. He had realized that there were many other things he was interested in, most especially English. He said that this was something he'd noticed in many second-generation Asian Americans: "There is almost a certain amount of rebellion in embracing English if it's the language that was not spoken predominantly by your parents. You work hard to erase any trace of accent from your voice and embrace literature, instead of the technical arts that parents basically claim as the grounds for a stable life and future."

Breaking tradition

After Yang told his parents that he had decided not to follow the family tradition—and that he was going to switch his major to psychology and English—there was a brief spell of hard feelings that have since been mended.

While at Harvard, Yang was exposed for the first time to a community of Asian Americans, an experience he found very

Jeff Yang

diversity—at the same time—that I saw as being remarkable."

After graduation in 1989, Yang watched as most of his friends took jobs in management consulting and at Wall Street brokerage houses or went on to law school or other advanced training. None of these options appealed to the young man, who had come to enjoy writing and publishing. One day he and a group of friends from his work on *Eastwind* and on the humor-oriented *Harvard Lampoon* got together and decided to pool their money to start a new publication that "expressed not only issues of identity and concern to Asian Americans, but also celebrated in many ways the emerging culture we had discovered at college." Yang said this was an especially ripe time for such a magazine to start, because America was in a sense just then beginning to "discover" its Asian minority, so conspicuously absent from view for so long. Asian faces were appearing on movie screens in non-demeaning, non-stereotypical roles, and novels by Asian American writers were making it onto bestseller lists, most notably **Amy Tan**'s 1989 hit *The Joy Luck Club.*

A. Magazine

Yang and his friends took the money they collected, moved to New York City, and spent three months putting together the bare bones of a start-up magazine, including materials for a subscription mailer, a test issue of the magazine, and an advertising media kit. All the tedious initial work paid off; Yang and his friends found out that there was a vast potential market for just the sort of magazine they envisioned. They put together a premiere issue in the summer of

heartening. He became involved in Asian American activist groups in the Boston area and on Harvard's campus. He started a publication called *Eastwind,* a biannual undergraduate magazine. Being involved with community organizations and working on an ethnic magazine with other Asian Americans gave Yang a sense of belonging that he had not really experienced before. "All of a sudden I wasn't someone outside looking inside; somebody who was with my family Asian but to the people outside something alien.... It was a sense of commonality and

1990 and sold out all 5,000 copies in a matter of weeks. Two more test issues were produced in 1991 to build the subscriber list and further fine-tune the product.

In June of 1992, Phoebe Eng, a mergers and acquisitions lawyer in New York who had from the beginning provided the young publishers with legal advice, left her law office to become the magazine's full-time publisher. Not long after that, *A. Magazine* opened its first permanent office in Lower Manhattan. Since then, *A. Magazine* has attracted significant attention. Major media outlets like the *New York Times, Crain's New York Business,* CNN, ABC, NBC, and PBS have all done stories on it. Eng retired as publisher in 1994, and Yang, who had been editor-in-chief, assumed the role of publisher, too. As of 1995, *A. Magazine* was distributed by the Time Warner communications company and boasted a circulation of over 100,000. It has a full-time staff of 16 and in 1994 went from publishing four issues a year to publishing six.

Yang also continues to write for the *Village Voice* and other national publications. He is currently working on a book of non-fiction about second-generation Asian Americans.

Sources:

A. Magazine, promotional material, February 1995.
Yang, Jeff, telephone interview with Jim Henry, February 3, 1995.

Laurence Yep

Writer
Born June 14, 1948, San Francisco, California

"In the 1950s when I was growing up, there were no books on being Chinese American.... I really liked science fiction because kids from the everyday world were taken to another world, and had to learn another language, another culture. Science fiction was about adapting and that's what I was doing every time I got off the bus."

L aurence Yep is best known as an author of children's books, although he is a multitalented writer who has written historical fiction, short stories, and novels. His two most famous books, *Dragonwings* and *Dragon's Gate,* were both named Newbery Honor books, the highest distinction awarded to children's books in the United States. In addition to his writing, Yep holds a Ph.D. in English and for a time taught creative writing at the University of California at Berkeley. In the mid-1980s he began writing plays. One of his most successful was a stage adaptation of *Dragonwings,* which was produced at such noteworthy venues as New York's Lincoln Center and Washington, D.C.'s Kennedy Center for the Performing Arts.

Growing up between two slums

Yep is the son of second-generation Chinese Americans. He grew up in an apartment above the grocery store his parents owned in the Western Edition District, a predominantly black neighborhood in San Francisco, California. For school, however, Yep left this neighborhood, taking a bus to Chinatown. He described this experience for *Asian American Biography (AAB):* "Going back and forth between those two ghetto areas is why I got interested in science fiction. In the 1950s when I was growing up, there were no books on being Chinese American. And I couldn't identify with the standard children's books because in all of them, the kids lived in houses where the front door was always unlocked and they all had bikes. I didn't know anyone like that. I really liked science fiction because kids from the everyday world were taken to another world, and had to learn another language, another culture. Science fiction was about adapting and that's what I was doing every time I got off the bus traveling between my two worlds."

Yep went to high school at a private religious school run by the Catholic order of Jesuits, famed for the rigor of their instruction. Here Yep went through two important changes: he was exposed to the white majority culture for the first time, and he became interested in writing. Initially, he planned to become a chemist, the career his father was pursuing when the Great Depression of the 1930s—during which America was gripped by massive unemployment and the economy slowed almost to a standstill—forced him to leave school and work. But then a teacher convinced Yep to pursue his writing. "In my senior year, I had an English teacher who told me that if I wanted an A in the course, I had to get something accepted by a national magazine," Yep reported. "So I started sending in stories, and started getting serious rejections. The teacher eventually retracted

Laurence Yep

the demand, but I had already gotten into the habit of sending in my stories."

Higher education

After graduating from the Jesuit high school, Yep enrolled in Marquette University in Milwaukee, Wisconsin, another Catholic school. While there, he had his first story published by the now-defunct science-fiction magazine *Worlds of If.* A few years later Yep's story was republished in an anthology called *The World's Best Science Fiction of 1969.* Yep did not finish his studies at

DRAGONWINGS
by Laurence Yep

Cover of *Dragonwings*

Marquette; he eventually returned to school at the University of California at Santa Cruz (UCSC), from which he earned a degree in literature in 1970. He also continued writing and working on his stories and novellas and saw more of his work published.

Shortly after graduation, Yep was asked by a friend who worked in the children's division of a large publishing house to write a science fiction novel for children. In 1973, his first novel, *Sweetwater,* was published. "I didn't realize it at the time, but the aliens in the book are based on the bachelor society in Chinatown," Yep explained, referring to the large numbers of unmarried Chinese immigrant men in the early part of this century. Strict anti-immigration laws barred Chinese women from entering the United States at the time and, with mixing of the races being illegal, Chinese men were unable to marry. Thus a whole culture of Chinese men lived a sort of alien existence in the United States, in government-enforced isolation. Much of Yep's fiction expresses alienation, recalling his childhood feelings of being between two cultures and having to adapt to unfamiliar surroundings.

Yep continued writing and working on his education; he enrolled in the doctoral program in literature at the State University of New York at Buffalo, earning his Ph.D. in 1975, the same year that saw the publication of *Dragonwings.* The young adult novel tells the story of a Chinese American aviator who built and flew a flying machine in 1909, a true story. The book enjoyed wide success: in addition to being chosen a 1976 Newbery Honor Book, it received numerous awards, including the 1976 IRA Children's Book Award, being named Notable Children's Book of 1971–1975 and the Best of Children's Books for 1966–1978, as well as winning the 1976 Carter G. Woodson Award. The *New York Times Book Review* called *Dragonwings* "an exquisitely written poem of praise to the Chinese American people" and "a triumph."

Return to California

Armed with a Ph.D. and a couple of novels to his credit, Yep returned to California hoping to find work as a teacher, but due to budgetary cutbacks, teaching jobs had become scarce. He decided instead to concentrate on his writing. Although Yep often writes of alien and futuristic worlds, he draws many of his ideas from his own life; the inspiration behind two works, *Sweetwater,* about the first colonists from Earth sent to the star Harmony, and *Dragon's Gate,* about the use of immigrants, notably the Chinese, in the construction of the transcontinental railroad, is essentially the same. Yep explained the process behind his writing for *AAB,* noting, "When I write a Chinese piece that I haven't completely explored, I begin by first writing science fiction. I use the science fiction as a testing and experimenting ground to explore the psychology and dynamics of a potential subject before I actually write it."

Yep continued writing throughout the 1980s. In 1984 he added plays to his repertoire but continued writing novels as well. In 1989 he published *The Rainbow People,* a compilation of 20 Chinese folktales told by immigrants and retold by Yep. Two years later he published another collection of such tales, *Tongues of Jade.* Yep has also written novels that tell the story of his family; in 1991 he published *The Star Fisher,* the remarkable story of his maternal grandmother's life in rural West Virginia.

As of the mid-1990s, Yep was at work on a number of projects, including two children's books, *Dream Soul* and *Thief of Hearts,* sequels to *The Star Fisher* and *Child of the Owl,* his 1977 novel about a young girl coming to terms with her dual American and Chinese heritage in San Francisco's Chinatown. He was also developing picture books based on Chinese folktales, as well as an adult novel based on one of his one-act plays. Yep says that he has no preference for a particular genre, insisting, "Every one of the different styles brings new interesting challenges."

Sources:

Authors & Artists for Young Adults, volume 11, Detroit: Gale, 1992.

HarperCollins, promotional material for *Dragonwings,* April 1994.

Yep, Lawrence, telephone interview with Terry Hong, August 1, 1994.

Shirley Young

Business executive
Born May 25, 1935, Shanghai, China

General Motors hired Shirley Young in hopes that her expertise as a strategic marketing planner would help the giant auto manufacturer regain its share of the domestic auto market, which had slowly but steadily eroded throughout the 1980s.

S hirley Young is the vice president for consumer market development with General Motors (GM), a post she has held since 1988. GM hired Young in hopes that her expertise as a strategic marketing planner would help the giant auto manufacturer regain its share of the domestic auto market, which had slowly but steadily eroded throughout the 1980s. This loss of market share was due in large part to GM's efforts at retooling its plants and reorganizing its management to more effectively compete with the growing import market. During this period of restructuring, GM and the other two major American automakers

(Ford and Chrysler), suffered from low consumer ratings, and Young was hired to reverse this trend. Prior to her work at GM, Young worked for more than 25 years at New York-based Grey Advertising, an internationally renowned agency. There she held a variety of positions, including executive vice president, and was a member of the agency policy council before being named president of Grey Strategic Marketing—a subsidiary of Grey Advertising—in 1983.

War refugee

Young's father was a career diplomat with the Nationalist Chinese government, which ruled China prior to the Communist takeover in 1949. This was a tumultuous time for China. Japan had occupied Manchuria for some time and was fighting the Chinese government for control of the huge country. During World War II, Young's father was stationed in the Philippines, a country Japan had also occupied. In 1942, as a representative of the government of China, Young's father was executed by the Japanese, who left a legacy of terror and brutality throughout their Asian empire. Following the war, Young and the remainder of her family fled to the United States where she has lived ever since.

Young was educated at Wellesley College in Massachusetts, where she studied economics. She graduated in 1955 with a bachelor's degree. After graduation, her first job was as a project director with the Alfred Politz Research Organization, a market research firm, where she worked for three years before joining the Hudson Paper Corporation as a market research manager. In 1959, she was hired as a researcher by the prestigious Madison Avenue agency, Grey Advertising.

In her first position at Grey, Young helped pioneer what is referred to in the advertising field as "attitudinal studies." As described in a *Business Week* profile of Young, "her method, Market Target Buying Incentive Studies, helps packaged goods companies such as Procter & Gamble Company and General Foods Corporation understand how consumers go from thinking about a product to actually buying it." This sort of innovative thinking marked Young's career at Grey and continues to have a profound impact on the way advertisers court consumers. Young continued her market research at Grey, assuming various marketing positions before being named executive vice president. In 1983 she became president of Grey Strategic Marketing; five years later she was elevated to chairperson.

An introduction to GM

Young began working with General Motors in 1983 on a consulting basis. One of her first accomplishments was the initiation of a roadside assistance program and a toll-free hotline for Cadillac owners, two programs meant to restore the air of exclusivity to Cadillac buyers. This was done as the historic quality of the cars diminished along with their size and distinctiveness of design. In 1988 Young was hired full time by GM chair Roger Smith. Since then Young has concentrated her efforts on enhancing the giant company's responsiveness to consumers, an acknowledged flaw in the past.

In 1990, Young initiated a marketing campaign with the tagline "Putting Quality

Shirley Young

base that is proud of what it produces, she told *Business Week,* "A lot of this job is what I call persistent evangelism."

Another project of Young's at GM has been to establish distinctiveness among the automaker's five divisions, a recurring problem with the company. It has often been suggested that GM eliminate one or two of its divisions, which are frequently criticized as repetitive and inefficient. In this program Young was working less on selling than on creating brand recognition and loyalty with consumers, her specialty. The marketing image she laid out for each of the divisions, as reported in *Business Week,* attempts to lock in the mind of the car-buying consumer specific images or ideas with each of the division's names. A Buick, for example, is the "Premium American motorcar"; a Cadillac, "The standard of luxury worldwide"; a Chevrolet, "More than the customer expects"; an Oldsmobile, "Innovative technology"; and Pontiac, "Performance-oriented [automobiles] for young people."

Corporate and community leadership

Young has earned a reputation at GM as an intense and demanding worker. Although she has a powerful position, she works out of a fairly small and simple office—a few doors from that of the chairman—and employs only one assistant. In addition to her work at GM, Young sits on the board of directors of Bell Atlantic and the Promus Companies. She also served for 12 years as a consultant director for the Dayton Hudson Corporation and in 1980 served as a vice chair of the nominating committee for the New York Stock Exchange.

on the Road." It was her first corporation-wide campaign, and it was a risky one. As *Business Week* said, "The new ads have an unmistakable implication: That for years GM's cars fell short of its customers' expectations." In addition to convincing consumers that GM was back from the crisis times of the late 1970s and early 1980s—when by anyone's standards the entire American auto industry fell far behind its foreign competitors—Young's campaign was meant to reinvigorate the GM workforce. In acknowledgment of the importance of having a motivated employee

In addition, Young is involved in several community service and cultural organizations. She is chair of the Committee of 100, a national Chinese American leadership resource, and is a founding member of the Committee of 200, an international organization of leading businesswomen. She also serves on the national board of directors of Junior Achievement and is trustee of Wellesley College and member of the board of directors of the associates of the Harvard Business School. She was awarded an honorary doctorate of letters from Russell Sage College and in 1986 was given the Wellesley College Alumna Achievement Award.

Sources:

General Motors, "Shirley Young," press release, resume, Detroit, Michigan.

Lander, Mark, "Shirley Young: Pushing GM's Humble Pie Strategy," *Business Week,* June 11, 1990, pp. 52-53.

Teddy Zee

Entertainment executive
Born May 15, 1957, Liberty, New York

"I always felt special—which is a nice way of saying I always felt different. I see this as an advantage, not a disadvantage."

Teddy Zee is one of the top producers working in Hollywood today. From his position as executive vice president of movie production at Columbia Pictures, he has produced such films as *Indecent Proposal,* starring Robert Redford, Demi Moore, and Woody Harrelson, and *My Girl,* starring Macauley Culkin. More recent projects include *First Knight,* starring Sean Connery and Richard Gere, and *Blankman,* starring Daman Wayans and David Alan Grier. Zee brings to his projects a sense of fun and a Harvard business education—a combination that has proven valuable to a Hollywood film industry that is obsessed with profits but that relies on meaningful fantasy to make its money.

The "Borscht Belt"

Zee's father, Charles A. Zee, immigrated to the United States from his native China in the 1940s. He had worked for a time in the Chinese merchant marine, and when he arrived in the United States he enlisted in the navy. After leaving the navy, the elder Zee worked in the restaurants along the New Jersey coast, a popular vacation spot for New Yorkers, and for a while at the famous Algonquin Hotel in New York City. He saved his money and was eventually able to begin paying for the rest of his family to join him in his new country. He first brought over his wife, Chu Yue, and their eldest son, Richard. Two more children were born in New York before the Zee family moved to Liberty, New York, where Charles Zee sought employment at Grossingers Hotel. Grossingers is one of the best known and oldest of the resorts that loosely form what is referred to as the "borscht belt." (Borscht is a soup made of beets popular among people of Eastern European Jewish background, many of whom frequented hotels like Grossingers.) These were resorts that were favored by middle-class New Yorkers in the 1950s and 1960s, featuring "lounge" singers and classic stand-up comedians like Jackie Mason and Sheckie Greene. Into this culture Teddy Zee was born.

Zee remembered what it was like growing up in the borscht belt environment in an interview with *Asian American Biography (AAB)*: "It was very strange growing up in Liberty. I was the all-American boy who fit in everywhere, but didn't fit in anywhere—not even at home, because Chinese was spoken there. In fact, as I grew older a real language barrier developed between my mother and me. My Chinese deteriorated because I only spoke it at home, and when I communicated at home everything had to be spelled out very carefully to be sure we all understood." Increasing the isolation, Zee added, was the fact that "we didn't belong to a church, we weren't a part of the community except through the school."

A scholarship to Cornell

As soon as Zee was old enough, he began working at Grossingers, as did his brothers and sister. He was an excellent student, and while in high school he entered a scholarship competition sponsored by the Hotel and Restaurant Workers and Bartenders Union—to which his father belonged. The contest attracted applicants nationwide, and from this immense pool, Zee was selected. In 1975 he enrolled at Cornell University in upstate Ithaca, New York, on a full scholarship to study industrial and labor relations. Going to such a prestigious school with all the opportunities it afforded had a great impact on Zee. He began to see that the world spread far beyond the limited horizons he had known, and that there were

Teddy Zee

tremendous possibilities for success. "Before I went to Cornell, I had never traveled—never been south of the Jersey Shore or West of Buffalo [New York]. While I was at Cornell, I felt my horizons expanding," Zee told *AAB*.

Zee graduated from Cornell in 1979 with a bachelor's degree. His first job was as a management associate with NBC-TV in New York. The management associates spent about six months working in a variety of departments to give them a feel for the overall operations of the network. One of Zee's positions at this time included preparing for the broadcast of the 1980 summer Olympics, to be held that year in Moscow, Russia. The planning ended up being in vain, however, when President Jimmy Carter announced that the United States would boycott the games in protest of the Soviet Union's invasion of Afghanistan in 1979. This was a highly controversial decision, and due to the U.S. pullout, the games were not broadcast in the United States.

Zee's next assignment with NBC took him to Los Angeles. There he became director of compensation and also headed an experiment with "teletext," a technology that, it was hoped, would broadcast magazines and newspapers to homes via the television set. At this time, teletext technology was seen as the wave of the future, and Zee was fascinated by it. Much of the work he participated in has now been transformed to home computer technology and today people can access magazines and newspapers via their computer screens.

On to Harvard

Zee was dissatisfied with his career options at this point and decided to further his education. He applied to Harvard Business School and was accepted. After completing his master's degree in business administration, Zee returned to Los Angeles, where he hoped to find a job with a film production company. Such jobs are highly difficult to secure, however, even for someone with as impressive a resume as Zee's. After a long, unproductive search, he took a job as a management consultant, which left him miserable.

Rather than completely giving up, though, Zee continued looking for work in the entertainment industry, landing interviews with the Disney and Paramount film studios. Paramount offered Zee his golden opportunity; in 1985, Dawn Steel, at that time Hollywood's highest-ranking woman studio executive, became intrigued by Zee's unique combination of talents and hired him as a creative executive. "She liked my 'borscht belt' background, and she gave me a shot," Zee remembered. In five years at Paramount, Zee advanced to senior vice president of production. In 1990 he left Paramount for Columbia Pictures, where he is executive vice president of production.

When asked what it was like to make such a dramatic career change—from management consultant to movie producer—Zee replied, "We should all do what we love doing. I didn't want to do what was expected of me: I wanted to meet *my* expectations. I didn't want to deal with life and death situations—I wanted to bring joy and happiness—to help people enjoy themselves."

Zee married his wife, Elizabeth, a former classmate at Harvard Business School, in 1986. They have two children.

Sources:

"Power Brokers," A. *Magazine,* vol. 2., no. 3, December 15, 1993, pp. 25-34.

Zee, Teddy, telephone interview with Susan Gall, July 21, 1994.

FIELD OF ENDEAVOR INDEX

TELEVISION
Barry, Lynda **1**
Carrere, Tia **1**
Chao, Stephen **1**
Chen, Joan **1**
Cho, Margaret **1**
Chung, Connie **1**
Hattori, James **1**
Kashiwahara, Ken **1**
Lee, Ming Cho **1**
Lone, John **1**
Mako **2**

McCarthy, Nobu **2**
Morita, Pat **2**
Quo, Beulah **2**
Salonga, Lea **2**
Takei, George **2**
Tomita, Tamlyn **2**
Toyota, Tritia **2**
Wong, B. D. **2**
Zee, Teddy **2**

THEATER
Gotanda, Philip Kan **1**

Hwang, David Henry **1**
Kim, Willa **1**
Lee, Ming Cho **1**
Lone, John **1**
Mako **2**
McCarthy, Nobu **2**
Morita, Pat **2**
Quo, Beulah **2**
Salonga, Lea **2**
Tomita, Tamlyn **2**
Wong, B. D. **2**